THE HIDDENNESS OF GOD

Michael C. Rea is Rev. John A. O'Brien Professor of Philosophy and Director of the Center for Philosophy of Religion at the University of Notre Dame, where he has taught since 2001. He is also a Professorial Fellow at the Logos Institute for Analytic & Exegetical Theology at the University of St. Andrews. He has written or edited more than fifteen books and fifty articles in metaphysics, philosophy of religion, feminist philosophy, and analytic theology, and he has given numerous lectures in the United States, the United Kingdom, the European Union, Russia, China, and Iran. He was the 2017 Gifford Lecturer at the University of St Andrews. His publications include *Analytic Theology: New Essays in the Philosophy of Theology* (co-edited with Oliver D. Crisp; 2009), *Philosophical and Theological Essays on the Trinity* (co-edited with Thomas McCall; 2009), and *The Oxford Handbook of Philosophical Theology* (co-edited with Thomas P. Flint; 2009). He is also the series editor of Oxford Studies in Analytic Theology with Oliver D. Crisp.

D1600659

The Hiddenness of God

MICHAEL C. REA

OXFORD
UNIVERSITY PRESS

OXFORD
UNIVERSITY PRESS

Great Clarendon Street, Oxford, OX2 6DP,
United Kingdom

Oxford University Press is a department of the University of Oxford.
It furthers the University's objective of excellence in research, scholarship,
and education by publishing worldwide. Oxford is a registered trade mark of
Oxford University Press in the UK and in certain other countries

Published in the United States of America by Oxford University Press
198 Madison Avenue, New York, NY 10016, United States of America

British Library Cataloguing in Publication Data
Data available

Library of Congress Cataloging in Publication Data
Data available

ISBN 978–0–19–882601–9 (Hbk.)
ISBN 978–0–19–284516–0 (Pbk.)

To
Eleonore Stump

Preface

This book is a significantly expanded and revised version of my 2017 Gifford Lectures at the University of St. Andrews, entitled *"Though the Darkness Hide Thee": Seeking the Face of the Invisible God*. It is a book that I have been wanting to write for a very long time.

My first real confrontation with the problem of divine hiddenness as a challenge to faith came from a friend during my first or second year in college. We had gone to church together and afterward, sitting in my parents' kitchen, we got to talking about various kinds of faith struggles. Eventually she broke down in tears, saying "God is supposed to be my heavenly father. So why can't he just whisper 'I love you' once in a while?" Later, during my first semester in graduate school (in fall 1991, just two years before the publication of J. L. Schellenberg's landmark book on the topic), Tom Morris introduced me to a philosophically more rigorous version of the problem to which my friend had given voice just a few years previously. It has been on my mind in one way or another ever since—sometimes in its guise as a purely philosophical objection to theistic belief, but more often as a kind of pastorally and existentially important theological problem for religious believers (friends, loved ones, and, often enough, myself as well) stricken by unsatisfied longing for some kind of experience of the love and presence of God.

I began work in earnest on the hiddenness problem about a decade ago, shortly after the publication of the private writings of St. Teresa of Calcutta under the title *Come Be My Light*. I now think that my earlier efforts on this topic (two scholarly papers and one tailored more for popular audiences, all listed in the references at the end of this book) embody some important misunderstandings and misreadings of the philosophical work that had been done (most notably by J. L. Schellenberg) in appealing to divine hiddenness as evidence against the existence of God; but the theological ideas in those earlier papers, underdeveloped as they were, I still mostly stand by. The most substantial of these theological ideas have found their way in more developed form into various chapters of the present book. And, thanks to some significant help from some of the friends and colleagues listed in the acknowledgments, I am hopefully optimistic that I have now managed to correct my earlier misreadings and misunderstandings.

For quite some time now it has seemed to me that the hiddenness problem needs to be approached, by Christians anyway, with attention not just to relevant issues in epistemology, ethics, and philosophy of religion (the philosophical sub-disciplines whose literatures most substantially intersect with the literature on the hiddenness problem) but also with attention to scripture, tradition, and matters theological. Accordingly, I am inclined to prefer an interdisciplinary approach to the hiddenness problem—one that is informed not just by ideas and insights in the relevant philosophical literature, but also ideas and insights drawn from theology and biblical studies. I hope that I have managed to do justice to this preference in this book.

In the part of his will that designated his intentions for the Gifford Lectures, Lord Gifford stipulated that the lectures are to treat the topic of natural theology "in the widest sense of that term"; and he expressed the desire that lecturers "treat their subject as a strictly natural science, the greatest of all possible sciences ... without reference to or reliance upon any supposed special exceptional or so-called miraculous revelation." A few people who know this about the Gifford Lectures, and who also knew that I was inclined to approach the hiddenness problem in the way that I just described, asked me how I would be presenting *that* kind of project as Gifford Lectures. Much has been written (mostly, but not entirely, in the prefaces and introductions of the books people have produced in the wake of their own Gifford Lectures) about what one must do, or is permitted to do, in trying to fulfill the task set for a Gifford Lecturer. Here, then, are my own thoughts about how the present project meshes with what is written in Lord Gifford's will.

Despite his stated desire that lecturers treat their subject "as a strictly natural science," neither philosophy nor theology are nowadays understood to be natural sciences. And, as other Gifford Lecturers (most notably, Alasdair MacIntyre) have pointed out, what Lord Gifford most likely envisioned in expressing this desire was, in any case, probably very different from what any contemporary reader of those words would envision. Be that as it may, philosophy as done in the so-called "analytic" style *is* nowadays often regarded as being at least *methodologically continuous* with the natural sciences; and the burgeoning field of analytic theology aims to treat *its* subject matter, the subject matter of theology, with precisely the same science-like, theory-building ambitions and methods that characterize the best instances of analytic philosophy. Insofar as they represent the best that their discipline has to offer, analytic theologians are, in the first instance, "sincere lovers of and earnest inquirers after truth" about God, just as Lord Gifford hoped that his lecturers would be; and they aim to build, or contribute to building, robust explanatory theories about theological matters by way of methods that in many ways resemble those of the natural sciences, especially in their prioritization of precision, logical rigor, and theoretical virtues like simplicity, explanatory power, fit with relevant data, and the like. It is my hope, therefore, that insofar as my lectures in 2017, and the book you have before you now, count as instances of analytic theology, they will accordingly be recognized as importantly faithful to Lord Gifford's stipulations, even if our visions about what exactly it would be to treat theological matters scientifically are rather different from one another.

My invitation to give the lectures came in 2015 from Louise Richardson, who was at that time Principal and Vice Chancellor of the University of St. Andrews. I am grateful to her, to the Selection Committee, and to Lord Gifford for the opportunity provided by that invitation to work on this project. My work was partly supported by a generous grant from the John Templeton Foundation, under the auspices of the Experience Project, a three-year multimillion dollar interdisciplinary initiative led by Laurie Paul, Sam Newlands, and myself. I am grateful to the John Templeton Foundation for their support; and, as is typical, I note that their financial support and my acknowledgment of it imply no endorsement on their part of the views in this book. I am also grateful to the University of Notre Dame for approving research leave for me a year earlier than I would otherwise have been eligible. I would have had a very hard time completing this project in time without that.

Virtually none of this book has appeared elsewhere in its current form; but some of it draws on my earlier work, and some has been given in lecture form on various occasions. A small portion of Chapter 8 was published (almost verbatim) by the *Huffington Post* in 2017 under the title "A Lenten Reflection on Job;" and Chapter 5 will appear in a volume published by T&T Clark entitled *Love, Human and Divine: Contemporary Essays in Systematic and Philosophical Theology*, edited by James Arcadi and Jordan Wessling. Chapters 3 and 4 draw on my 2015 paper, "Hiddenness and Transcendence"; and

Chapter 5 draws a bit on both "Narrative, Liturgy, and the Hiddenness of God" and "Divine Hiddenness, Divine Silence." Bibliographical material for these latter three works is just where you would expect to find it—in the bibliography.

I have been helped by many friends and colleagues in writing this book. I would like to begin by thanking the audiences at various conferences and institutions where this material has been discussed. My William P. Alston Memorial Lecture at the 2016 meeting of the Society of Christian Philosophers at the Central Division Meeting of the American Philosophical Association was an early draft of the material in Chapters 3 and 4. Other portions of this book have been given as lectures or discussed in reading groups at Fuller Theological Seminary, the California Metaphysics Workshop at the University of Southern California, the University of York, the University of Leeds, the University of Cambridge, and the University of Notre Dame (both in the Philosophy Department colloquium and in several meetings of the weekly discussion group in the Center for Philosophy of Religion). A draft of the entire book was read by the members of a graduate seminar taught at Baylor University by Charity Anderson, and then discussed with me in a question–answer session over Skype. I am grateful to the audiences on all of these occasions for helpful comments and discussion.

Additionally, I am grateful to the referees for Oxford University Press, most notably the ubiquitous and ever-challenging Reader 2. The press commissioned three readers for this book, one of whom delivered a sparse but complimentary report (thank you, Reader 1), another of whom delivered a couple of pages of helpful comments mostly on Chapters 4 and 5 (thank you, too, Reader 3), and the third of whom—in fact labeled by the press as "Reader 2"—delivered a glowing single-page report recommending publication, followed by some forty-eight single-spaced pages of detailed, often exasperated, and occasionally...well...colorful critical comments. These comments ultimately turned out to be some of the most helpful comments I have ever received on a manuscript, and I am deeply grateful for the generous investment of time and effort they represent. I doubt that I will have satisfied Reader 2 at every turn. (The common lore in academia, in any case, is that Reader 2 is *never* satisfied.) But I do know that the book is much better—particularly as regards my interpretation of some of the authors I discuss in it—as a result of this person's help.

I would also like to thank the following people for their comments on drafts of various portions of the book, some of which came in the context of one or more of the presentations and reading groups mentioned earlier, others of which came in response to requests from me for comments on individual chapters or portions thereof: Karl Ameriks, Robert Audi, Max Baker-Hytch, Matt Benton, Rebecca Chan, Nevin Climenhaga, Dustin Crummett, Kristen Drahos, Kate Finley, Andrew Helms, Jack Himelright, Erin Kidd, Liz Jackson, Anne Jeffrey, Pat Kain, John Keller, Lorraine Keller, Sam Lebens, Jeff McDonough, Chris Menzel, Joe Milburn, Andrew Moon, Carl Mosser, Sam Newlands, Michelle Panchuk, Caroline Paddock, Callie Phillips, John Schellenberg, Jeff Snapper, Eleonore Stump, Alli Thornton, Kevin Timpe, Sameer Yadav, and Christina Van Dyke. I would also like to thank Jessica Wilson for suggesting, as I was first beginning this project, that I look into the literature on cognitive penetration with an eye to its possible applications to the topic of religious experience. Chapters 6 and 7 might have looked rather different had I started elsewhere in exploring that topic.

Among those just mentioned, I am especially grateful to Jeff Snapper, who read and commented in detail on all of the chapters, and fairly quickly, shortly before I gave the Gifford Lectures. I also owe a special debt of gratitude to Michelle Panchuk, who, in addition to commenting on most of the chapters in one context or another, also spent a considerable amount of time talking and corresponding with me about the ideas in the book, and also about some intersecting ideas in her own work.

Special thanks are due also to several friends who generously took time out of their schedules to prepare for and attend two small workshops (one funded by the Experience Project, and one funded by research money from the University of Notre Dame) dedicated to intensive discussion of whatever draft material had been completed by the time of the workshop. The first was in fall 2015, covered material that is now in Chapters 1–7, and was attended by Charity Anderson, Sarah Coakley, Terence Cuneo, Trent Dougherty, Amber Griffioen, Daniel Howard-Snyder, Cristian Mihut, Kathryn Pogin, and Meghan Sullivan. (Charity, Kathryn, Cristian, and Trent each read and commented on additional material later on, too.) The second workshop was in fall 2016, covered drafts of everything except for Chapter 9, and was attended by Michael Bergmann, Jeff Brower, Oliver Crisp, and Hud Hudson. The voluminous comments that emerged from and in the wake of these workshops were tremendously helpful, making a substantial difference to the final form of the book. Words can hardly express how grateful I am to these friends for their time and effort.

Writing a book generally imposes demands upon and requires support from one's family. I am grateful to mine—to Chris, my wife, and to Aaron, Kristina, Gretchen, Matt, and Penelope, my kids, for all that they have given (knowingly or not) to make it possible for me to finish this project. I am most deeply grateful to Chris, who sacrificed her time and energy in all manner of different ways, large and small, to facilitate the various activities associated with this project and to support me through them and their attending stresses. She also read and commented on drafts of most of the chapters; so I thank her for that as well.

The book is dedicated, with admiration and gratitude, to Eleonore Stump. For most of my career, Eleonore has been among the people I would first turn to for professional and sometimes personal mentoring; and by this point in my career I think that she has also been the most influential of these. She and her work have significantly impacted many of my philosophical and theological views; and I have also sought to emulate in the ways that I can what, for lack of better terminology, I might simply describe as her general "way of being" in the profession. For all of this, too, I am thankful.

Contents

1

Hidden God

I was about four years old when I attended the first adult church service that I can remember. Until that time, the sanctuary of our church—the place that I knew from my parents to be God's house—had been shrouded in mystery. But on this day the mystery would be revealed. On this day, so I expected, I would come into the presence of God.

The author of the Epistle to the Hebrews reminds us that it is a dreadful thing to fall into the hands of the living God. As a small child, I knew this by pure instinct. I was terrified of our church's sanctuary. I thought *God himself* would be there. I was afraid that when I entered, the powerful and majestic, stern and sometimes angry authority of the universe might see me and, for reasons wholly his own and beyond all comprehension, bring me to my end. I approached with dread, and was glad when my parents wisely sat in the last row of the church balcony. I did not doubt that God could see me from his vantage point on the stage, but I figured that he would surely, for convenience, select someone sitting a lot closer to him for arbitrary and instant death.

My balcony seat afforded much-needed relief but, ironically, it also prolonged the mystery. It was hard to see what was actually taking place in the service. The stage was bathed in light; I also heard a Voice. Eventually I made out what seemed to be a man standing on the stage. After a while, I was pretty sure that God inhabited neither the light nor the Voice. The owner of the Voice seemed to be none other than the man on stage, and that man seemed to be old and balding, unlike the pictures of Jesus that I had seen in the halls. By the end of the service, I concluded that God had skipped church. I remember walking out with a sense of relief. But there was also disappointment. Church, the mysterious house of God, had turned out after all to be quite familiar and ordinary.

God is everywhere, we are told. *Where can I go from your Spirit?* asks the psalmist. *Where can I flee from your presence?* The implied answer is, *Nowhere.* God is anywhere and everywhere we might choose to go. Thus, Psalm 139 continues:

> If I go up to the heavens, you are there;
> if I make my bed in the depths, you are there.
> If I rise on the wings of the dawn,
> if I settle on the far side of the sea,
> even there your hand will guide me,
> your right hand will hold me fast.[1]

There is no escaping the divine presence; *and so*, the psalm seems to say, *divine guidance and support are always everywhere readily available.*

Perhaps God is everywhere; but God is not *any*where in the way that a child might expect. We do not find God sitting in our sanctuaries. He does not inhabit the light. He does not speak with a Voice for all to hear. Not to most of us, anyway; not today. Seeing no signs of God up in the heavens or down in the depths, many question God's existence; receiving no tangible guidance from God, and finding no divine hand to hold them fast in times of trial, many question God's love.

Job, in the midst of his suffering, demanded an audience with God. After a time, God appeared and spoke from the whirlwind: "Brace yourself like a man; I will question you, and you shall answer me."[2] But the only questions that come from our whirlwinds are those we ask in the wake of their destruction. Where was God? Where is God now? Why doesn't God save the dying, or speak comfort to those suffering loss? If God truly loves the frail creatures of Earth, why do so many of us find ourselves seeking with frustration and tears what the author of Psalm 139 seemed to find always ready at hand?

In 2007, about ten years after her death, some of the private writings of St. Teresa of Calcutta were published under the title *Come Be My Light*. The journal entries revealed a woman celebrated for her faith and devotion to God but at the same time tormented by

---

[1] Except where indicated otherwise, all scripture quotations in this book are from the New Revised Standard Version Bible, copyright © 1989 the Division of Christian Education of the National Council of the Churches of Christ in the United States of America.

[2] Job 38:3, Holy Bible, New International Version ®, NIV ® Copyright © 1973, 1978, 1984, 2011 by Biblica, Inc. ® Used by permission. All rights reserved worldwide.

pain and doubt for lack of the felt presence of God in her life. In one of the most moving passages of the book, she writes:

> Lord, my God, who am I that You should forsake me? The child of your love—and now become as the most hated one—the one You have thrown away as unwanted—unloved. I call, I cling, I want—and there is no One to answer—no One on Whom I can cling—no, No One.— Alone. The darkness is so dark . . . The loneliness of the heart that wants love is unbearable. . . . My God—how painful is this unknown pain. It pains without ceasing. . . . I am told God loves me—and yet the reality of darkness & coldness & emptiness is so great that nothing touches my soul. . . . What are You doing My God to one so small?
>
> (Teresa 2007: 186–7)

What indeed? What are we to make of the hiddenness of God?

The term "divine hiddenness" evokes a variety of different phenomena—the relative paucity and ambiguity of the available evidence for God's existence, the elusiveness of God's comforting presence when we are afraid and in pain, the palpable and devastating experience of divine absence and abandonment, and more.[3] Many of these phenomena are hard to reconcile with the idea, central to the Jewish and Christian scriptures, that God is deeply lovingly concerned with the lives and emotional and spiritual well-being of human creatures.

Nevertheless, as Samuel Balentine observes at the end of his classic study of divine hiding in the Old Testament,[4] "the experience of

---

[3] In conversation about an early draft of this chapter, Hud Hudson helpfully distinguished at least seven different ways in which God might be said to be hidden. God might be hidden (from someone, on some occasion) by virtue of (i) being absent from a place; (ii) being unavailable to someone's awareness; (iii) being unavailable to someone's *reflective* awareness, so that even if she is aware of God, she cannot recognize God *as such*, or be aware that she is aware of God; (iv) failing to speak to someone; (v) failing to satisfy someone's relational desires; (vi) someone's lacking insufficient evidence for God's existence; or (vii) being incomprehensible (in the sense that theologians typically have in mind—a sense that will be discussed in more detail in later chapters).

[4] In the course of working on another volume (Bergmann, Murray, and Rea 2011), I learned that there is no unproblematic term for referring to the texts that Christians call the "Old Testament." Part of the problem is summed up nicely by James Sanders as follows:

> Another problem [arising around the middle of the twentieth century] was what Christians should call the first of their double-testament Bible. Most wanted to drop the sub-title, Old Testament, out of respect for the continuing existence and variety of Judaism . . . Some Christians began to say "Hebrew Bible" instead of Old Testament, but this is clearly inaccurate and inappropriate since "Hebrew Bible," or *Biblia Hebraica*, is a time-honored term for the Jewish tri-partite Bible,

God's hiddenness, just as the experience of his presence, [was] an integral part of Israelite faith."[5] The same has been true of Christian faith throughout the centuries. (It is also true of important strands of Common Era Judaism and Islam; but I will not comment further on these religious traditions since I am not well equipped to talk about their theologies in detail.) Such experience is given voice in the lamentations and protests of the Old Testament, and in the language of divine "darkness" that pervades the theology of the Christian mystical traditions. Despite the manifest tension between divine love and divine hiddenness, both occupy a central place not only in Christian theology, but also in the scriptures and religious traditions that gave it birth.[6] The loving and faithful partner of Israel is a God who hides, a God who loves human beings intensely and yet is all too often disturbingly and painfully absent.

"[A]n important component of ancient Israel's worship," writes Joel Burnett, "was the engagement of divine absence."[7] Whereas Psalm 139 affirms the ubiquitous presence of God, many other psalms grapple with and lament God's absence. The problem is partly experiential: the psalmists desire union with and comfort from God. But it is also partly evidential: the world is not at all as one might expect under the governance of God. Neither in the psalter nor in other biblical texts that wrestle with divine hiddenness, however, is the *reality* of God called into question.[8] The same is true of ancient

the Tanak, and not for the Old Testament (besides there being a few Aramaic portions in it). The unfortunate designation persists even in sophisticated circles despite the fact that the Christian First Testament and the Hebrew Bible are significantly different from one another in shape and even contents. Another suggestion, my own in fact, was to refer to it as the First Christian Testament, but some object to this because it apparently suggests that Jews should have a Second Testament as well. ... In Jewish institutions it is called simply "Bible" to distinguish it from Talmud and Responsa.   (Sanders 2005: 7–8)

In that other volume, my co-editors and I opted for the term "Hebrew Bible" because that seemed to be the best and most convenient of the "faith-neutral" terms available for referring to the texts we were interested in. However, in the present book it seems appropriate to use the term "Old Testament," since the book is written from a Christian theological perspective.

[5] Balentine 1983: 172.

[6] On the importance of the hiddenness motif in scripture see (again) Balentine 1983: 164–7, Burnett 2010, and (more controversially) Friedman 1995.

[7] Burnett 2010: 149.

[8] As Burnett notes, in ancient Israel "the sense of divine absence [and the sorrow and suffering that goes along with it] is regarded as a normal part of human experience" (2010: 117). For fuller discussion, see Burnett 2010: 116–20, as well as G. A. Anderson 1991: 59–97.

Near Eastern religious texts more broadly: divine hiddenness is a pervasive and distressing reality, but not, in and of itself, a challenge to the reality of the gods.[9] It is also true of the various and diverse strands of patristic, medieval, and modern theology that emphasize different aspects of God's hiddenness—from the idea of divine darkness that stretches from the writings of Philo and Gregory of Nyssa on through the medieval spokesmen and spokeswomen for the Dionysian mystical tradition, to the Sanjuanist idea of the "dark night of the soul" as a vital stage in a person's spiritual development,[10] to the *Deus absconditus* in Lutheran theology, and so on. Divine hiddenness in one form or another looms large in these theologies, but God's love and existence remain unchallenged.

The idea that divine hiddenness counts against the existence of God is largely a twentieth-century phenomenon.[11] In the late nineteenth century, Friedrich Nietzsche remarked that it would be quite cruel of God, if God existed, to leave human beings wondering and debating about how to secure salvation, thus tacitly suggesting a connection between a certain kind of divine hiddenness and disbelief in the God of traditional Christianity.[12] At the very end of the nineteenth century, Robert Anderson, reflecting on the persistent silence of God, drew an explicit connection between divine silence and difficulty maintaining faith in God:

> It is no novel experience with men that Heaven should be silent. But what is new and strange and startling is that the silence should be so absolute and prolonged; that through all the changing vicissitudes of the Church's history for nearly two thousand years that silence should have remained unbroken. This it is which tries faith, and hardens unfaith into open infidelity. (Anderson 1897: 62–3)

Nevertheless, clear and explicit challenges to God's existence on the basis of divine hiddenness are, at best, few and far between until the twentieth century.[13]

---

[9] Cf. Burnett 2010 and Korpel and de Moor 2011.

[10] I do not mean to suggest that all of St. John of the Cross's "nights" of the soul involve divine hiddenness; nor do I mean to suggest that any of the Sanjuanist nights can be *identified* with divine hiddenness as I am thinking of it in this book. I mean only to suggest overlap between what I am calling divine hiddenness and some of what has been referred to in the Sanjuanist tradition as the dark night of the soul.

[11] This according to G. Tom Milazzo (1991: 33).   [12] Nietzsche 1997: 52–3.

[13] Schellenberg finds the germ of the idea suggested as early as the eighteenth century in Joseph Butler's remark (at the beginning of the sixth chapter of the second part of *The Analogy of Religion*) that some have thought that "if the evidence of revelation appears doubtful, this itself turns into a positive argument against it:

The twentieth century witnessed an explosion of interest in the arts and across a variety of academic disciplines in the theme of divine hiddenness.[14] The final three decades in particular saw a tremendous increase in scholarly attention devoted to the topic. Among the more important books and articles discussing the theological significance of divine hiddenness (under some construal or other), often with attention to the challenge posed thereby to religious faith, we might list Samuel Terrien's *The Elusive Presence* (1978), Samuel Balentine's *The Hidden God* (1983), Thomas V. Morris's "The Hidden God" (1988), G. Tom Milazzo's *The Protest and the Silence* (1991), and J. L. Schellenberg's agenda-setting *Divine Hiddenness and Human Reason* (1993).[15] By the century's close divine hiddenness had become the foundation of a powerful family of arguments for the conclusion that God does not exist, and a variety of now standard responses were beginning to emerge.

The *problem of divine hiddenness*, which I will present in detail in Chapter 2, ranks alongside the problem of evil as one of the two most important and widely discussed reasons on offer for disbelieving in God. As we will see, however, the problem depends for its traction on contestable theological assumptions. Accordingly, one might just as easily take the problem not as a referendum on the existence of God, but rather on the viability of certain ways of understanding the nature of God and God's attributes.

After noting the centrality of divine hiddenness to Israelite faith, Samuel Balentine comments that "[b]oth experiences [i.e., the experience of divine presence and the experience of divine hiddenness] derive from the nature of God himself."[16] If true, this suggests that the key to addressing philosophical problems about divine hiddenness is not to treat the phenomenon as an anomaly, but rather to treat it as a natural result of God living out the divine life in relation to us and the rest of creation. Treating it this way will steer us away from the usual quest for potential benefits that human beings might derive

because it cannot be supposed, that, if it were true, it would be left to subsist upon doubtful evidence" (2015b: 25).

[14] This is compendiously documented in the first chapter of Korpel and de Moor 2011.

[15] As it happens, my own interest in this topic dates to this period as well. I was introduced to the problem of divine hiddenness in a graduate course at the University of Notre Dame taught by Thomas V. Morris in fall 1991.

[16] Balentine 1983: 172.

from divine hiddenness and toward a theory about the attributes of God, and particularly about the love of God and the way in which it is manifested to humans, that makes room for divine hiddenness in its various forms as a natural outgrowth of *who and what God is* rather than of *what God is doing to serve human needs and desires.*

My aim in this book is to develop such a theory—not completely, of course, but in enough detail at least to address what I take to be some of the most important challenges raised by divine hiddenness. I will take the basic tenets of traditional Christian theology as the framework within which my theory is to be developed, but I will try to avoid relying on assumptions that are hotly contested within the Christian tradition. Thus, one might reasonably construe my overarching goal as to provide a "generically Christian" response to challenges raised by divine hiddenness. Some of what I will say can be adopted by adherents of other religious traditions; but not all of it can be—at least not without substantial modification.

I will begin in Chapter 2 by explaining a bit more carefully what I mean, and what others have meant, by the term "divine hidden-ness." I will then go on to articulate the problem of divine hiddenness and explain its relationship to the problem of evil.

In accord with standard practice, I formulate the problem as an argument (or family of arguments) against the existence of God; but, as I have already indicated, I prefer to see it as a referendum on certain common ways of thinking about God.[17] In fact, to pitch the problem as an argument against the existence of God seems to me to reflect a misconception of the overall significance of the premises and reasoning patterns that enter into the various versions of the argu-ment. It takes a remarkable abundance of faith in human theoretical capacities to give up belief in God, or to decline to investigate the matter further, simply on the basis of one's alleged rational insight into the premises of the hiddenness argument. Given the importance and complexity of the question whether God exists, it does not seem right or reasonable to think that the matter could be decided by the hiddenness argument in the absence of detailed, historically and

---

[17] In stating this preference, I don't mean to suggest that the preference is novel. It is, in fact, quite common for theists to treat atheistic arguments as reasons to discard problematic ways of thinking about God rather than as reasons to reject theism. For two recent examples of this kind of approach to the problem of evil, see Dougherty 2014b: 7–15, and Perrine and Wykstra 2014.

theologically informed exploration and defense of the assumptions about God that are embedded in it. But such exploration and defense is precisely what has not yet been undertaken by defenders of the hiddenness argument over the past two and a half decades.[18]

My own view, then, is that the hiddenness problem is significant primarily as an invitation to and challenge for systematic theological reasoning about the nature of God and the proper understanding both of central divine attributes like love and goodness and also of what it might mean for human beings to enter into a relationship with God. This is not to say that it is primarily an academic problem. Far from it. People's hearts are broken, their spiritual lives left in shambles, over the phenomena that fall under the label "divine hiddenness"; people lose faith or refrain from embracing it in the first place, opting to live as agnostics or atheists, because of divine hiddenness. It is a problem with deep existential import that requires serious and sustained theological reflection to sort out properly.

My solution to the hiddenness problem comes in two steps. The first and most important step will be to show that it rests on unwarranted assumptions and expectations about God's love for human beings. Scripture and the Christian tradition provide overwhelming testimony in support of the idea that God loves us deeply and, indeed, perfectly. I affirm these claims, but I deny that they provide any reason for thinking that God's love would preclude divine hiddenness. Nor do they provide reason for thinking that God would permit divine hiddenness only if it contributed to some significant human good; nor, for that matter, do they even provide reason for thinking that divine love for us would lead God to permit horrendous suffering in our lives only for the sake of greater human goods. If this is right, then—as shall become clear from my characterization of the problem of divine hiddenness in Chapter 2—the central premises of the hiddenness problem stand unmotivated.

This first step is supported by two arguments. First, in Chapters 3 and 4, I explain how scripture and tradition bear testimony not only to God's love, but to God's transcendence; and I argue that God's transcendence should be understood as implying that *all* of God's intrinsic attributes—divine love included—elude our grasp in ways

---

[18] Schellenberg, in fact, seems now to think that theology and its history are irrelevant to the hiddenness argument. See his 2007: 197–8 and 2015b: 13–15, as well as my discussion of this issue in Chapter 4, pp. 58–61.

that should put us in doubt about any revelation-independent claim about how a perfectly loving deity would likely behave toward human beings. Establishing this conclusion undercuts the hiddenness argument by casting doubt on its underlying assumptions about divine love.

But even if one is inclined to resist the idea that God is transcendent (in the way I describe in Chapter 4), there is an independent reason for doubting such claims. In Chapter 5, I argue that even if we suspend belief in divine transcendence, the fact that God loves us perfectly provides, all by itself, no reason for thinking that God is so devoted to our well-being or to pursuing relationships with us as to prevent divine hiddenness altogether, or to permit it only for the sake of greater human goods. This conclusion, too, casts doubt on the assumptions about divine love that support the hiddenness argument.

But even as this first step of my solution undercuts familiar versions of the problem of divine hiddenness, it only raises a further problem. Key to that first step is the idea that our grasp of the attribute that we call "divine love" is deeply limited, so much so that we have no good reason to believe God is devoted to us in ways that would preclude divine hiddenness or intense human suffering except for the sake of greater human goods. But then, one might ask, how can we continue to cling to the idea that this attribute can profitably be understood on analogy with the most excellent of human loves? Fine and good, one might say, if divine hiddenness doesn't strictly license an inference to the conclusion that no perfectly loving God exists; but the Christian tradition is up to its neck in parental and spousal analogies put forth in scripture and elsewhere as characterizations of divine love. These analogies are not easily given up; for they are put forward precisely to motivate us toward the kind of trust, devotion, and abandonment of self to Father, Son, and Holy Spirit that are central to the religious life of a Christian. This is the problem that will be left lingering at the end of Chapter 5, and the one which the remaining chapters of this book will aim to address.

Part of the answer to this lingering problem will involve appeal to God's creative and sustaining activity—God's general goodness to all of creation—as well as to the life, death, and resurrection of Jesus. These indicators of divine love, to the extent that one believes in them, are undeniably significant. But in the present context, they are not quite enough to address the problem. God's creative and sustaining activity points to a kind of original love for all of creation; the incarnation and atoning work of Christ point to God's dramatically generous and loving willingness to supply a path by which God's own grievances with human beings might be addressed. No doubt these signs of divine love—perhaps in conjunction with apparently answered prayers and other providential "coincidences"—serve for many to buttress characterizations of divine love on analogy with that displayed by the most excellent of friends, spouses, or parents. But for many people the phenomena of divine hiddenness—especially in the face of intense human suffering—naturally suggest other analogies: a distant king who loves his kingdom generically but is rather indifferent to the daily lives of individual subjects; a professed friend to many who plays favorites and genuinely loves only a few; a mercurially abusive parent who greets his children sometimes with the open hand of welcoming love and sometimes with the closed fist of anger. How can such "counter-analogies" be neutralized? What entitles us to hang on to the positive love analogies and dismiss the negative ones?

The answers to these questions depend on which aspects of divine hiddenness we are considering. In some cases, there is misunderstanding; God appears to be hidden in ways that God actually is not. In other cases, there is misinterpretation: desires or motives (or their absence) are attributed to God without sufficient evidence. In such cases, responding to the questions will involve identifying or explaining away the relevant misunderstanding or misinterpretation. In still other cases, there is no misunderstanding or misinterpretation, but counter-analogies become salient as a result of (perhaps perfectly understandable) particular aspects of a plausible narrative about what God is doing or allowing in someone's life. The response in these cases will involve facilitating a different narrative, one that fits the problematic behavior into a larger story according to which God's relationship with certain kinds of people is much more loving than it initially appears.

The kinds of responses just described could, in some cases, take the form of a theodicy or defense aimed at identifying particular goods for the sake of which divine hiddenness occurs. But this will not be my approach. As I shall explain more fully in Chapter 5, I doubt that human beings are able to identify the goods for the sake of which God causes or permits the most puzzling cases of divine hiddenness. Instead, my focus will, in general, be on identifying ways in which God is reaching out in love to and facilitating relationships with various different kinds of people. Doing this will not, of course, address every possible counter-analogy that might be raised to salience by the many and various ways in which God's behavior violates human expectations. But it will directly address some of the most important ones, it will point the way toward addressing others, and it will help to cultivate both skepticism toward the idea that divine love is properly understood through some negatively valenced analogy, and greater openness to the idea that a more expansive understanding of God and God's purposes would ultimately vindicate the positive analogies prevalent in the Christian tradition.

Like most people working on the hiddenness problem, I take it that *access to presence* is an important feature of loving relationships. It is deeply desirable, and naturally expected from those who claim to love us; so it is hard to see how God's behavior could bear even analogical resemblance to excellent kinds of human love if experience of God's presence were wholly inaccessible, or absurdly difficult to access even for those who are open to it. Accordingly, in Chapters 6 and 7, I explore the metaphysics of divine presence with an eye to showing that experiential access to God's presence is more widely available than many suppose it to be, more similar even to the most dramatic biblical experiences of God than many suppose it to be, and more similar to our ordinary experiences of other human persons than many suppose it to be. Moreover, I argue that, in light of this, anyone who has the concept of God and whose relationship with God is not obstructed by intense conflict is able to participate in a positively meaningful relationship with God.

In Chapter 8, I turn my attention to those whose relationships with God *are* obstructed by some intense form of conflict, broadly construed—fear, significant doubt or distrust, anger, resentment, the perception of abuse or neglect or manipulation, and so on. For such people, negatively valenced love analogies, narratives according to which God's behavior is cruel or abusive, and the like become highly salient. The reason—or one very important reason—is that, whatever else God might be thought to be doing for such people, to the extent that their grievances against God persist unaddressed, it is hard to see how God is providing a way forward for them to continue to participate in their relationship with God in a positively meaning-ful way. My goal in Chapter 8 will be to cast doubt on the idea that God is doing *nothing* for such people, and to explain how attention to biblical revelation actually facilitates narratives according to which God *is* providing them with a path forward.

The final source of counter-analogies that I will consider comes from the case of people who lack even the concept of God, or people who have the concept of God but are incapable for one reason or another of taking a positive attitude toward the idea that God exists (much less desires a relationship with them). Here the important question will be whether such people are, so long as they remain in their condition, entirely cut off from participating in a positively meaningful relationship with God. If they are, it is very hard to see how divine love could plausibly be understood by way of analogy with the best human loves. This is the issue that will occupy Chapter 9.

2

The Problem of Divine Hiddenness

The task for this chapter is to articulate the problem of divine hiddenness, the family of challenges to traditional Christian belief to which I respond in this book. I will begin in the first section by explaining in more careful detail the meaning of the term "divine hiddenness." Then, in subsequent sections, I will present the hiddenness problem and discuss its relationship to the problem of evil.

1.

When theologians talk about divine hiddenness, most often what they have in mind is the attribute of transcendence, or incomprehensibility—the "darkness" of God.[1] On this construal, hiddenness is intrinsic to God. It is not a fact about how God is or is not known or experienced. It is not a fact about the available evidence for God's existence or attributes. It is not even the fact that God transcends creaturely concepts and categories. It is whatever intrinsic attribute of God partly explains or grounds, from God's side of the relationship, such facts and makes God, in relevant respects, inaccessible to creaturely cognition.

This concept of divine hiddenness can be found in many theological works. In Karl Barth's *Church Dogmatics*, to take just one famous example, it, or something quite like it, is laid out in explicit

---

[1] On divine darkness, see, e.g., Turner 1998.

detail. Toward the beginning of a chapter section entitled "The Hiddenness of God," Barth writes:

> God's hiddenness is not the content of a last word of human self-knowledge; it is not the object of a last performance of human capacity; it is the first word of the knowledge of God instituted by God himself... When we say that God is hidden, we are not speaking of ourselves, but, taught by God's revelation alone, of God.   (1957: 183)

Later, he goes on to say that:

> [t]he hiddenness of God is the inconceivability of the Father, the Son, and the Holy Spirit; of the one true God, our Creator, Reconciler, and Redeemer, who as such is known only to Himself and is therefore viewable and conceivable only to Himself and alone capable of speaking of Himself aright.   (1957: 197)

I take it that Barth's view here is not that God's hiddenness consists in the *fact* that God is inconceivable; rather it consists in what might be called God's *intrinsic* or *essential inconceivability*—in other words, the intrinsic attribute of God that partly explains or grounds, from God's side of the relationship, the fact that human beings must rely on divine revelation in order to have any grasp on the attributes of God. Moreover, as I understand Barth's view, it is not just that God *happens* to be the sort of being whom creatures conceive only with help from divine revelation. Rather, as he sees it, God *cannot* be viewed or conceived by creatures apart from divine revelation.

Construed in this way, divine hiddenness clearly has implications for how God can be known or experienced. The precise nature of these implications will depend upon just how we understand the attribute of transcendence. Barth's own understanding of it is expressed in the claim that God is "known only to Himself," and famously implies the impossibility of natural theology; but one might just as well adopt an understanding of divine transcendence that is somewhat more friendly to the enterprise of natural theology. So I don't mean to suggest that the notion of divine hiddenness as it commonly appears in theological writing is associated with Barth's or any other *particular understanding* of the attribute of transcendence, but rather simply that it tends to express that attribute, whatever it might be.

How exactly should we understand the attribute of transcendence? That is a topic I leave for Chapters 3 and 4. For now, suffice it to say that, although I will not use the term "divine hiddenness" as a synonym for "divine transcendence," a proper appreciation of the place of divine transcendence both historically within the Christian tradition, as well as in contemporary theology and spirituality, will be a vital component in my overall response to the challenges posed by divine hiddenness.

In contrast to the usual theological understanding of divine hiddenness, the characterizations that contemporary philosophers (and some biblical scholars) tend to work with primarily concern this-worldly facts about the occurrence of certain kinds of nonbelief in God, the apparently limited strength and distribution of evidence for God's existence, the limited availability of certain kinds of experiences of God (e.g., experiences of God's love or presence), and the like. These are the kinds of facts that tend to figure centrally in different versions of the problem of divine hiddenness, initial contemporary formulations of which are to be found in the works cited earlier by Milazzo (1991), Morris (1988), and Schellenberg (1993).

The characterizations offered by Morris and Schellenberg focus on what I will call the *doxastic* (belief-oriented) aspect of God's hiddenness. Morris's characterization is primarily concerned with our general evidential circumstances. For him, divine hiddenness consists in the fact that we live in a "religiously ambiguous environment," a world in which God's existence and concern for humanity are left unclear, God's presence is not readily accessible, and many people remain (at least) in doubt about God's existence.[2] Schellenberg's earliest characterization of divine hiddenness is similar. In *Divine Hiddenness and Human Reason*, he notes that the term is ambiguous and says that the sense most pertinent to the problem he wants to discuss is one having to do with the "obscurity of God's existence."[3] This way of putting it resembles Morris's talk of "religious ambiguity," and suggests that divine hiddenness is primarily a fact about the evidence for God's existence.

---

[2] Morris 1988: 6–8.
[3] Schellenberg 1993: 4. He notes that the term also might refer to divine incomprehensibility, or to human inability to detect God's pattern of working in the world. Furthermore, he goes on a bit later to say that perhaps the most natural understanding of "God is hidden" is one according to which it refers to God's deliberate activity in causing or allowing us to be in the evidential circumstances in which we find ourselves. In light of this, and because the problem he is interested in is focused on the implications for theistic belief of the occurrence of certain kinds of nonbelief, he initially resisted characterizing his problem as a problem *of divine hiddenness*, or as an argument *from divine hiddenness* (1993: 5–6; and see also 2015b: 15–16).

In his more recent work, however, Schellenberg indicates that the term, in the sense most pertinent to his argument, refers simply to the fact that the world includes certain kinds of nonbelief in God.[4] This is a sensible shift, since he has always formulated the *problem* of divine hiddenness by way of premises that reference the occurrence of nonbelief rather than specific facts about the evidence for God's existence. In *Divine Hiddenness and Human Reason*, and in much subsequent work on the topic, the salient kind of nonbelief was *reasonable*, or *inculpable* nonbelief.[5] In more recent work, the focus has moved to *nonresistant* nonbelief.[6]

In light of the characterizations offered by Morris and Schellenberg, I propose to capture the doxastic aspect of divine hiddenness with the following three theses:

INCONCLUSIVE EVIDENCE.   For some people, whatever evidence they possess in support of the existence of God is inconclusive in the following sense: even if they happen to see that this evidence at least weakly supports belief in God, it is not strong enough in relation to the rest of their evidence and background beliefs (however those might have been acquired) to produce in them rational belief in God.

REASONABLE NONBELIEF.   Some people inculpably fail to believe in God.

NONRESISTANT NONBELIEF.   Some people nonresistantly fail to believe in God.

INCONCLUSIVE EVIDENCE is the understanding of divine hiddenness suggested by Morris's talk of "religious ambiguity" and Schellenberg's

---

[4] Schellenberg 2015b: 14–18, esp. p. 17.

[5] In Schellenberg 1993, "reasonable nonbelief" and "inculpable nonbelief" are equivalent by stipulation; and he sometimes seems to assume that these are also equivalent to "nonresistant" nonbelief (1993: 31, 38). Under ordinary understandings of these terms, of course, they are not equivalent. For example, someone who is mentally ill might *inculpably* believe that she is Joan of Arc, or that her head is made of glass; but these beliefs will not be *reasonable*. Likewise, she might resist belief in God because she thinks (incoherently) that it is her supreme moral duty to resist having any theological beliefs whatsoever; but, obviously, she will not be culpable in this case for her nonbelief.

[6] In *The Hiddenness Argument: Philosophy's New Challenge to Belief in God*, Schellenberg writes: "I now see [the] focus on culpability and inculpability as a mistake" (2015b: 55).

talk of "obscurity."[7] The two NONBELIEF theses affirm the existence of the two kinds of nonbelief asserted by Schellenberg's various formulations of the hiddenness argument over the years. I do not, of course, suppose that these are the only three claims that might plausibly be taken to be part of the doxastic aspect of God's hiddenness;[8] but I think that the conjunction of these three will capture it sufficiently for the purposes of this book.

INCONCLUSIVE EVIDENCE is fairly uncontroversial. I find it plausible, and so I am happy to concede its truth, at least for the sake of argument. The two NONBELIEF theses, by contrast, are very controversial. I do not myself endorse them;[9] but I have no argument to offer

---

[7] See also McKim 1990 and 2001.

[8] For example, one might wish to include some thesis about the demographics of theism—the "geographic patchiness" of belief in God, as Stephen Maitzen (2006: 183) calls it—or about what Jason Marsh (2013) terms "natural nonbelief" in God. For my part, I would *not* want to include such theses, because I think that they assert more than just the hiddenness of God, and raise problems that are interestingly related to but not mere variations on the problem of divine hiddenness. But I see no reason to insist on or try to defend this view here.

[9] Schellenberg (2007: 206, n. 13) says that, in light of his arguments, "it would take something like willful blindness to fail to affirm that not all nonbelief is the product of willful blindness." This may be right if "willful blindness" (as a source of resistance to belief in God) is understood to be *conscious, deliberate* rejection of belief in God, conceived of under the familiar theistic concept of God. But there are other forms of resistance—and even of self-deceptive resistance, which is another concept Schellenberg sometimes invokes—to relationship with God besides willful blindness. In light of this, although I would accept NONRESISTANT NONBELIEF under an interpretation that simply equates nonresistance with lack of willful blindness, I am not inclined to accept it when the interpretation of 'nonresistant' is left wide open. In any case, my arguments in this book will not depend on any particular interpretation of "nonresistant" (especially since I will simply concede the truth of both REASONABLE NONBELIEF and NONRESISTANT NONBELIEF), but I did want to be clearer about the conditions under which I am not inclined to endorse these claims.

As to *why* I do not endorse them: the reason is simply that, Schellenberg's arguments on their behalf notwithstanding (cf. Schellenberg 2004: 200–3, 206–11; 2007: 205–6, ch. 10; 2015b: ch. 6), they seem to me to be theses for which nobody could have very good evidence. It would be too much of a digression to try to rebut Schellenberg's arguments in detail; but just think of what it would take to have good evidence—evidence sufficient to produce warranted belief—for the conclusion that someone's failure to believe in God is *nonresistant* (never mind inculpable). Among other things, you would have to be able to acquire good evidence for the conclusion that resistance to belief in God, bias against relationship with God, and the like have in no way colored her attention to or assessment of the available evidence for God's existence. We have such limited access to the minds of others that it is hard even to imagine how one might acquire good evidence for such claims. Even if the person has never entertained the concept of God, she might, for all you could tell, have self-induced, even self-deceptive, biases against relationship with a deity—*any* deity.

against them. So I concede their truth, too, for the sake of argument (and, accordingly, I will sometimes talk as if I endorse them).

But the doxastic aspect of divine hiddenness includes only part of the total body of phenomena grouped under the label "divine hiddenness." There is also an experiential aspect, which includes both the felt absence of God and related experiences that believers might describe as *the withdrawal of God's presence* or *the hiding of God's face*. These, too, are important sources of doubt and disbelief, and they generate problems even for believers who are untroubled by the doxastic aspect of divine hiddenness.[10]

St. Teresa of Calcutta, for example, struggled with divine hiddenness; but the greater part of her struggle seems not to have been oriented as much around her general evidential situation as around the ongoing felt absence of God's presence.[11] Some might be tempted

---

For all you could tell, such biases might also color her attention to and assessment of evidence that would otherwise point her toward the existence of God. So how could you ever be in a position to say whether someone else's failure to embrace theism is wholly free from influence by such biases? Perhaps we are each initially entitled to believe *of ourselves* that our assessment of the evidence for or against any given claim (theism included) is free from bias. But this entitlement seems to be undercut by a proper appreciation both of the tremendous existential import of believing or failing to believe in God and of ordinary human capacities for and dispositions toward self-deception and other bias-infected belief-forming practices. (Then again, the idea that we would be unreliable detectors of our own implicit biases is not uncontroversial. For discussion of this and related issues, see Brownstein 2016 and references therein.).

[10] This is not, of course, to suggest that the doxastic aspect of divine hiddenness generates no problems for believers. It does—not only because it gives rise to a well-known argument for atheism, but also because it raises some of the same existential concerns about divine love that are raised by the experiential aspect. (Cf. the introductory chapter of Howard-Snyder and Moser 2002.)

[11] In describing her struggles, Brian Koldiejchuk notes that, although "she no longer felt Jesus' presence," she also:

knew that her perception of her spiritual state with all its darkness was not the whole picture. She could catch a glimpse of her love for God: it was becoming more real, and "most strange tokens of love" arose spontaneously into her consciousness. And while she felt "as if" God was not caring for her, she knew she was "a child of his Love." (Teresa 2007: 213)

He also reports that, although she did not have "the sense of believing," she:

did have faith, a biblical faith, a blind faith, a faith that had been tried and tested in the furnace of suffering, and that traced the path to Him through darkness. Undeterred by feelings, she continued living by the faith she felt as lost.
(Teresa 2007: 239)

Note, too, that "having faith" contrasts here with lack of belief (insofar as lacking "the sense of believing" is taken to be evidence, in St. Teresa's mind, of lacking faith).

to say that her struggle with divine hiddenness posed a problem that was fundamentally existential, or pastoral, rather than theoretical. But it is easy enough also to identify a theoretical problem—one expressible in the question, "If God loved her, then why did God let her experience so much suffering and doubt as a result of her longing for some experience of God's love or comforting presence?"

Milazzo's understanding of divine hiddenness focuses on what I am calling its experiential aspect. For him, talk of divine hiddenness—or divine silence, divine absence, or divine darkness— seems primarily to refer to the experiential unavailability of God's *presence*, particularly in the midst of suffering. So, for example, at the end of a section discussing divine hiddenness in the Old Testament and the Hebrew verb used to express the concept, he sums up by saying:

> God is hidden because God has willfully turned away, intentionally concealed itself and turned its back. YHWH has purposefully withdrawn into the darkness, covered its face, and chosen to isolate itself from Israel. (1991: 35)

He goes on to associate the notion of God "hiding its face" with the withdrawal or concealment of divine presence;[12] and he expresses the problem posed by this aspect of divine hiddenness forcefully as follows:

> The God that chooses to be silent in the presence of suffering and death is a God whose face is darkened by our agony and whose hands are covered with our blood. If the face of God is darkened by our suffering, a God whose reason and purpose is unknown to us, the faithful cannot but protest God's injustice, hiddenness, and absence. Yet inasmuch as this lament is a protest against God's silence, it is also a call to God to come out of the darkness that God might absolve itself of complicity in our suffering and tragedy. ...Either God is not there, and God's hiddenness is really absence, or the God who is there is a cruel, angry, brutal God that seems to relish human suffering. Either God is absent, or God is implicated in, if not responsible for our death. (1991: 44–5)

The problem expressed here is similar to the one Schellenberg raises; but, importantly, this one would remain even if inculpable and nonresistant nonbelief were eliminated from the world.

---

[12] Cf. Milazzo 1991: 35ff.

I propose to capture the experiential aspect of divine hiddenness by way of the following thesis, whose truth I not only concede but positively affirm:

LIMITED RELIGIOUS EXPERIENCE.   Some people have strong but persistently unfulfilled desires to have experiences that seem clearly to them to be experiences of the love or presence of God as such.

In affirming LIMITED RELIGIOUS EXPERIENCE, I do not mean to deny that many people have—and have with some frequency—experiences that they would describe as experiences of the love and presence of God. Reports of vivid, intense experiences of God's presence—visions, voices, "ecstasies," and the like—are common in the writings of the medieval mystics, for example; and many of those writings seem to presuppose that the having of such experiences is quite common and familiar in monastic circles. There are numerous contemporary reports of such experiences as well. They are, for example, reportedly widespread among contemporary American evangelicals, and they are also commonly reported within various kinds of religious populations (Christian and not) in such places as India, Africa, and Latin America.[13] But many people never have such experiences, and even those who sometimes do have them often also find themselves bereft of them in ways that cause serious doubt or spiritual turmoil. Although the literature on divine hiddenness has tended to focus on the problems raised by the doxastic aspect of God's hiddenness, it seems to me that the theological problems posed by the experiential aspect are relevantly similar, and no less severe.[14]

2.

Having now characterized divine hiddenness in some detail, let me turn in this section and the next to the business of formulating the problem it raises.

---

[13] Cf. Luhrmann 2012: esp. chs. 1, 2, 7, and 8.

[14] Although Schellenberg's focus over the years has been on the challenge to theistic belief generated by the existence of a certain kind of nonbelief, he does not disagree with this point (personal correspondence), and has himself made a very similar claim (2002: 34–5).

The initial formulations of the problem presented by Morris, Milazzo, and Schellenberg are all quite similar. All three present divine hiddenness as standing in tension with divine love; all three present arguments that purport to show that the existence of a perfectly loving God is incompatible with some kind of divine hiddenness that manifestly exists in our world.[15] The main differences concern the particular kind of divine hiddenness that is in view, and the level of rigor and detail with which the argument is presented and defended. Schellenberg's argument, as I have said, is the version that has come to dominate the literature; and—especially if one takes account not only of the presentation in *Divine Hiddenness and Human Reason* but also of Schellenberg's copious subsequent work on the topic—it is by far the most rigorously formulated and carefully explored version as well.[16] Accordingly, that is the one I shall take as my starting point.[17]

As I have already indicated, what we might call "the Schellenberg problem" takes the form of an argument for the conclusion that God does not exist. In his most recent book, *The Hiddenness Argument: Philosophy's New Challenge to Belief in God*, Schellenberg formulates the argument as follows:[18]

> S1. If a perfectly loving God exists, then there exists a God who is always open to a personal relationship with any finite person.

---

[15] However, interestingly, in *Divine Hiddenness and Human Reason*, Schellenberg emphasizes that his *goal* in presenting the hiddenness argument is not to defend atheism, but rather simply to identify an argument for atheism that may or may not be outweighed or defeated by later, pro-theistic arguments (1993: 12).

[16] In his most recent book on the topic, Schellenberg says that, although "[t]he idea that weak evidence for the existence of God or the presence of nonbelief might count against the truth of theism does appear here and there in the history of philosophy—though quite rarely... it took until 1993 [with the publication of his own work] for it to be fully developed into an explicit argument against the existence of God" (2015b: 23). I think that this, like other similar statements throughout the book, underappreciates the contributions of Schellenberg's "precursors" to the problem of divine hiddenness; but he is certainly correct that nobody writing on the topic prior to him had developed and defended the argument in the sort of careful and extensive detail that he did in *Divine Hiddenness and Human Reason*.

[17] For Morris's statement of the problem, see Morris 1988: 6; for Milazzo's, see his 1991: 53.

[18] Schellenberg has expressed the argument in several slightly different ways over the years. The version presented here, from Schellenberg 2015b: 103, is a simplification of the version that appears in his 2015a.

S2. If there exists a God who is always open to a personal relationship with any finite person, then no finite person is ever nonresistantly in a state of nonbelief in relation to the proposition that God exists.

S3. If a perfectly loving God exists, then no finite person is ever non-resistantly in a state of nonbelief in relation to the proposition that God exists (from S1 and S2).

S4. Some finite persons are or have been nonresistantly in a state of nonbelief in relation to the proposition that God exists.

S5. No perfectly loving God exists (from S3 and S4).

S6. If no perfectly loving God exists, then God does not exist.

S7. God does not exist (from S5 and S6).

This formulation of the argument differs in some ways from his original formulation in *Divine Hiddenness and Human Reason*. But, so far as I am concerned, the differences are unimportant—my replies to all versions of it will be substantially the same. Note that the aspect of divine hiddenness that is pertinent for this argument is the doxastic aspect, as captured by NONRESISTANT NONBELIEF.

Schellenberg characterizes his argument as an argument "from above" (2015b: 37), one that starts not from facts about the empirical world and their evidential bearing on the existence of God but rather from non-empirical, rationally discoverable truths about the concepts involved in the argument. The most important of these are the concepts of *God, perfect love,* and *openness to personal relationship.* Accordingly, we might expect that an examination of these concepts would shed light on both the strength and the scope of the Schellenberg problem.

Let us start by asking whose god, exactly, is in view in Schellenberg's argument. In earlier work, his answer to this question is quite explicit: the argument targets belief in "the personal God of traditional the-ism." (2005a: 209) But what god is that? Theism itself is not a religious tradition in its own right; and the various religions that are paradig-matically theistic—Judaism, Christianity, Islam, and a few of their offshoots—embrace very different conceptions of God, very different views about how God is to be worshiped, and very different views on a wide range of other theological topics.

Granted, all three of these religious traditions share *some* common views about God. Indeed, they have traditionally overlapped on a small family of theological claims that together comprise the philosophical–theological position known as *classical theism*. Classical theism, notoriously, is largely the product of philosophical reflection on the concept of *perfect being*; but a survey of the tradition makes it clear that there is no uniform commitment on the part of classical theists to theses about divine love and personality that are robust enough to support Schellenberg's argument.

In his more recent work, Schellenberg is clear that the concept of God in play in his argument is not so much one that is tethered to the scriptures or traditions of the great theistic religions, but rather one that arises simply out of philosophical reflection on the concept of a *perfectly loving person*.[19] It is certainly tempting to think that this is a good concept of God to work with if your ultimate goal is to provide a philosophical argument against belief in the personal God of Judaism, Christianity, and Islam; and most philosophers working on the hiddenness problem have been happy to concede as much. By contrast, my own view, which I will defend over the course of Chapters 3–5, is that, insofar as the argument relies on this concept of God, it actually *fails* to target belief in the Christian God.[20]

But first we need to understand what is centrally involved in Schellenberg's idea of a perfectly loving person, and in his concept of a personal relationship with God. We can begin to shed some light on these things by examining his understanding and defense of what he calls the "main premise," i.e., S1, the thesis that if a perfectly loving God exists, then there exists a God who is always open to a personal relationship with any finite person.

Let us start by unpacking the idea of *openness to personal relationship*. For Schellenberg, a personal relationship with God is to be understood as an *explicit* (or *conscious*), *reciprocally interactive*, and *positively meaningful* relationship.[21] A conscious relationship, according to Schellenberg, is "a relationship one recognizes oneself to be in."[22] It is clear enough independently of Schellenberg's discussion what it is

---

[19] Cf. Schellenberg 2015b: 18–22, 88–101.

[20] I do not, of course, mean to deny that the Christian God is a perfectly loving person. Rather, the point is that, as I see it, the Christian God does not conform to any concept that arises out of *mere philosophical reflection* (unaided by divine revelation) on the concept of a perfectly loving person.

[21] See Schellenberg 1993: 18ff.; 2005: 202, 208; and 2015b: 38. In earlier work he tends to use the term "explicit" rather than "conscious" in his characterization of personal relationship with God. His more recent work uses the term "conscious." It does not seem to me that much hangs on the difference, so hereafter I will simply use the term "conscious."

[22] Schellenberg 2015a: 23. See also 2015b: 59.

for a relationship to be (reciprocally) interactive; but over the years Schellenberg has brought further clarity by way of illustrative examples. On God's side, such a relationship with a human being might involve giving guidance, support, forgiveness, and consolation; on the human side, it might involve acts of worship, obedience, gratitude, and trust. The relationship counts as interactive at least in part because what God gives in the relationship is relevantly connected to what the human being gives, and vice versa.[23]

On the meaning of *openness* to relationship, Schellenberg has this to say:

> [Openness at a certain time] means *not through one's own actions or omissions making it impossible* for the other whom one loves to partici-pate in personal relationship with one at that time should the other wish to do so. Alternatively, and applying this now to God, it means that it will be *possible* for creatures who haven't made it impossible themselves through their own God-obscuring resistance to the divine, to participate in relationship with God; if they want to, they will be able to do so simply by *trying* to do so (notice that this doesn't mean that trying will be easy: perhaps what one would need to do to further a meaningful relationship with God would often be difficult).
>
> (2015b: 41, emphasis in original)

If God is truly *always* open to personal relationships in the way just described, nonresistant nonbelief should never occur, and every non-resistant person should *always* be in a position to participate in a personal relationship with God just by trying. This gives us S2.

But why think that S1 is true? Why think that a perfectly loving being would *always* be open to relationship with every finite creature? Schellenberg has sometimes defended claims relevantly similar to S1 by appeal to the fact that participating in a personal relationship with God would greatly benefit human beings,[24] or by way of analogies with the best forms of human love (of which *parental* love is a paradigmatic instance), all of which are typically understood to include a strong disposition to seek ongoing personal relationship with one's beloved.[25] He has also argued that a perfectly loving being

---

[23] Schellenberg 1993: 18–21; 2002: 41–2.

[24] Schellenberg 1993: 18–21. He emphasizes, however, that it is *not* his view that a loving God would seek, or be always open to, relationship *mainly* or *only* because it benefits us. (Cf. 1993: 21–2; 2005: 207, 210; 2015b: 43.)

[25] See, e.g., Schellenberg 2002: 43; 2003: 32–5; 2015b: 41–2.

would value personal relationships for their own sake, would desire "to come close, allowing [her beloved] explicitly to share in her life," and would love created persons "fully" and in an "unlimited and unsurpassable" way; and, moreover, God would have no limits in resources or power that would force corresponding limits upon God's capacity for openness.[26] His most recent defense, however, and the one that he has seemed to prefer for over a decade now, is to say that S1 (or something very much like it) is simply a self-evident conceptual truth.[27] "Love is deeply relational," he says; in light of this, "[s]uch minimal openness as we've identified seems self-evidently to belong to divine love."[28]

3.

So much, then, for the Schellenberg problem. That is certainly *a* problem of divine hiddenness; but it does not all by itself deserve to be called *the* problem of divine hiddenness. The reason is that the Schellenberg problem is driven by just one aspect of the phenomenon of divine hiddenness (the truth of NONRESISTANT NONBELIEF) and it emphasizes just one way in which NONRESISTANT NONBELIEF is problematic—namely, it seems to constitute evidence against the existence of God. But there is more to divine hiddenness than NON-RESISTANT NONBELIEF, and more ways in which God's hiddenness raises theological problems.

The problem of divine hiddenness, like the problem of evil, is fundamentally a problem of violated expectations. We expect certain things of God in light of what we know about God and in light of a wide range of background assumptions about the world—about the nature of love and goodness, various human needs and the ways in which they can normally be met in a world like ours, and so on. But God does not deliver on our expectations; so, we are conflicted: Is something wrong with our expectations? Is God not as we thought? Does God not exist? As with the problem of evil, different *versions* of the problem can be formulated by replacing one problematic

---

[26] Cf. Schellenberg 1993: 21–2; 2015b: 41, 43, 45–6.
[27] Cf. e.g., Schellenberg 2005a: 207, 212–13 and 2015b: 41.
[28] Schellenberg 2015b: 41.

phenomenon with another, and by bringing out the conflict with our expectations in different ways.

In the case of the problem of evil, some versions take *evil in general* as the problematic phenomenon; others focus on *gratuitous suffering*, or *horrendous evil*, or some other more specific kind of evil. Some aim to show that the problematic phenomenon is *inconsistent* with the existence of a perfectly powerful, knowledgeable, and good God; others aim to show that it renders improbable the claim that God is perfectly loving, or perfectly good; others have different aims. The arguments reach different conclusions; they differ in logical form; and what counts as a reply to one of the arguments won't necessarily carry over as a reply to the others.[29] But they all count as versions of *the problem of evil* because they all focus on facts about the world that are supposed to be instances *of evil*, and each treats evil *as such* somehow as evidence against important beliefs about the existence, nature, and attributes of God. So far as I can tell, these are the *only* interesting features that the different versions of the problem of evil share in common; and it seems to me that any problem or argument that shared those features would likewise plausibly be construed as a further version of the problem of evil.

Similarly, then, any argument or problem wherein some aspect of divine hiddenness is treated as evidence against the existence of God or against important beliefs about the nature and attributes of God will count as a version of the problem of divine hiddenness. The Schellenberg problem is one version; but we can easily construct another version that focuses on LIMITED RELIGIOUS EXPERIENCE (for example) rather than NONRESISTANT NONBELIEF. Or we might pose the truth of NONRESISTANT NONBELIEF, LIMITED RELIGIOUS EXPERIENCE, or some other hiddenness thesis not as evidence against the *existence of God* but rather as evidence against a particular traditional conception of divine love or divine goodness or divine power or some other attribute. These variations are not trivial; they represent differences in what, if anything, the various aspects of the phenomenon of divine hiddenness tell us about the existence *and* nature of God. *The* problem of divine hiddenness seems really to be a family of sub-problems, all of which trade on apparent tensions between traditional theological doctrines and the phenomenon of divine hiddenness.

---

[29] For concrete examples, just compare, for starters, the formulations offered in Draper 2008 and Draper and Dougherty 2013: 71–2.

Is the hiddenness problem itself a version of the problem of evil? Many have said that it is; some say that it is not.[30] By the standards articulated here, the problems overlap just to the extent that divine hiddenness is plausibly construed on its own as an instance of evil. Whether it is or not will depend partly on what sort of divine hiddenness is in view, and partly on what other assumptions are taken as background. Is it necessarily a bad thing to have one's strong desires for religious experience go persistently unfulfilled? Is it necessarily a bad thing to lack belief in God—even if, say, God were to make it possible to have a relationship with God in the absence of such beliefs? To the extent that these and similar questions are to be answered negatively, the problems of evil and divine hiddenness come apart; to the extent that they are to be answered affirmatively, the problems start to converge.

One might wonder why, if divine hiddenness is *not* an instance of evil, it still would count as evidence against the love and goodness of God. But it should be easy to see that a phenomenon need not be bad in itself in order to count against the love or goodness of someone. If all of your friends belong to a single race or gender, that might—in a certain context—constitute evidence of sexism or racism on your part, and this even though it is not intrinsically bad for all of one's friends to belong to a single race or gender. If you are discovered to own two cell phones, that might, in a certain context, constitute evidence of your marital infidelity (as it did, misleadingly, in an early episode of *Breaking Bad*), and this despite the fact that there is nothing intrinsically bad about owning two cell phones.

4.

My initial solution to the two versions of the problem of divine hiddenness that I have explicitly identified here—the first part of what, in Chapter 1, I called the "first step"—is to contest the "violated expectation" claims, the claims asserting that if a perfectly loving God

---

[30] Those who say that it is include Kvanvig (2002), Schellenberg (1993: 6–9), and Swinburne (2004: 267–72). Those who say that it isn't include Dougherty (2016), Dougherty and Parker (2015), Schellenberg (2010 and 2015b), and van Inwagen (2002).

exists then NONRESISTANT NONBELIEF or LIMITED RELIGIOUS EXPERIENCE is false. I imagine I would solve other versions in much the same way. I contest these violated expectation premises because I think that a proper appreciation of divine transcendence undercuts whatever reasons we might have for affirming them. Chapters 3 and 4 are devoted to explaining why this is so.

3

God and the Attributes

Biblical texts employ a wide range of images to teach us about God. God is our shepherd and counselor; a mighty man of war who piles the waters with a blast from his nostrils; the owner of a still, small voice; Israel's king, bridegroom, and betrayed lover; a consuming fire. God appears as a lone anonymous wrestler, and a trio of afternoon visitors; he is the Ancient of Days, riding the fiery chariot throne on the clouds of heaven. He calls from a burning bush, interrogates from a whirlwind, and thunders his paternal love from the clouds as a dove descends upon the Jordan. She is the maternal comforter of Jerusalem, and a bear robbed of her cubs, threatening to tear Israel apart. He is the stern employer of the parable of the talents, a hard man who reaps where he has not sown and who punishes his steward for failing to invest wisely, and the generous employer who pays even latecomers a full day's wage. He is the betrayed vineyard owner who sends his only son to make peace with and ultimately die at the hands of disloyal fieldworkers. But above all in the Christian tradition, the one who is imaged in all of these various ways is our heavenly Father, one who loves his children with the reckless abandon of a patriarch who would be so undignified as to *run* to greet a wastrel son upon his return, and to kill the fatted calf in celebration.

The image of God as father looms large in the Christian tradition. The image of God—and especially of Jesus—as *mother* also has a remarkably important place.[1] Within a large segment of contemporary Christendom, God has been increasingly portrayed as, in effect, a doting suburban helicopter parent whose entire day is structured around the interests and needs of his or her child. "If God had a

---

[1] See, e.g., Bynum 1982, ch. 4 for some details.

refrigerator," writes bestselling author Max Lucado, "your picture would be on it. If he had a wallet, your photo would be in it."[2]

It is hardly surprising, then, that believers whose theology is driven by parental imagery would find the hiddenness of God deeply puzzling. As we saw in Chapter 2, the problem of divine hiddenness trades on violated expectations; and nothing short of outright abuse violates our parental expectations more than persistent hiddenness even in the face of desperate longing. What loving father would intentionally leave his children wallowing in a state of doubt and uncertainty as to his love or his very existence? What loving mother would withhold comfort from children who are suffering, and assurance of love from children who sorely need it? Loving parents *tell* their children— repeatedly—that they love them. They don't leave them to infer it from the presence and orderly arrangement of toys in the basement.

Parental imagery is not essential to generating the hiddenness problem. Thinking of God as a concerned monarch or as some other kind of benefactor might equally lead one to cry out in anguish or protest over perceived divine absence.[3] What is most salient is the simple fact that God is supposed to be perfectly loving. When we imagine divine love on analogy with the best, most noble kinds of human love and concern we can easily find ourselves arriving at expectations for divine behavior that are persistently violated.

But why take the expectations seriously? Why think that we know what divine love *ought* to look like? Here is one answer—an answer that many philosophers and theologians will find congenial.[4] We know from scripture and tradition that God is *loving*, *good*, and *perfect*.[5] We also know a lot about the nature of parental love and

---

[2] Lucado 1995: 122, quoted in Brenneman 2016: 617.

[3] Cf. Burnett 2010: 14–26.

[4] Something like this answer described in the remainder of this paragraph (minus the appeal to the authority of scripture and tradition, of course) also seems to underlie the expectations that drive the Schellenberg problem, and particularly Schellenberg's defense of S1 (see Chapter 2, pp. 23–5).

[5] For scriptural declarations of the goodness, love, and perfection of God, we might look to Psalm 25:8, Psalm 103, Mark 10:18, Matthew 5:48, and 1 John 4:8–12. Admittedly, these and other texts notwithstanding, plenty of scholars have denied that the Bible on the whole depicts God as loving, good, and perfect. But that is neither here nor there for the present point, which is just that many philosophers and theologians will agree that, in these and other texts, scripture speaks in favor of the perfection, love, and goodness of God. Traditional declarations of these attributes can be found in many of the major symbols and confessions of the various denominations of Christianity (see, e.g., the *Catechism of the Catholic Church*, Prologue and part

other kinds of human love—if not enough for a full-blown conceptual analysis, then at least enough to be able to identify some necessary conditions on certain kinds of human love, and on love in general. From these bits of knowledge, we are therefore also able to identify necessary conditions on divine love—which conditions, in turn, comprise some of the most important expectations that fuel the problem of divine hiddenness.

Congenial though it may be, this answer to the "How do we know?" question embodies a concept of God and an approach to theology both of which deserve close scrutiny. The concept is one version of the familiar *theistic* concept of God—God understood as a perfect being—that is central to Judaism, Christianity, and Islam. The methodology is continuous with the method of analytic theology, which relies heavily on rational intuition and conceptual analysis as sources of evidence for theological claims.[6] But it is hardly inevitable that analytic theological development of a theistic concept of God should deliver expectations that generate the problem of divine hiddenness. The problem arises out of a union of concept and method that involves assumptions extraneous to both—assumptions that, as we shall see, are both optional and at odds with important strands of the Christian tradition.

"Theism" is a technical term in contemporary philosophical theology that typically refers to at least one of the following views: (i) that God exists; (ii) that there exists a *perfect being*, who is (among other things) omnipotent, omniscient, and omnibenevolent; or (iii) that there exists a *greatest possible being*—one who is unsurpassable in knowledge, power, goodness, love, and other salient "great-making" features. For purposes here, I will identify theism with the third of these views, and I will assume without argument that it implies each of the first two.[7] It is commonly held that, whatever their other differences might be, Christianity, Judaism, and Islam are all theistic religions; and it is likewise commonly held that the God whose existence is implied by theism is identical to the God who figures

---

1.2.1; the *Westminster Confession of Faith*, ch. 2; the *Belgic Confession*, articles 1 and 20; and the *Augsburg Confession*, article 1), as well as in many of the most important theological works produced over the past two millennia.

[6] On analytic theology, cf. Crisp and Rea 2009 and McCall 2015.

[7] I will also assume that "God" is a name rather than a title, and that God exists only if that name, in traditional Christian usage, has a referent.

most centrally in the Hebrew and Christian scriptures. *Classical* theism fleshes out the idea that God is *perfect* with a list of attributes that many now take to be not so much the result of a natural (and suitably historically informed) reading of scripture as of purely philosophical reflection upon the nature of perfection—the method of *perfect being theology.*[8] The concept of God arrived at by this method is sometimes disparagingly referred to as "the God of the philosophers." I prefer Janet Martin Soskice's term, to which the title of this chapter gives a nod: "the God of the attributes."[9]

The God of the hiddenness problem is *most saliently* a perfectly good and loving being. But the God of the attributes is more than just perfectly good and loving. That God is also immutable, impassible, *a se* (or absolutely independent), and transcendent. Why are these latter attributes commonly ignored when it comes to theorizing about the expectations we might reasonably impose on God's manifestation of perfect love? The answer, I suspect, is twofold. First, it is initially very hard to see how to reconcile attributes like immutability, impassibility, and transcendence with the image of God as our loving heavenly parent, or with various other images of God as a lover or benefactor. At any rate, it is hard to see how a God with these other perfections (as they are most commonly understood) could count as personally loving and parental in the *ordinary* sense of those terms.[10] Second, the other perfections are more controversial than the three omni-attributes, partly because of the first reason just mentioned, but also because they are often taken to be less well grounded in scripture.

---

[8] Against the idea that classical theism arises out of a natural and appropriately historically informed reading of scripture, see, for example, the essays in Pinnock et al. 1994.

[9] Soskice 2002: 61. I prefer her term because I think that classical theism is not so much the product of *philosophy* per se as it is the result of an interdisciplinary method that proceeds under the assumption that philosophical theorizing about individual *attributes* is our primary avenue to theological understanding. I am on board with this method insofar as it treats such theorizing about the attributes as *a* route to theological understanding; but, as I hope will become clear over the next few chapters, I would deny that philosophical theorizing about individual attributes should be given pride of place.

[10] Hard, but not necessarily impossible. In my opinion, the most successful contemporary efforts at reconciling classical theism with the claim that God is personally loving and parental in the ordinary senses of these terms are to be found in the work of Eleonore Stump—especially Stump 2012, 2016, and 2018.

Here, then, we have the "extraneous assumptions" underlying our congenial answer to the "How do we know?" question. In determining which attributes are salient to our expectations on divine love, the answer first sets aside certain attributes that have historically had an important place in Christian theology. It then takes for granted a literal, ordinary language understanding of the allegedly salient ones, and arrives at necessary conditions on their manifestation through empirically informed analytic reflection on paradigms (e.g., parental love, romantic love, etc.). My goal in this chapter and Chapter 4 is to call these moves into question.

In the present chapter, I argue that the attribute of transcendence in particular ought also to be considered salient in our theorizing about divine hiddenness; and, after highlighting some of the core ideas underlying the notion of transcendence, I describe a continuum on which characterizations of this puzzling attribute generally fall. In Chapter 4, I make a case for a "mid-range" characterization of transcendence, and I show how attention to this attribute ought to impact our theorizing about divine love, divine parenthood, and, ultimately, divine hiddenness.

1.

Let me begin by talking about the biblical portrayal of God and, more specifically, the portrayal we find in the Old Testament. Perhaps, though, it is better to speak of *portrayals*. There is widespread agreement among biblical scholars that the Old Testament texts suggest multiple, sometimes apparently competing, conceptions of God. Some see this multiplicity as evidence of disagreement among biblical authors as to the nature of God. Others see it as evidence of evolution in Israelite (and maybe pre-Israelite) thinking about God.[11] Still others see it as evidence of nothing more than the fact that God is very difficult to understand, much less to characterize in an accessible way. Perhaps some divine mysteries are best revealed by way of assertions and images that, while ultimately perfectly coherent, inevitably present reflective creaturely minds with intractable theoretical

---

[11] Cf., e.g., Bellah (2011: esp. ch. 5) and Uffenheimer (1986). But there is a real debate to be had here. Kugel, e.g., argues that the different concepts of God found in the Torah can't plausibly be seen as different evolutionary stages because "the sources seem ... to be grouped too closely together [in time]" (2008: 306).

difficulties. One's views about what we should infer from the multiplicity of ideas about God in scripture will obviously depend heavily upon one's beliefs about the nature and goals of divine revelation, and about the extent to which scripture counts as divine revelation.[12] But regardless of what one thinks about these matters, it is hard to deny that the multiplicity is there.

Scholars disagree about the exact number and character of the conceptions of God that can be teased out of the Old Testament texts. These disagreements depend largely on differences of opinion about how to date the biblical texts, about how the texts have or have not influenced one another, and about the extent to which the texts we have are edited compilations of prior source material. Despite these controversies, however, some basic points of general agreement can be identified, and these points are all I will need to move forward with the main argument of this chapter.

Biblical scholars tend to identify at least three different conceptions of God within the Old Testament. First, there is a highly anthropomorphic conception that portrays God in ways suggestive of an extremely powerful human person and emphasizes God's immanence in the world. Second, there is a less anthropomorphic conception that treats God as transcendent rather than immanent, but nonetheless emphasizes God's personhood and God's concern with morality and with being the sole object of Israel's worship. Third, there is an entirely non-anthropomorphic conception that is consistent with divine immanence (e.g., God's presence in the temple) but treats God more as an abstract, impersonal force.[13] The first conception is usually associated with what scholars regard as the earliest biblical texts, most especially those portions of the Torah that are commonly

---

[12] Here then I disagree with Kugel, who says:

accepting the Documentary Hypothesis in any form means retreating substantially from the most basic idea of Scripture itself, that the Bible represents words given by God to man. If God had something to say to different writers in different periods, He ought nonetheless to be basically the same God and say basically the same things: however many "bottles" there were, they ought still to contain the same wine. Then why should he say to one prophet that He is essentially a divine humanoid while saying to another that He is an abstract, distant deity who dwells in heaven?   (2008: 299)

Why indeed? But it follows that God didn't say these things only if they are irreconcilable, which hasn't been shown. Note, too, that the documentary hypothesis itself is no longer the dominant paradigm in pentateuchal studies. For references, see note 14.

[13] Cf. Geller 2000; Kugel 2008: ch. 20; and Uffenheimer 1986.

attributed to the Jahwist and Elohist sources.[14] The second and third conceptions are usually associated with what people take to be later texts—the second with the portions of the Torah commonly attributed to the Deuteronomist source, and also with Second Isaiah; the third with Old Testament wisdom literature and those portions of the Torah commonly attributed to the Priestly source.[15]

These three conceptions are not exactly all on the same footing, however. There is broad agreement that pre-Israelite and perhaps early Israelite religion was henotheistic, with the absolute monotheism of Judaism being a later theological development. A fairly standard view is that Jewish monotheism was rooted most fundamentally in the Deuteronomistic conception of God. This conception, furthermore, might be seen as living within the tension between the first and third conceptions mentioned in the previous paragraph: God is personal, in accord with the Jahwist/Elohist conception; but God is also deeply "other," in accord with the Priestly/wisdom conception.

In any case, the picture that emerges from a survey of the literature on Old Testament conceptions of deity and on the evolution of the concept of God in ancient Israel is that the biblical portrayals of God taken together emphasize two key attributes: personality and transcendence.[16] Contemporary popular piety tends to downplay divine transcendence in favor of God's personal attributes. So also does most of the philosophical literature on the hiddenness problem. But it is important to recognize that *both* divine transcendence and divine personality are scriptural ideas central to the theology that lies at the very root of the Jewish and Christian traditions.

Transcendence and personality do not easily fit together. As I mentioned earlier, many contemporary scholars take the emphasis

[14] The "Song of the Sea" (Exod. 15:1–18) is one such text. Note that my way of referring to the pentateuchal sources here presupposes some version of the documentary hypothesis, which is no longer the dominant paradigm and is regarded by some scholars as wholly discredited. (Cf. Wenham 1970 and 1999, and Rendtorff 1993.) Nothing substantive here depends on the documentary hypothesis being true; I am simply casting my discussion in terms of the presuppositions of the secondary sources I am referencing.

[15] Cf. Geller 2000: 278–81. But see also Sommer 2011: 64. Sommer embraces a very minimalist conception of transcendence, according to which it implies little more than that God does not dwell on Earth (though God visits occasionally).

[16] A variety of scholars have highlighted the unique way in which divine transcendence is asserted alongside, rather than over against, divine personality in biblical texts. See, e.g., Muffs 2009: ch. 6; Smith 2002: 207; and Sommer 2011: 124, 251 n. 1.

of both in scripture to be evidence of disagreement among the biblical authors about the very nature of God. Since one would hardly expect that *God* is of divided mind as to the divine nature, the appearance of serious disagreement within the canon about the attributes of God is naturally seen as a challenge to the divine authorship and inspiration of scripture. Accordingly, traditional believers face pressure to discount, reinterpret, or ignore those parts of the Bible that advocate one or the other of these two attributes. If the contours of evangelical theology and analytic philosophy over the past century are any guide, this is a contest in which personality tends to win out.

In fact, however, the perceived threat is only illusory. For most of its history, the Christian tradition has sought to hold the attributes of personality and transcendence in tension with one another, and to understand God's personality in light of divine transcendence, and vice versa. This, I think, is the proper theological response to the mix of assertions and images that we find in the Old and New Testaments; and I see no reason to doubt the possibility that God allowed apparently competing visions of the divine nature to make their way into scripture precisely to encourage this sort of theological response.

So even if one does think that there is substantive theological diversity among the authors of scripture, one might still think that all of the various theological claims and images that we find in scripture have been included—indeed, inspired—by the divine author to teach us something important and true about God, and that it is the task of systematic theology to figure out just how they are to be woven together. But the key point is that they are *meant* to be woven together, which means tempering the expectations engendered by the more anthropomorphic threads in scripture with those that are more naturally engendered by the less anthropomorphic threads, and vice versa.

The classical theistic enterprise might well be regarded as one attempt—or, better, a diverse family of attempts—to accomplish precisely this task. The attributes, and the different available accounts of each, have emerged from a theoretical process that tries at once to do justice to the idea that God is a (perfect) person as well as to the idea that God is importantly set apart from creation. The hiddenness problem, by contrast, seems, in its various incarnations, to emerge from a theoretical process that significantly downplays divine transcendence and takes for granted both the ordinariness and familiarity of divine love, personality, and parenthood, as well as the in principle direct availability of God to human experience. The god of the Schellenberg problem is one whose love for creaturely persons satisfies all of the necessary conditions delivered by (empirically informed) philosophical reflection on the best kinds of *human* love. But, as shall emerge more fully in what follows, there is no good reason to think that the god of the Schellenberg problem is the transcendent personal God of scripture or traditional Christian belief. Arguably, matters will be similar with the gods of other versions of the hiddenness problem.

In light of this, it is easy to see why, in the contemporary literature, the problem of divine hiddenness, and particularly the Schellenberg version, has received attention almost exclusively from analytic philosophers rather than from theologians. Academic theology has, for the past couple of centuries, been captivated by its appreciation of divine transcendence and by increasingly strong understandings thereof, whereas analytic philosophy of religion has, for the most part, downplayed that attribute. The god of the hiddenness problem is, in important respects, foreign to contemporary (and much historical) theology. Analytic philosophers, by contrast, have tended to take it for granted that terms like "loving," "powerful," "personal," and so on mean the same thing in theological discourse as they do in ordinary, literal discourse, whereas theologians have tended to insist that theological sentences containing such terms are to be understood analogically or metaphorically.

There are pitfalls on both sides of this divide. Those who severely downplay divine transcendence, as well as those who overemphasize it, run the risk of paying mere lip-service to important swaths of both scripture and tradition. At one extreme, we risk denying God's personality, maintaining that God is not really wise, does not really love us, and so on. At the other extreme, we risk portraying God as little more than an extremely powerful, knowing, and benevolent human. At both extremes we risk a kind of idolatry. Weaving the attributes of transcendence and personality together and understanding them in light of one another is therefore key both to the larger task of developing a correct theology and to the narrower task of solving the hiddenness problem.

Talk of extremes suggests, correctly, that conceptions of transcendence lie on a continuum. In Section 2, I highlight two core ideas underlying the notion of transcendence, and in so doing I identify the poles on the continuum of characterizations.

2.

Transcendence is related to and often equated with ineffability, incomprehensibility, unknowability, or some combination of these. For purposes here, I will talk as if the latter three attributes go hand in hand—not because I think it is impossible for them to come apart, but rather simply because they are commonly treated as belonging together (or as outright equivalent) and there is no advantage to be gained in the present discussion by trying to keep them separate.

As I indicated in Section 1, there is widespread agreement that the crucial turning point in Israel's movement from henotheism to monotheism was the transition from thinking of God as akin to a very powerful humanoid who inhabits this world and is intimately involved with natural phenomena and human affairs to a concept of God as in some sense transcendent. Israel's religion, like many others, is thought to have undergone this transition during the so-called "Axial Age," which spanned roughly three centuries, from 600–300 BCE; and, indeed, the transition from immanent to transcendent conceptions of divine reality is generally taken to be one of the defining features of the Axial Age.

Despite the importance of the idea of transcendence in the literature on the evolution of religion, however, one is hard-pressed to find any precise characterization of it there. Likewise in the literature on divine attributes, in the literature on mystical theology, and in pretty much every other body of literature in which the notion of transcendence has been significant. In fact, I would venture to say that transcendence is among the least understood of the divine attributes, in no small part because of the abundance of different and often paradoxical characterizations of it that have been given throughout history. But there is some unity within this diversity. The different conceptions of transcendence seem to arise out of different ways of understanding its two most central components.

One core idea within the concept of transcendence is that of God's *difference* from creation, God's "otherness," or *alterity*. The claim that God is holy is often taken to express not so much God's moral perfection as God's radical alterity.[17] The question, of course, is just

---

[17] See, e.g., Otto 1958; Mittleman 2015.

how far to take the idea that God is other. In other words, we must ask just how unlike creation, how conceptually foreign, God really is.

Minimally, God's otherness has been understood to imply God's separateness from creation—God is somehow outside or in other ways separate from the world we inhabit, or outside creation entirely.[18] So, at the very least, transcendence contrasts with earthly presence: God's dwelling is not down here on earth—though perhaps God occasionally visits—but rather up there, in the heavenly realm. It is also generally taken to contrast with *spatiotemporal* immanence: God is not material; God is outside spacetime. Moreover, God stands apart from creation in the sense that God is uncreated, neither depends on creation nor is bound by it, but rather has dominion over it.[19] These attributes—spatiotemporal distance, immateriality, independence, and mastery—obviously represent very different ways in which something might be "separate" from the earthly, human realms. One might think of God as separate in some of these senses but not others, or as separate in one or more of these senses to varying degrees.

God's otherness has also been understood to imply more than mere separateness, more than mere exaltation; it has been understood to imply both that God's *thoughts*—most saliently, God's values, and whatever reasons and reasoning processes might explain God's actions—are very different from human thoughts, and that God's intrinsic character is very different from anything with which we are acquainted. The idea that God's thoughts differ from human thoughts is explicit in Isaiah 55:8–9 (said in reference to the magnitude of God's love and mercy):

> For my thoughts are not your thoughts, nor are your ways my ways, says the LORD. For as the heavens are higher than the earth, so are my ways higher than your ways and my thoughts than your thoughts.

---

[18] The doctrine of the incarnation obviously complicates matters here; but I will, for present purposes, leave those concerns aside. Also, as noted earlier, Sommer (2011: 64) maintains that the Deuteronomistic conception of transcendence amounts to nothing more than the very minimal claim that God is separate from creation. He relies on this interpretation in developing and defending his view that the Old Testament portrays God as multiply embodied rather than as entirely lacking a body.

[19] Yehezekel Kaufmann (1972) goes so far as to say that the ideas of independence and mastery comprise the "basic idea" of Israelite religion. But see also Levenson 1994 for a slightly different perspective.

But, of course, these verses on their own leave the question of *how* different God's thoughts are from ours mostly to our imagination. Likewise for God's intrinsic otherness. Scripture says that "God is not a human being that he should lie, or a mortal that he should change his mind," (Num. 23:19) and that God, unlike human beings, does not dwell in houses (Acts 7:48). God is spirit, not flesh (John 4:24), and far beyond human beings in wisdom and might (Job 38–40, Isa. 40). But even these vast differences yet leave room, in principle, for a great deal of similarity.

For many theologians, doing justice to the grandeur of God means ratcheting up the notion of divine otherness as far as possible, well beyond anything conveyed by a natural reading of the verses just quoted from Deutero-Isaiah; and it is here that we start to get some of the more puzzling conceptions of transcendence in the literature. For example, one finds both theologians and biblical scholars saying that God is *not a thing in the world alongside other things in the world*, or that God is *completely ontologically detached* from the world.[20] Many want to say that, although it is certainly *apt* to characterize God in personal and other creaturely terms, God is so wholly other than creation that there is an important sense in which God simply cannot be characterized except (perhaps) by way of analogy or metaphor.[21]

The second core notion is that of *inscrutability* or *unknowability*. At the very least, the idea here is, again, one suggested by a natural reading of Isaiah 55:8–9: the mind of God and the patterns of divine valuing are beyond our full comprehension. But most apophatic theologians want to say much more than this—e.g., that God's *essence* is unknowable, or, most radically and paradoxically, that God entirely eludes human conceptualization.[22]

These two core ideas are obviously related to one another. Divine alterity might be thought to explain the fact that language is

---

[20] Cf., e.g., Uffenheimer 1986: 146, and the discussion and references in Ticciati 2013: ch. 1, and Trakakis 2015.

[21] The idea that God can be characterized only via analogy is, of course, ubiquitous in the tradition. (Cf., e.g., Turner 1998 and White 2010.) As I shall discuss further in Chapter 4, the idea that God can only be characterized via metaphor is ubiquitous in contemporary theology. (Cf., e.g., Johnson 1984 and McFague 1987.)

[22] The less radical view, that God's essence is unknowable, is a mainstay of Patristic and medieval philosophical theology. For statements of more radical views, see, e.g., Caputo 1992, Marion 2012, and (attributing a more radical view also to ancient Egyptian theologians and the authors of the Hebrew Bible) Korpel and de Moor 2011: 67–9.

inadequate to the task of literally and univocally characterizing God; and this fact, in turn, might be thought to explain our fundamental inability to know important, substantive things about God. They are also, as we have just seen, badly underinterpreted: both admit of weaker or stronger interpretations, thus yielding a continuum of possible understandings of divine transcendence.

At the lightest end of the spectrum, God's transcendence is just the fact that God is uncreated, non-spatiotemporal; different from creatures in the sense of having a unique, non-creaturely nature, and perhaps some additional attributes that are not shared with any creature; and unknowable in the sense of not being *fully* knowable by creatures, so that at least some of God's attributes lie forever beyond our ken. At the darkest end of the spectrum, God's transcendence is God's absolute otherness; human concepts and predicates—including the predicate "exists"—have no literal application to God. God is, accordingly, deeply unknowable and ineffable. The lightest understandings place God objectionably close to the familiar and mundane; the darkest ones defy explication to such a degree that one might reasonably doubt whether they are even meaningful. My own inclination, unsurprisingly, is to locate the correct understanding somewhere in the middle. In Chapter 4, I explain why.

4

Hiddenness and Transcendence

At the end of Chapter 3, I described a continuum on which characterizations of divine transcendence generally fall. In the present chapter, I make a case for avoiding both poles, thus locating the correct understanding of transcendence somewhere in between. I will not ultimately advocate for any particular understanding of this puzzling attribute; there is no need to do so for my purposes in this book. But I will identify several theses that I take to be consequences of any theologically adequate understanding of divine transcendence. I will then conclude the chapter by showing how these theses bear on the problem of divine hiddenness.

1.

The sixth-century theologian, Pseudo-Dionysius the Areopagite, is probably the most frequently cited historical spokesman for the darkest interpretations of divine transcendence. Famously, toward the end of his *Mystical Theology*, Pseudo-Dionysius says that God is "beyond every denial, beyond every assertion" and that God "lies beyond thought and beyond being." (Pseudo-Dionysius 1987: 136) By far the most common gloss on these beyondness affirmations is the view that God can only be truly characterized by way of images, or metaphors. Just as the portrayal of God as the chariot-riding Ancient of Days is nothing more than an image, so too even the portrayal of God as the omnipotent, omniscient, omnibenevolent creator is a mere image.

William Alston applied the term *pan-metaphoricism* to this view; others (including Alston) have called it *pan-symbolism*.[1] For reasons

---

[1] Alston 1989b: 35 and Rowe 1962: 278, citing Urban 1940: 35–6.

to be explained shortly, I will use the latter label. Pan-symbolism is not only widely affirmed among contemporary theologians, but is also routinely described as a traditional view.[2] According to Alston, it is an "article of faith" in contemporary theology;[3] and, indeed, it seems that one can hardly pick up a text in theology or biblical studies in which divine transcendence is characterized without finding something like a blanket, unqualified assertion to the effect that God cannot be spoken of in literal terms.

Pan-symbolism is not, as it happens, the *most* extreme understanding of divine transcendence on offer. That prize goes to views according to which the bare application of concepts to God, metaphorical or not, is seen as problematic. Jean-Luc Marion, for example, takes the application of concepts to God to be inherently idolatrous, and so maintains that God can only be praised, not described.[4] John Caputo does him one better, objecting even to praise on the grounds that it, like description, involves the idolatrous *and violent* application of concepts to God.[5] Views like these, I think, involve their proponents in performative contradiction and so ought to be dismissed out of hand. But even if I am wrong about this, the objection I will raise against pan-symbolism will apply equally to these views as well.

Before objecting, however, let me begin with three clarifying remarks. First, pan-symbolism, as I understand it, is not a theological claim but a metatheological claim. Theology takes *God* as subject; metatheology does not. Instead, it takes *theology* as subject. So pan-symbolism does not directly attribute anything to God; it simply says that all true theological discourse is metaphorical. As Daniel Howard-Snyder (2017) points out, understanding pan-symbolism this way saves it from implying, implausibly, that pan-symbolism itself is mere metaphor.

Second, although I have glossed it as the thesis that all true theological discourse is metaphorical, strictly speaking pan-symbolism should be understood as the conjunction of two logically independent theses: (i) all true theological discourse is metaphorical, and (ii) no theological claim is literally true.[6] Pan-symbolism is commonly

---

[2] See, e.g., Hampson 1996; Hick 2000; Johnson 1984; and McFague 1987.

[3] Alston 1989b: 17.   [4] Marion 1994; Hector 2011: 16; Jones 2011: 9.

[5] Caputo 1992; Hector 2011: 20–1.

[6] For purposes here, I will say that a sentence is "literally true" just if it has a true proposition as its semantic content. For more on this, see the discussion of metaphor later on.

understood to include both claims; but often the second is treated (mistakenly, in my opinion) as if it is a logical consequence of the first.[7]

Third, I take pan-symbolism to be distinct from the thesis that all theological discourse is *analogical*. Some people draw sharp distinctions between analogy and metaphor; others do not.[8] I think it is clear that analogy and metaphor are not exactly the same thing; but, beyond affirming that very minimal claim, I do not want to take a stand on whether or to what extent the categories of analogy and metaphor might overlap. I do, however, want it to be clear that I do not take my objections here to carry over automatically to the claim that all true theological discourse is analogical.

Having made these clarifications, I now want to raise two objections against pan-symbolism as an account of divine transcendence. These are hardly the only objections one might raise against the view.[9] But they are the only two I can think of that are clearly independent of what I take to be objectionable theories of metaphor.

The first objection begins with the observation that pan-symbolism is not even the right *sort* of thesis to serve as an account of divine transcendence. The claim that God is transcendent is a theological claim; pan-symbolism is a metatheological claim. So *whatever* it means to say that God is transcendent, pan-symbolism can be, at best, only a consequence of divine transcendence rather than an account of it.

This by itself is no big problem for the pan-symbolist. She will naturally deny that there is *any* divine attribute of which we possess a proper (literally true) account.[10] So it should come as no surprise to

---

[7] The second claim does not follow from the first because some metaphors are literally true. Borrowing an example from Cooper 1986: "a work of art is not an egg" is both literally true and yet metaphorical.

[8] Soskice (1992: 82–3) for example, seems to treat metaphor and analogy as at least partially overlapping categories. She characterizes Aquinas as treating the term "father" as applying *metaphorically* to God, despite the fact that Aquinas denies this, saying instead that it applies analogically (ST 1.13.3, 6; ST 1.33.2). This makes sense on the supposition that, on her understanding of metaphor, some analogical uses of terms are also metaphorical. In her book on metaphor and religious language, however, she seems to draw a sharp distinction between analogy and metaphor (Soskice 1985: 64–6, esp. p. 65); and Burrell (1973), Jenson (1992), and Cox (2015) similarly insist on the distinction.

[9] See Alston 1989a, Alston 1989b, Rowe 1962, Van Woudenberg 1998, and especially Howard-Snyder 2017.

[10] Why does it follow from the fact that talk about *God* is non-literal that talk about God's *attributes* is non-literal? In short, the answer is that if talk about God is

anyone that her position provides no proper account of the attribute of divine transcendence. The problem, however, comes when we ask about the *link* between pan-symbolism and divine transcendence. Grant that pan-symbolism is both true and distinct from the thesis that God is transcendent. Why, now, should we think that it is a *consequence* of the thesis that God is transcendent?

As I see it, a pan-symbolist can't give a good answer to this question. The reason is that identifying *any* non-trivial consequence of a sentence requires knowing the logical form of the proposition expressed by the sentence, and deriving anything other than trivial and purely formal consequences requires the ability to express both the target sentence and the sentence that allegedly follows from it in a way that clearly exposes the conceptual connections between the propositions they express. But the pan-symbolist has to deny that we can do either of these things with the claim that God is transcendent.

Suppose you say, upon being arrested, "it's a fair cop"; and suppose I want to identify consequences of your claim. I cannot even begin to do this unless I first figure out whether the proposition you aim to express is indeed a simple predication—from which I could at least infer that *something is a fair cop*—or some other kind of proposition. Without knowing the logical form of the proposition you aim to express, I can't make the inference.

Suppose I reflect on Romeo's claim that *Juliet is the sun.* It is reasonable to think that Romeo intends to predicate something of Juliet; so it is reasonable to think that the proposition he intends to convey is a simple predication.[11] But I can't go very far with this bit of knowledge; and, importantly, I can't identify any of its interesting consequences unless I am in a position to expose the connections between Romeo's sentence and whatever properties he aims to attribute to Juliet. Is it a consequence of his statement that Juliet is *beautiful*? I cannot say, unless I am somehow in a position to affirm that the property *being beautiful* is among the properties expressed by the predicate *is the sun* in Romeo's metaphor.

---

non-literal, then any sentence attributing a property to God is non-literal too; and if we have no literally true account of what it means to say (e.g.) that God is wise, then we have no literally true account of what *divine wisdom* consists in.

[11] On the distinction between "conveying" and "expressing," see note 14.

So likewise with "God is transcendent." We can identify pan-symbolism as a consequence only if we know the logical form of the proposition expressed by it and are in a position to expose conceptual connections between the predicate "is transcendent" and other predicates whose literal meanings we understand. But if *all* theological discourse is non-literal, I see no reason to think that we can identify the logical form of whatever "God is transcendent" expresses. (Why think that sentence is any more a simple predication than "It's a fair cop"?) And if we could *clearly* expose conceptual connections between the predicate "is transcendent" and other predicates whose literal meanings we understand, then there should be no obstacle to saying literally true things about God, which the pan-symbolist denies that we can do. So, in short, there is no way to identify the consequences of the proposition expressed by "God is transcendent" unless pan-symbolism is false—which is to say that pan-symbolism cannot be identified as a consequence of divine transcendence. At best, pan-symbolism can only be offered as a partial and contestable *interpretation* of the claim that God is transcendent.

The second objection is that pan-symbolism is inconsistent with theism. Theism implies that something is God, or that something is divine. (Maybe those two claims are equivalent, maybe not; it depends on what the content of "is God" is.) Either way, it is a theological thesis; so pan-symbolism implies that theism is not literally true. Theists, then, have positive reason to think that pan-symbolism is false.[12]

One might reply to this objection by denying that theism is a theological thesis. Perhaps it is a thesis about the world, or things in the world (e.g., that the world is *created*, or *has a cause*, or something like that); or perhaps it is the assertion that a certain role (e.g., *creator*) is occupied.[13] This reply works, of course, only if the thesis with which theism is identified is not equivalent to the claim that God exists (lest it be a theological thesis after all); and it is hard to see why any theist would want to make such a move. But let us simply grant that this problem can be overcome. Still, to make this reply is, in effect, to say that all of the important elements of Christian doctrine

[12] Cf. Howard-Snyder 2017.
[13] Cf. Turner 2004: chs. 9, 11. As I read him, Turner's suggestion in these chapters is that theism amounts to the claim that the creator role is occupied; but I confess that I am unsure that I am reading him correctly on this score.

can be faithfully paraphrased by sentences that do not employ the terms "God" or "is divine." I cannot hope to prove that this claim is false; but accepting it requires a leap of faith that is well beyond me. How could one possibly expect to paraphrase the ecumenical creeds, or the doctrines of the trinity and the incarnation, for example, without recourse either to the name "God" or to predicates that are equivalent in meaning to "is divine"? The task seems utterly hopeless.

But there is a second reply available to the pan-symbolist. There is a distinction to be drawn between what is *said* by a metaphor and what is *literally meant* by that metaphor; and, in light of this, one might insist that theism is to be identified with what is *said* by "God exists" rather than with what is literally meant. On the view of metaphor that I favor, the literal meaning of a metaphor is whatever proposition is its semantic content; what is said by the metaphor is whatever proposition is pragmatically conveyed in the relevant context.[14] So this reply blocks the objection that theism is inconsistent with pan-symbolism by identifying theism with a proposition different from whatever proposition, if any, might be the literal content of "God exists." Accordingly, it is open to the pan-symbolist to say that "God exists" is true, but not literally true, and theism is the metaphorical content, rather than the literal content, of "God exists."[15]

But even if this is the pan-symbolist's *best* reply, it is not a *good* reply. The problem is that it is completely unmotivated. The claim that "God exists" is true but not literally true cannot be identified as a consequence of divine transcendence unless pan-symbolism is false, for reasons already discussed. Nor is it plausible on independent grounds. So far as I can tell, the most likely motivation for affirming that "God exists" is true but not literally true is parity with other important claims that proponents of darker interpretations of divine transcendence often want to take non-literally: for example, that God

[14] See Camp 2006a; Camp 2006b; and Reimer and Camp 2006 for details. Following what I take to be standard conventions, I say that a proposition is (semantically) expressed by a sentence just if the proposition is the semantic content of the sentence; and I say that a proposition is (pragmatically) conveyed by a sentence, or sentence user, just if it is among the propositions not semantically expressed by the sentence but somehow still communicated by way of context or other aspects of the occasion of use.

[15] Howard-Snyder (2017) considers this reply, provides a preliminary argument for the conclusion that it is incoherent, but then ultimately offers a way of recovering it on the pan-symbolist's behalf.

is loving, wise, good, etc. But I think it can be shown that, in fact, the claim that God exists is *not* on a par with these other sorts of claims.

Scripture and tradition together exert a great deal of pressure toward taking affirmations like "God is good" or "God is loving" as somehow involving what we might call *semantic deviance*—usage of words that is not strictly in accord with their semantic values. The pressure from scripture comes from the often noted fact that the biblical texts attribute thoughts and actions to God that seem wholly irreconcilable with God's being good or loving in any ordinary sense of those terms. The pressure from tradition comes from the explicit and widespread endorsement by leading theologians in most of the major strands of Christianity of the view that such claims are analogical or metaphorical.

It is commonly held that the deviance in question consists in *non-univocal* usage of words like "good" and "loving." Saying that the word "good" is not univocally applied to both God and creatures implies that the word *has a different meaning*, a different semantic value, when applied to creatures than when applied to God. But this is not what the pan-symbolist says. The pan-symbolist says that the semantic deviance consists in a failure of literality. On this view, words like "good" have the same semantic value when predicated of human beings and of God, but a sentence like "God is good" counts as true not because God possesses the property that "goodness" refers to, but rather because the sentence has a (true) metaphorical content that is different from its (false) literal content.

So, on this way of thinking, a sentence like "God is good" functions like "Juliet is the sun" as uttered by Romeo. The predicate "is the sun" has in that metaphor the same semantic value that it always does, something like the property *being the star around which Earth is in orbit*. So there is no failure of univocity in Romeo's speech. But, in context, "Juliet is the sun" does not *say* that Juliet is the star around which Earth is in orbit. The sentence is semantically (and so literally) false; but it still says something true because it is being used to say a proposition that is different from its semantic content. This is part of what makes it a metaphor.

Of course, the view does have the awkward consequence of committing its adherents to the view that it is literally false that God is good. But, as the view is typically developed, this consequence is mitigated by the supposition that human words can take only properties applicable to creatures as their semantic values, and the divine properties that we are trying to capture with our words are generally far better than or otherwise beyond the properties that those words have as their semantic values. So, on this way of thinking, it is literally false that God is good *not* because God is somehow bad, but rather because God is somehow *better than* or (in some positive and praiseworthy way) *beyond* being good.

If this is right, however, then there is motivation to understand claims like "God is good" as metaphors rather than as failures of univocity only to the extent that there is reason to think that words like "good" always have mere creaturely properties as their semantic values. And the same goes for "God exists": there is motivation to understand it as a metaphor only if there is reason to think that the word "exists" always has a mere creaturely attribute as its semantic value. But in fact there is no reason at all to think this—at least not apart from some very substantive assumptions about being and existence that are entirely optional from the point of view of theology.[16]

So whatever divine transcendence amounts to, it should neither be identified with nor taken to imply pan-symbolism. The darkest pole on the continuum is to be avoided; we ought to acknowledge that we can say literally true things about God. Likewise, however, the lightest pole should also be avoided.

According to the lightest interpretations of divine transcendence, God is *different* from and beyond the comprehension of creatures in important respects; but many of God's intrinsic attributes—especially those, like divine love, goodness, power, and knowledge, that have historically been most salient for Christian theology—can, even apart from divine revelation, be deeply understood and characterized in literal, univocal terms and be made the literal semantic content of human words and concepts. From a purely philosophical point of view, one might take the hiddenness argument itself as reason to reject very light interpretations of divine transcendence. As shall become clear later on, the hiddenness argument rests in part on the

---

[16] In particular, it will depend on what one thinks about (i) whether a language that expresses existence via a predicate is more ontologically perspicuous than a language that expresses existence via quantifiers, (ii) whether a language with multiple existential quantifiers is more ontologically perspicuous than a language with just one, (iii) whether absolutely unrestricted quantification is possible, and (iv) whether the most ontologically perspicuous language will include a (possibly disjunctive) quantifier that subsumes all other quantifiers that are restricted to particular modes of being.

supposition that God is (at most) lightly transcendent. So some-body who arrives at theism by way of natural-theological reasoning might then take the fact that light interpretations of divine tran-scendence support an argument *against* theism as reason to reject those interpretations.

That said, however, it is also worth noting that, insofar as we might also be interested in the question whether the *Christian* God is only lightly transcendent, there is a strong scriptural case to be made against that view as well. The Bible is repeatedly explicit about the fact that God's ways, thoughts, and values are very different from ours. In the Old Testament, we might again point to Isaiah 55:8–9; in the New Testament, we might point to 1 Corinthians 1:25–7:

> For God's foolishness is wiser than human wisdom, and God's weakness is stronger than human strength. Consider your own call, brothers and sisters: not many of you were wise by human standards, not many were powerful, not many were of noble birth. But God chose what is foolish in the world to shame the wise; God chose what is weak in the world to shame the strong.

On their own, such texts prove nothing very significant about the relationship between divine and human love, divine and human wisdom, divine and human mercy, and so on. But read against the backdrop of the jarring apparent inconsistency between, on the one hand, grand biblical claims about the love, compassion, mercy, and parental care and concern that God showers upon both the nation of Israel and individual people who are devoted to God, and, on the other hand, biblical claims about God's apparently harsh treatment of both Israel and particular individuals, the pressure starts to emerge.

To put it mildly, it is very hard to see how the God of the Christian Bible can sensibly be described as unfailingly good, loving, merciful, and parental toward Israel, toward all of God's individual children, or toward humanity as a whole if divine love, goodness, and mercy are understood according to what might be called "human" or "crea-turely" standards.[17] Grant the (traditional) assumption that biblical narratives provide deep insight into the character of God; and hold fixed the (traditional) view that God is in fact perfectly loving, good, and merciful. It is then hard to resist the idea that, for example, texts describing God's commands in relation to the conquest of

[17] Cf. Brueggemann 2012: 359; Crenshaw 2013; and O'Connor 2002: ch. 9.

Canaan, God's treatment of Israel (particularly during the Babylonian destruction of Jerusalem and conquest of Judah), and God's treatment of particular individuals (historical or fictional) like Job, Jephthah, and Ananias and Sapphira (to name just a few), provide very strong reason for thinking that whatever exactly divine love, goodness, and mercy amount to, they cannot be very well understood (much less analyzed, or literally characterized) by human reason alone, without aid from divine revelation. Furthermore, insofar as "ordinary" or "creaturely" love and goodness *can* be well understood, analyzed, and literally characterized without aid from divine revelation, we thus also have reason to think that divine love and goodness are, at best, only analogically related to ordinary human love and goodness.

Let me not overstate the case: I am not here claiming that the witness of scripture *forces* us away from the lightest pole on the continuum of accounts of divine transcendence. One might respond to the pressure I have just described by looking all the harder for an account of love, mercy, and so on that both satisfies our intuitions about the nature of human love and also readily accommodates the sort of harsh treatment that we find reported in the pages of scripture. One might seek other strategies instead. Historically, however, the most popular theological strategy—which accommodates both the data of scripture *and* historically entrenched views about the catalog of other divine attributes—has been to embrace a doctrine of transcendence that is at least somewhat darker than what I have characterized as the lightest pole on the continuum.

2.

For the reasons just identified, then, my own inclination is to endorse a doctrine of transcendence that falls somewhere in the middle of the continuum between what I have been calling the "lightest" and "darkest" understandings. The view I am inclined to adopt is the following:

> (DT)   Divine transcendence is whatever intrinsic attribute of God explains the fact that *intrinsic substantive predications of God* or of the divine nature that express *non-revealed concepts* are, at best, analogical.

A concept is non-revealed just if its content is not given entirely by divine revelation. I assume that most of our concepts are like this, though I grant that it is possible that some are not. Intrinsic predications are, roughly, those that aim to say how God is independently of God's relations (if any) to contingent beings.[18] Omnipotence, for example, is intrinsically predicated of God, whereas being the object of Christian worship, or having become incarnate, are not. Likewise, transcendence is intrinsically predicated of God; but the attribute that (according to DT) it explains—being such that intrinsic substantive predications of God or of the divine nature are, at best, analogical—is not. Substantive predications are, roughly, those that neither apply to everything nor are trivial logical consequences of truths about God. So, for example, "God exists" and "God is self-identical" are non-substantive predications, as are "God is omnipotent or grass is green" and "God is omnipotent and $2 + 2 = 4$."

DT is not itself an intrinsic predication of anything, so it does not imply of itself that it is non-literal.[19] Nor, obviously, does it preclude literal theological discourse. But, at the same time, it implies that, if God is transcendent, then God is not *wholly* characterizable in literal, univocal terms. So it falls appropriately in the middle of the spectrum.

In Chapter 3, I noted that *alterity* is one of the core concepts in the notion of divine transcendence, and that part of what is wrapped up in the idea of God's alterity is God's *separateness* from creation in various senses. But DT does not obviously capture this aspect of

---

[18] Here I loosely follow the Langton and Lewis (1998) definition of "intrinsic." As subsequent discussion in the literature has shown, their definition is not problem-free; but I'll stick with my present characterization because I do not think that further effort in the direction of precisifying the definition will make a significant difference to my discussion here.

[19] DT does imply that God has an intrinsic attribute that plays a certain role—namely, explaining a particular fact about intrinsic substantive predications of God. Is this a problem? One might think so, because one might think that DT thereby tells us something non-analogical about the divine nature. But I think that in fact there is no problem here. DT offers no analysis of transcendence, no account of what it is in and of itself; and so I see no reason for thinking that DT says anything substantive about how God is intrinsically. In fact, DT is relevantly similar to other claims that apophatic theologians have been willing to make about other divine attributes (like *love*). For example, just as there is no problem (so far as respect for divine transcendence is concerned) in saying that divine love is the attribute that explains the aptness of "excellent parent" analogies in characterizing God, so too there is no problem saying that divine transcendence is the attribute that explains some of the limitations on what we can literally say about God.

divine transcendence. Is that a problem? For my purposes, no. I find it quite plausible to think that whatever attribute explains the limitations on our ability to talk about God in the ways described by DT is also the attribute that explains God's separateness; and if this is right, then DT is a true statement about transcendence, even if it is not a fully perspicuous explication of it.[20]

The understanding of divine transcendence that I have just sketched is not one that I am prepared to defend here; nor is it even one upon which I want to insist for purposes of this book. Rather, I offer it merely as an *example* of an understanding of divine transcendence that I take to have the consequences that any suitable account—any account that strikes the right balance between light and dark, modesty and robustness—will have; and it is these consequences, rather than any particular account of transcendence, that will be doing the heavy philosophical-theological work in the remainder of the book. I will focus on just two of them.

First, I take it that one consequence of even a very modest doctrine of divine transcendence is that we have no *fully transparent, nonrevealed* concept of any intrinsic attribute of God. A concept is fully transparent to a subject S if, and only if, (a) it occurs in a proposition *p* that S understands, and (b) S understands *p* in a mode that gives rise to reliable intuitions about the concepts that occur in *p*.[21] Fully transparent concepts are ones that facilitate reliable classificatory judgments—i.e., we can reliably tell whether or not something satisfies the concept. They are also our best candidates for being concepts about which we can have a *warrantedly assertible* philosophical account. One might try to theorize philosophically about a concept that is not fully transparent; but, precisely because it isn't a concept

---

[20] Of course, if God is simple, then there is a sense in which what I have just said here is trivially true. But, obviously, that is not the sense I have in mind when I indicate that the same attribute explains both God's separateness and the limitations on our ability to think and speak about God. I should also note that for those who believe I am wrong about this—for those who think that the attribute picked out by DT would *have* to be different from whatever attribute is or explains God's separateness—I would be happy to concede, just for the sake of moving forward with the points that most interest me, that there has been some equivocation in the literature with respect to the term "transcendence," with people sometimes using it to pick out attributes connected with God's separateness (which I am less interested in here) and on other occasions using it to pick out the attribute DT describes.

[21] Here I am adapting George Bealer's notion of *determinate concept possession*. See Bealer 1996 and 1998, and Rea 2002: 203–4.

that one understands in a way that gives rise to *reliable* judgments about what does or does not satisfy the concept, one will have good reason to doubt—and so insufficient warrant for asserting—the truth of the account that emerges.

Does DT have this first consequence? Yes. Our fully transparent concepts are the ones most firmly in our possession—the ones we understand best, and most clearly. So if we are able to think and speak non-analogically at all, we should be able to do this by way of thoughts and sentences that express fully transparent concepts. Accordingly, insofar as DT says that we cannot predicate *anything* non-analogically of God except by way of thoughts or sentences that express revealed concepts, DT implies that we have no fully transparent, non-revealed concept of God.

So consider some particular intrinsic attribute of God—*divine love*, for example.[22] I am not denying that we can arrive at a revealed concept of *love*; nor am I denying that we can arrive at a *fully transparent* concept of *divine love*. No doubt it would be difficult to arrive at such concepts; but I am not committed to thinking it is impossible. What I am denying, however, is that we can arrive at a fully transparent concept of divine love *without deriving it somehow from divine revelation*, simply by analyzing *love* in general, or by reflecting on creaturely paradigms of love. One's only hope for arriving at a fully transparent concept of divine love is to reflect on, and come to understand, divinely revealed truths in which the concept of love occurs, or—as both Alan Torrance and Kevin Hector have argued, in very different ways—somehow allow ourselves and our ways of thinking about things to be taken up into and transformed by the divine revelation that is the life and work of Jesus Christ and his church.[23]

Karl Barth, toward the beginning of his discussion of the perfections of divine freedom, affirms a stronger point that I do *not* intend

---

[22] God's *love for me* is not an intrinsic attribute, nor is God's *particular expression* of love to any of God's creatures. These are states of affairs that depend partly on God's intrinsic dispositions but also on God's relations to contingent beings. Together they comprise what we might call the "topography of divine love." (The term is due to Jeff Jordan (2012), although I am not sure that he means by it exactly the same thing that I do.) But the general character of God's love, the ways in which the divine persons love and are disposed to love one another and whatever creatures might be created, *are* independent of God's relations to contingent beings; so it is in that sense that divine love is intrinsic.

[23] Torrance 2001: 137; see also Hector 2011: esp. ch. 4.

to assert, and that I do not take to be a consequence of just any suitably modest doctrine of divine transcendence.[24] Having already asserted that divine hiddenness (which, for him, is the attribute of divine incomprehensibility) is "the first word of the knowledge of God instituted by God himself" (1957: 183), Barth writes:

> The recognition of divine attributes cannot be taken to mean that for us God is subsumed under general notions, under the loftiest ideas of our knowledge of creaturely reality, and that He participates in its perfections. It is not that we recognize and acknowledge the infinity, justice, wisdom, etc. of God because we already know from other sources what all this means and we apply it to God in an eminent sense, thus fashioning for ourselves an image of God after the pattern of our image of the world, i.e., in the last analysis after our own image … God is subordinate to no idea in which He can be conceived as rooted or by which He can be properly measured. There are not first of all power, goodness, knowledge, will, etc. in general, and then in particular God also as one of the subjects to whom all these things accrue as a predicate.
>
> (Barth 1957: 333–4)

The idea here and in the surrounding context is that our knowledge of divine attributes like wisdom, power, goodness, and love, *and of their creaturely counterparts*, is subordinate to what we learn by way of revelation, rather than the other way around. On this way of thinking, apparently, we have no non-revealed concept *whatsoever* of the intrinsic divine attributes; and even our knowledge of their creaturely correlates is importantly dependent on divine revelation. This is a view that I find in many ways theologically amenable; but it is a strong doctrine with deeply controversial consequences for natural theology, for the time-honored doctrine of the analogy of being, and no doubt for other important doctrines as well. Accordingly, it is not something to be affirmed lightly, and is certainly no consequence of a *modest* doctrine of transcendence.

The second consequence is what we might call "humility about expectations":

HUMILITY ABOUT EXPECTATIONS. Suppose F is an alleged intrinsic attribute of God; and suppose we have formed expectations about the manifestation of F-ness on the basis of our grasp of a *non-revealed* concept of

---

[24] I did assert this in Rea 2015; but I now think that I was not sufficiently attending to some of the more radical consequences of Barth's doctrine.

F-ness. In that case, the violation of those expectations does not by itself support (i.e., imply, render probable, or justify belief in) the conclusion that sentences predicating F-ness of God are not true.[25]

So, for example, consider *goodness*, and suppose our commonsense concept of goodness, or our best philosophical account of whatever non-revealed concept of goodness we possess, yields the expectation that if God is good, God would never permit suffering of a certain kind. In that case, perhaps the existence of the relevant kind of suffering supports the conclusion that God does not strictly conform to *that* concept of goodness. But, if HUMILITY ABOUT EXPECTATIONS is correct, it does not support the more general claim that "God is good" does not express a truth.

DT implies HUMILITY ABOUT EXPECTATIONS because it implies that intrinsic substantive predications of God that involve non-revealed concepts are, at best, analogical. Analogies break down; so it is to be expected that, if (e.g.) "God is good" is *at best* analogically true, divine behavior will violate at least some of the expectations we form by way of philosophical reflection on our non-revealed conceptions of good-ness. At most, then, from the fact that our expectations are violated we can conclude that either God is not good (at all) or that God's goodness is importantly different from creaturely goodness; and then we can issue a challenge to those who affirm divine goodness: *explain* how God is aptly described as good, given that God does not

---

[25] The parenthetical material is meant just to clarify my present usage of the term "support," not to supply a definition or analysis of it. Note, too, that I am leaving aside complicated questions about how different ways of assigning probability to divine transcendence or its consequences might impact the support we get from violated expectations about divine love for the conclusion that God is not loving. How, for example, should one think about the question whether God is loving if she thinks it is *very* likely that no perfectly loving being would allow nonresistant nonbelief, and only *somewhat* likely that God is transcendent in a way that supports HUMILITY ABOUT EXPECTATIONS? Trent Dougherty (2014a) offers a helpful discussion of roughly this sort of concern as it arises with regard to the so-called "skeptical theist" strategy for responding to the problem of evil. The discussion is relevant in no small part because skeptical theism is a natural extension of HUMILITY ABOUT EXPECTATIONS, insofar as the latter also implies that the existence of apparently pointless evils does not support the conclusion that no perfectly good or loving God exists. (Cf. Howard-Snyder 2009 and Rea 2013.) For purposes here, however, the questions in view in Dougherty's article can be left aside because my overall response to the hiddenness problem does not depend solely on appeal to divine transcendence and its consequences. For those who have high confidence in a form of divine transcendence that implies HUMILITY ABOUT EXPECTATIONS, the response offered in this chapter will suffice. For those who do not, I offer the arguments of Chapter 5.

conform to creaturely standards of goodness. The challenge will not be toothless. But neither will failing to meet it have the same atheological import as the conclusion that *there is no good God*; and the same holds, *mutatis mutandis*, for the other intrinsic attributes of God.

3.

In light of this chapter's discussion of divine transcendence, I draw the following preliminary conclusion about the problem of divine hiddenness. If God is transcendent, then the Schellenberg problem is unsuccessful as an argument against the existence of God, as is any other version of the hiddenness problem that trades on the violation of expectations arising *simply* out of philosophical or commonsense conceptions of attributes like "love" and "goodness." Divine transcendence implies HUMILITY ABOUT EXPECTATIONS; and HUMILITY ABOUT EXPECTATIONS implies that violated expectations on divine love and goodness do not support claims like "no perfectly loving God exists," except insofar as those expectations can be defended by appeal to revelation-based systematic theological considerations. But no such defense is forthcoming for the expectations in play in the Schellenberg problem.

Let me be clear that my point here is *not* that there is some in-principle problem with philosophical theorizing about God and the attributes of God; nor is it that there is anything suspect about our intuitions about the application conditions for commonsense or philosophical conceptions of love, goodness, and the like. Rather, the point is that, in light of the fact that divine love is importantly *different from* human love—in light of the fact that divine love transcends human love—arguments like Schellenberg's require for their rational believability a certain kind of defense of their salient theological premises that Schellenberg has not yet produced.[26] In particular, we can take the theological premises seriously only if and

---

[26] Note, in connection with this, pp. 202–4 in Schellenberg 2007, where Schellenberg is explicit about the fact that he is "making a conceptual point" about love based on "our everyday understanding of the language of love," and that the picture of divine love in play in his argument is one that may emerge for a person only after acquiring some distance from "religious teachings." (Cf. also pp. 217–18 of the same book.)

to the extent that we have warrant for believing that they are affirmed or implied by the overall body of (putative) divine revelation that has been made available to us. For, if God is indeed transcendent, it is only in light of *that* body of evidence, rather than (solely) on the basis of (empirically informed) philosophical reflection on non-revealed concepts, that we can reason our way to general principles about the nature of divine love, goodness, and the like.

None of this is to say that trying to use scripture to arrive at revealed concepts, or recognizing them as such once we have arrived at them, is straightforward or unproblematic. The interpretation of scripture is a complex matter, fraught with difficulty; and I have no convincing argument for the conclusion that we can expect even the best, most divinely guided interpretation to provide us with revealed concepts of goodness, love, and the like. Perhaps, then, no one has or ever will acquire such concepts. In that case, as many in the Christian tradition have already been happy to affirm, analogy is the best we will ever achieve in our substantive theorizing about God's intrinsic attributes; and in that case the best scripture can do for us in our theoretical efforts is to steer us toward ever better analogies. Moreover, even this limited use of scripture will be fraught with difficulty, for precisely the same reason: the interpretation of biblical texts is no easy task.

That said, however, I also have no convincing argument *against* the conclusion that it is possible to glean from scripture revealed concepts of important divine attributes; nor do I see any good reason why we should not strive in faith to understand the texts of scripture in a way that will allow us to acquire such concepts. As I see it, the interpretation of scripture and the derivation of concepts therefrom is relevantly analogous to the "interpretation" and "derivation of concepts" from the book of nature: we have no guarantees of success but, at the same time, we have only familiar skeptical worries to counsel despair.

The analogy with the book of nature is not given lightly. As I see it, the study and interpretation of (putative) divine revelation properly plays a role in theorizing about God that is strongly analogous to the role played by empirical observation and the interpretation of empirical data in our theorizing about the natural world. As I noted in Chapter 3, then, understanding divine love, or any other divine attribute, will be a matter of reasoning about the various scriptural characterizations of God *together*, in a way that preserves the tensions among them, rather than arbitrarily privileging one over the other or relying wholly on philosophical theorizing. How best to do this is a complicated question to be sorted out in dialogue with research in biblical studies and systematic theology.

Schellenberg himself seems to think that theology has little to contribute to discussion of his argument from hiddenness (and I assume that he would pay a similar compliment to the field of biblical studies). Toward the beginning of his discussion of hiddenness arguments in *The Wisdom to Doubt*, for example, he warns against a "potential confusion of theology and philosophy," and then continues as follows:

> We have—all of us—been influenced by the many attempts of theology to make God fit the actual world. Theology starts off by accepting that God exists and so *has* to make God fit the world: in a way, that is its job. But our job as philosophers, faced with the question of God's existence, is to fight free from the distractions of local and historical contingency, to let the voice of authority grow dim in our ears, and to think for ourselves about what a God and a God-created world would be like. [footnote omitted] When we think at the most fundamental level about the idea of God, we cannot assume that probably God's nature is in accord with the actual world, *and so we cannot take as our guide a picture of God fashioned by theology over the centuries on that assumption.* (2007: 197–8, emphasis in original. Cf. also 2015a: 13–15)

Schellenberg's view here seems to be that our reflections on divine hiddenness ought to be guided by (and only by) our grasp of whatever theology- and revelation-independent concepts of love, perfection, God, and so on that we have, rather than by our grasp of concepts that have been substantially shaped by theology and divine revelation.

To my mind, these remarks of Schellenberg's and the view that I understand them to be expressing seem to me to be neither plausible nor well motivated. Imagine offering the following speech as advice to would-be philosophers of *time*:

> ADVICE. It is our job as philosophers to *think for ourselves* about what a temporal world would be like; and so when we think at the most fundamental level about the idea of time, we cannot assume that probably the *nature of time* is in accord with the actual world; and so we cannot take as our guide a picture of time fashioned by *physics* and *empirical results* over the past hundred years on that assumption.

Advice like this is not absurd; and research that proceeds in accord with it would surely be valuable. But its value will be limited; for research in accord with this advice will not shed much light on the nature and existence of *what physicists call "time,"* but only on the nature and existence of a certain kind of commonsense or philosophical conception of time. It is an interesting question, of course, how what physicists call "time" relates to our commonsense and philosophical conceptions of time; and research in accord with ADVICE may shed interesting light on this question. But if our goal is, primarily, to find out *about the nature and existence of what physicists call "time,"* we need to pay attention to the physicists, their empirical data, and their theories, and we need to conduct our theorizing at least to some extent within whatever conceptual framework might be "revealed" by physical research.

So likewise, I think, with research into the nature and existence of God. Applying Schellenberg's methodological principles to one's theorizing about divine hiddenness will no doubt yield some interesting results. In particular, it may tell us some interesting things about the relationship between certain commonsense or philosophical conceptions of God and the God of Christianity. But if our goal is to shed light on the nature and existence of the *God of Christianity*— which must be at least part of our goal, if we are concerned with the question whether divine hiddenness counts in favor of *atheism*—then we need to pay attention to theologians and their data (most notably, the contents of scripture and tradition), and we need to conduct our theorizing at least to some extent, if possible, within a framework of concepts that are revealed by these sources.[27]

Accordingly, I think it is misguided to rely exclusively on philosophical intuitions about the nature of love in trying to figure out what would have to be true if the *God of Christianity* were perfectly

---

[27] In doing this, will we thereby slip from doing philosophy to doing theology? Perhaps yes, at least on some conceptions of the boundaries between those disciplines. But I think I am much less concerned about disciplinary boundaries than Schellenberg is. In a footnote, he writes:

> I take it that the recent rise of "analytic theology" is symptomatic here [of the increasingly narrow focus on and preoccupation with the exploration of theism in contemporary philosophy of religion]—and this primarily because its proponents and practitioners appear to think it doesn't matter whether what they are doing is called theology or philosophy.   (2015a: 14 n. 2)

One gets the sense that Schellenberg thinks we *ought* to think it matters whether what we are doing is called "philosophy" or "theology." For my part, however, I don't—at least not so long as what is done by analytic theologians is recognized (as I think it clearly ought to be) as deeply relevant to both theology and philosophy of religion.

loving; and it is likewise misguided to rely on the conclusions that those intuitions lead us toward in constructing an argument for atheism. Even if one were to establish beyond doubt that nothing instantiates our own twenty-first-century philosophical conception of perfect love, it would be premature at best to conclude that there is no such thing as the God of classical theism, the God of theism in general, or (even more contentiously) the God of Judaism, Christianity, Islam, or any other religion that claims to worship the God of the biblical texts. For this reason, then, I think that the Schellenberg problem fails on its own terms, as does any version of the hiddenness problem that reproduces its basic structure.

Of course, not everyone will be on board with my affirmation of divine transcendence. For them, then, the hiddenness problem still lingers. But in Chapter 5, I will argue that, even apart from considerations involving divine transcendence, there is good reason to believe that *divine* love would not satisfy an idealized conception of human love. This will complete my case for the conclusion that the Schellenberg problem fails as an argument against the existence of God.

It might be tempting to stop at that point, declaring the hiddenness problem to be solved. The solution thus arrived at would be akin to the skeptical theist solution to the problem of evil, which appeals to God's ability to appreciate goods and relations among possible goods and evils that are far beyond our ken to block inferences from the fact that some evil *appears* to be pointless to the conclusion that it *is* pointless.[28] In the present case, the solution on offer is, in effect, that we are not entitled to conclude that God is *unloving* from the fact that the existence of divine hiddenness appears to involve a failure of love.

I do think that this conclusion is true, and that it constitutes a genuine solution to the hiddenness problem. At the same time, however, I acknowledge that it needs to be supplemented if it is going to be a *satisfying* solution. By cultivating skepticism about conclusions drawn about divine love on the basis of philosophical reflection on our concept of love, the solution I am offering raises to

---

[28] Cf. n. 25. Indeed, it is often said that our limitations are so severe that we are not entitled to the claim that some evil *appears* to be pointless—just as someone who does not speak Farsi is not entitled, upon walking into a room where Farsi is being spoken, to say that nothing meaningful is being said in the room.

salience a challenge of the sort that I mentioned at the end of Section 2—namely, the question of what justifies calling God loving, or *perfectly* loving, *at all*. What *signs* of divine love are there in God's treatment of suffering human beings? This is the question that will linger at the end of Chapter 5, and the remaining chapters in this book will be aimed at addressing it.

5

Divine Love and Personality

God is transcendent, vastly different from anything we might encounter in the world. As I explained in Chapter 4, the more we attend to this fact, the easier it is to see that we cannot have much confidence in our own preconceptions about what the love of God might look like. As confidence in those preconceptions diminishes, the problem of divine hiddenness dissolves.

But perhaps your own confidence remains undiminished. Perhaps you weren't persuaded when I argued against the lightest understandings of transcendence; and perhaps, like most philosophers working on the hiddenness problem, you have a great deal of confidence in the power of reason to discover the nature and scope of divine love. If so, then this chapter is for you. In this chapter, I temporarily set aside the arguments of Chapter 4 and proceed on the assumption that God is, at most, lightly transcendent.

It is widely assumed that divine love is simply an idealized version of one of the best kinds of human love.[1] That is the consensus among people writing about the problem of evil and the problem of divine hiddenness; it is also the consensus in the pews. God's love is the love of an ideal parent, an ideal spouse, an ideal friend. It is commonly held that this is what reason tells us the love of God is like; and it is also commonly held that reason can give us a pretty good idea of what it would mean to love like an ideal parent, spouse, or friend.

In fact, however, careful reflection on the concept of ideal human love gives us good reason to *doubt* that it is the same as divine love.

---

[1] See, e.g., Schellenberg 1993: 18–25; Wessling 2012: esp. 338–41; Talbott 2013: 304; and Jordan 2015: 183–4. Note, incidentally, that within the confines of the assumption just mentioned, Jordan reaches very different conclusions from these other authors about the scope and intensity of divine love for human beings.

In fact, once it is clear what we can reasonably expect (independent of divine revelation) from a perfect being in regard to love for human beings and pursuit of relationship with them, we should be quite surprised to find that God loves and desires relationships with us to the degree depicted in the Christian scriptures.

The bulk of this chapter is devoted to explaining why divine love should not be identified with idealized human love. The upshot, as I will explain more fully toward the end, is that the hiddenness problem can get no rational purchase on us by way of philosophical reflection on the nature of love. At best, the problem gains a foothold only through the negatively valenced love analogies that are suggested by certain characterizations of how God is behaving toward various kinds of people. I conclude by explaining in brief outline how this latter issue will be addressed in subsequent chapters.

In the course of defending my primary conclusion, it will also become clear in this chapter why divine hiddenness does not have to serve greater human goods in order for God to be justified in permitting it or bringing it about. By "human goods" I mean good states of affairs that centrally involve human beings. For example, human pleasure and friendship among human beings are human goods; so likewise are human relationships with God. By contrast, divine pleasure or friendship among dolphins are not human goods, since they do not centrally involve human beings. Of course, this characterization falls well short of rigorous definition; but I think it conveys the concept with sufficient precision for present purposes.

Much of the literature on the problem divine hiddenness has focused on trying to identify human goods for the sake of which divine hiddenness might be permitted—goods like freedom of choice, or the cultivation of various kinds of virtues.[2] My general opinion

---

[2] Some of the best work along these lines is still to be found in Howard-Snyder and Moser 2002—especially Garcia 2002, Moser 2002, Murray 2002, and Wainwright 2002. Schellenberg responds to these essays in his 2005a and 2005b; and Dougherty and Parker (2015) provide a very helpful survey of the variety of greater-human-goods solutions that have been developed since the publication of the Howard-Snyder and Moser volume. Among the valuable interventions along these lines *not* discussed in the Dougherty and Parker article, I would like to call attention to Crummett 2015 and Dumsday 2012. Note too that one might posit greater human goods without attempting to identify them. For example, Paul Moser (2002, 2008) identifies various God-justifying goods that might result from divine hiddenness, but he also denies that the goods he identifies explain every case in which God is hidden from someone. Nevertheless, his view seems to be that every case in which God is hidden from

about the views defended in this literature is that, although divine hiddenness often does contribute to securing the goods posited therein, it is deeply implausible to think that *every instance* of divine hiddenness (or suffering as a result of it) contributes to such goods, or is permitted to make room for the cultivation of such goods. I have very little stake in defending this opinion, however; for my own response to the problem of divine hiddenness does not depend on there being no human goods toward which divine hiddenness always contributes.[3] It implies only that there *need not* be any such goods in order for God still to count as perfectly loving. Accordingly, the greater-human-goods literature will not receive much discussion in this book.

1.

Love comes in many different varieties—romantic, erotic, filial, parental, and so on. Let us focus our attention on the best kinds, the purest and most noble versions of love, the ones that are the most plausible candidates for being identified with divine love. Parental love is surely one candidate; perhaps spousal love, or the love that obtains between the closest of friends will be good ones as well. Perhaps the very best kind of human love is some amalgam of these, and perhaps that one will be the best candidate of all. In any case, let it be understood that when I talk without qualification about "love," "human love," or "ideal love" the kinds of love I have in view are these "best" kinds, and, in particular, whichever among them is most apt to be identified, in its ideal form, with divine love.

There is a great deal of controversy about what exactly is involved in love. Despite the controversy, however, there are at least two points of widespread general agreement, and affirming these is all that I will need to move forward with the argument of this chapter. First, it is widely held that at least one of the following two desires belongs to the very essence of love: desire for *the good* of the beloved, and desire

someone is justified by some human good that God aims to promote (see especially Moser 2002: 135).

[3] For my own early attempts to develops a solution along these lines, see Rea 2009a and 2011a.

for *union* with the beloved.[4] That is to say, one does not count as displaying love toward someone unless one has for that person at least one of the two desires just mentioned.

One might doubt this claim if one's attention is focused on kinds of love—erotic love, for example—that are not likely candidates for being identified with divine love. Or one might doubt it if one thinks that love has no well-defined essence.[5] But neither of these two reasons for doubting is pertinent for the purposes of this chapter. The first is irrelevant because our focus here is on kinds of love that *are* candidates for being identified with divine love. The second I am setting aside for the sake of argument because affirming it would only cast further doubt on the soundness of the hiddenness problem. The expectations that drive that problem are predicated on the assumption that God desires union with us, desires our good, or both.[6] If this assumption were false, the key premise in the hiddenness argument (S1) would be much harder to motivate.

This brings us to the second point of widespread agreement, namely, that divine love includes not just one but *both* of these desires: God desires union with us, *and* God desires our good. The idea that God desires our good is central to the tradition. The idea that God desires—indeed, longs for—unitive relationship with human beings is also prevalent, especially in contemporary evangelicalism (which I think has, for sociological reasons, had a rather significant impact on the literature on the hiddenness problem). For example, in their bestselling devotional guide *Experiencing God*, Richard and Henry T. Blackaby write:

> God created you for a love relationship with Him. He yearns for you to love Him and respond to His immeasurable love for you. God's nature is perfect, holy, total love. He will never relate to you in any other way although you may not always understand His actions.   (2014: 11)

---

[4] See, e.g., Frankfurt 2004, Murphy 2017, and Stump 2011.

[5] Carrie Ichikawa Jenkins (2015) affirms this about romantic love. On her view, romantic love is a functional kind, and is present wherever one person *x* is prompted "to a sufficient degree, to engage in sufficiently many things on [some] list" of defining characteristics with respect to another person *y* (2015: 360). One might say something similar about other kinds of love.

[6] As we saw in Chapter 2 (pp. 23–5), Schellenberg's defenses of the claim that a perfectly loving God would not permit reasonable nonbelief to occur trade explicitly on the assumption that perfect love includes a desire for what is best for the beloved, and that perfect love includes a desire to "come close" and "share [one's] life"—in other words, to enjoy a kind of union—with the beloved.

The idea is also to be found in the work of process theologians and some who have been influenced by them.[7] This is not to say that the idea is a twentieth-century invention—Eleonore Stump attributes it to St. Thomas Aquinas, for example[8]—but it has certainly been prevalent in the twentieth and twenty-first centuries.[9]

One might worry that attributing desires to God is problematic on the traditional assumption that God is impassible. One might also worry that attributing desire for union with creatures to God portrays God as objectionably dependent upon creatures, suggesting that God needs something from us in order to be fully content.[10] But the idea that God *wills* our good is prevalent in the tradition, as is the idea that God wills union with us; and the fact that God wills something seems sufficient for at least the analogical attribution of desire for it to God. So I think that these concerns can also safely be set aside.

For purposes here, then, I will affirm both of the two widely agreed upon claims that I have just identified—that God desires union with human beings and desires their good, and that human love would, in its idealized form, *have to* include at least one of the two desires. If God loves us at all and these claims are not true, then solving the hiddenness problem is easy; for, in that case, one of two conclusions would follow. Either divine love is radically different from human love in its idealized form (a claim I hope to establish by other means in this chapter); or those working on divine hiddenness over the past quarter century have been importantly mistaken about what ideal human love might look like (a claim I reject, but whose truth would cast serious doubt on the premises that drive the hiddenness problem).

What I now want to show is that *perfect love*, or *divine love*, cannot plausibly be identified with idealized human love. In a somewhat misleading slogan: perfect love is not the same as love perfected. By *divine love*, I mean whatever kind of love a perfect being might have for another person or group of persons. Since any instance of divine love will be in accord with God's absolute perfection, any instance of divine love will also appropriately be described as a case of *perfect love*. *Ideal*, or *idealized* love is the kind of love that one person would have for another person or group if she were to have for that person

[7] Cf. Oord 2010; Sanders 1998: 87–8, 175–81.   [8] Stump 2012: ch. 5.
[9] For a very helpful survey and discussion of different views of divine love in the tradition, see Peckham 2015a and 2015b.
[10] Cf. Nygren 1969.

or group an idealized version of one of the best kinds of human love. We shall see that there are strong reasons for thinking that a perfect being *would not* have this latter kind of love for human beings (either individually or as a group). The upshot, then, will be that there is strong reason to doubt that divine love is equivalent to ideal love.

2.

Let me begin by explaining what it means, in general, to have an attribute in an ideal way. Some attributes are primitive; they can't be analyzed into simpler component ones. If *existence* is an attribute, it is plausibly like this. Maybe *concreteness* and *abstractness* are like this as well. In the case of traits like these, it is hard to say exactly what we mean when we speak of their idealization; but usually, if it is meaningful at all, it involves at least (and maybe no more than) the removal of all relevant limitations. So, for example, the idealization of existence is (plausibly) just necessary existence, since one way for something's existence to be limited is for it to be temporary or otherwise contingent. Or, if there are modes of existence corresponding to the most general kinds of things, then the idealization of (generic) existence might involve the removal all limitations that would be imposed under any particular mode of existence.

For complex attributes, idealization will likewise involve the removal of relevant limitations. But it will also involve idealization of component properties. So, for example, if being human is analyzed as being a rational animal, the ideal human would be ideal with respect to rationality and ideal with respect to animality (whatever exactly that would mean). Perhaps obviously, the idealization of a property—simple or complex—will involve *only* the removal of limitations that are consistent with still having the trait. So an ideal human will *not* be an ideal being, and vice versa, since (I assume) no human being is omnipresent in spacetime.[11]

---

[11] Close attention to this fact reveals some thorny problems with the method of perfect being theology. On this, see Speaks 2018. It also stands in *prima facie* conflict with the doctrine of the incarnation, since one wants to say that, as God, the incarnate Christ is an ideal *being* and, as a man, he is an ideal human being. This concern, however, can be addressed by noting that the ideal *being*, according to Christian doctrine, is the triune God, with whom the incarnate Christ is not strictly identical.

Consider, then, the idealization of love, understood as including desire for the good of the beloved or desire for union with the beloved. In light of what has just been said, a person who loves an individual or group of individuals in an ideal way would be unlimited in her desire for union with her beloved, unlimited in her desire for the good of her beloved, or both. But now consider what it would mean to be unlimited in these ways. One who limitlessly desires the good for an individual or group would desire their good in a way that eclipses in priority and strength any desires focused on anyone or anything apart from that individual or group, including desire for one's own good. Likewise for someone who limitlessly desires union with their beloved.

So, for example, imagine two parents, one of whom desires the good of her children to some particular degree, and the other of whom desires the good of her children ever so slightly more. Perhaps the second parent is slightly less focused on her own good; perhaps she is slightly less focused on the good of others. Clearly, whatever else we might say about the virtues and vices of these two parents, it is the second parent who (for better or worse) comes closer to the least limited, most idealized form of *desire for the good of her children*. Likewise if the desire in question were desire for union.

In reflecting on this example, one might already find reason to doubt that what I am calling *ideal* love could sensibly be identified with *perfect* love. One might also think that it is not aptly called "ideal" love. Mark Murphy, en route to defending conclusions similar to those I will be defending here, raises the same concern. As he puts it, "our ordinary conception of being excellently loving involves appropriateness conditions, so that the extent to which one is motivated toward the good of another and seeks union with that other is fitting to the relationship between them."[12] I agree, and will say more

For further explication of my views on the trinity and incarnation, see Rea 2009b and 2011b.

[12] Murphy 2017: 36. I said that Murphy defends conclusions *similar* to those I will be reaching here. (See also Murphy 2014.) At first glance one might think that he is defending the *same* conclusions. In particular, he argues that God would neither be maximally devoted to the pursuit of human welfare nor maximally devoted to the pursuit of union with human beings. Superficially, this is *exactly* the conclusion I will be reaching. So why not just help myself to Murphy's arguments and move on?

The answer, in short, is that Murphy and I differ in our concept of *maximal love*. Murphy's goal is to show that one cannot reason from the belief that God is perfect to the conclusion that God is *loving*. He thinks that scripture provides reason to believe

about this as the chapter unfolds. But for now, let us hold this objection in abeyance and suppose that, at least for God, it is *not* obvious that excellence in loving would diverge from what I am calling ideal love; and let us entirely set aside, because they are wholly insubstantial, any objections to the label, "ideal."[13]

In addition to wondering whether ideal love would be a good thing, one might also wonder whether it is even possible. There are at least two reasons why one might think it is not.

First, desire for union with someone and desire for their good can conflict. There are limits on how much interpersonal union human beings can endure, and from whom, and under what circumstances. So one person's limitless desire for someone else's good might well conflict with or force limits upon her desire for union with them, and vice versa. Perhaps this is how it would be with God's desires toward us. If so, then it follows immediately that if God is a perfect lover, God would not, indeed could not, love anyone in a way that is ideal with respect to both desires.

It is not obvious to me that a *perfect* being's unbounded pursuit of union with some individual or group would inevitably conflict with

---

that God is loving, but he denies that *love* is included in the concept of perfection. His reason for denying this is that, on his view, perfections—attributes included in the concept of perfection—have *intrinsic maxima*, whereas love does not. The intrinsic maximum for a property is "a point beyond which one cannot more valuably realize that property, either because the property cannot be realized more fully, or if it can be realized more fully, its realization would not be more valuable" (2017: 35). But, he argues, pursuit of human welfare and pursuit of union do not have intrinsic maxima; so neither does love. It is in *just this sense*, for Murphy, that God fails to be maximally devoted either to our good or to the pursuit of union with us.

As I am conceiving of it, however, maximal devotion does not require that there be an upper limit on the realization of the devotion in question. Rather, it requires only that *nothing else is of equal or higher priority*—the maximally devoted person is not disposed to sacrifice the object of devotion for the sake of any other object or goal. Murphy does not seem interested in ruling out the possibility that God is *in this sense*, maximally devoted to our good or to pursuing union with us. His concern lies elsewhere. Thus, his arguments do not establish the conclusion I aim to establish.

[13] Objections to the label are insubstantial because the label is not meant to convey a *view* about excellence in loving. The kind of love I have in mind needs *some* label to facilitate discussion, and "ideal" is reasonably well motivated. But we could easily change the label without affecting the substance of the discussion. The first objection, that my conclusion is already obvious, I hold in abeyance because I think that it is not antecedently obvious that excellence in loving diverges from what I am calling ideal love, even if that conclusion starts to seem obvious as the discussion goes on. As shall emerge over the course of the chapter, many seem to identify perfect love with ideal love as I have characterized it here.

pursuit of their good; but I think this possibility should not be ruled out by a characterization of ideal love. So let me qualify the characterization of ideal love as follows: ideal desire for the good of a person or group, and ideal desire for union with them, are as I have already characterized them; but ideal *love* that includes both desires will hold and pursue the two desires in balance with one another. To put it in other words: if someone ideally desires the good for a person or group, then that desire is motivationally predominant for her, and likewise for ideal desire for union; but ideal *love* that includes both desires will accord motivational predominance not to either desire on its own, but to the pair, in balance.[14]

Second, one might worry that ideal love toward *everyone* is impossible because ideal desire for the *good* for everyone would be precluded by conflicts between what is in various people's best interest. Jeffrey Jordan (2012), for example, maintains that God loves everyone with equal intensity only if God equally "identifies" with each person's interests, or equally takes each person's interests as God's own; and he goes on to argue that this, together with the obvious fact that people's interests often conflict with one another, implies that God does not love everyone with equal intensity. On the assumption that limitlessly desiring the good for someone implies identifying with their interests in the relevant sense, Jordan's conclusion also implies that it is impossible for God to desire, in an unlimited way, the good for two individuals whose interests conflict.

Jordan's argument is vulnerable to plausible criticism on at least two points: first, it is unclear that love for a person requires identifying with their interests; second, it is unclear that God cannot maximally identify with the interests of two individuals whose interests conflict.[15] But even if his argument is correct, his conclusion remains consistent

---

[14] I thank Robert Audi for the suggestion to understand the idealization of the desires of love in terms of motivational predominance. If a definition of motivational predominance is wanted, I tentatively offer the following: a desire d is motivationally predominant for a person $s =_{df} d$ provides s with a reason to act with the aim of fulfilling the desire, and s has no reason of equal or greater strength not to act with the aim of fulfilling d. Note that this definition allows for multiple non-competing desires to have motivational predominance for a person; but it does not allow for competing desires to be motivationally predominant, except in the case where they are held in balance with one another as components of a larger desire.

[15] Parker 2013. Talbott 2013 raises additional objections, one of which is that there are no genuine conflicts of interest in a theistic universe. This objection is relevant to my own argument, so I'll deal with it later. Jordan's own reply is in Jordan 2015.

with the thesis that a perfect being would love *some* human beings—indeed, might love *very many* of them—in an ideal way. His conclusion is also consistent with the claim that a perfect being would love human beings *collectively*, even if not individually, in an ideal way; for all that would be required for this would be a limitless desire for the good of humanity (which would sidestep the worry raised by human beings whose interests conflict) together with a limitless desire for union with all of humanity.

My own view, by contrast, is that a perfect being would love *no* particular human being in an ideal way; nor would God love human beings collectively in an ideal way. Furthermore, unlike Jordan's argument, mine depends on no controversial theses about the necessity of God identifying with someone else's interests. So I will set aside the dispute between Jordan and his critics, and I will simply stipulate that, considerations of goodness and rationality aside, it is at least possible for an otherwise perfect being to love human beings ideally—to be maximally oriented toward them, according motivational predominance both to the desire for union with them (individually, or collectively) and to the desire for their good, or to the pair in balance with one another if they happen to conflict.

3.

I turn now to my argument for the conclusion that divine love is not ideal love. I will start by challenging the idea that a perfect being might ideally desire the good for human beings.

Jordan Wessling uses the term "supreme love" to describe this kind of devotion:

> [W]hen God has supreme love for a person, He desires her highest good, and His character generates no contradictory desire of equal or greater strength; God therefore does all that is morally permissible and metaphysically possible to fulfill this desire.[16]

Wessling himself affirms that God has supreme love for every human being, and he furthermore acknowledges (by way of trying to explain why it makes sense to *argue* for that claim, as he does in his paper)

---

[16] Wessling 2012: 338.

that the view is "widely assumed" among contemporary philosophers of religion.

If this view is correct—if God does have supreme love for everyone—then God is something like what Susan Wolf would call a *(loving) moral saint*, someone who is maximally committed to improving the welfare of other people or of society as a whole, to the exclusion of the promotion of her own interests or welfare and even to the exclusion of the promotion of other competing goods.[17] However, Wolf argues persuasively that moral sainthood as she conceives of it is not a state toward which it would be at all rational, good, or desirable for a human being to strive. For similar reasons, so I shall argue, neither would it be rational, good, or desirable for a perfect being to strive for moral sainthood so conceived.[18] Thus a perfect being would not love any human being, or group of human beings, in an ideal way.

At the heart of Wolf's argument is the idea that it is genuinely good to cultivate and embrace love for goods other than the well-being of others, and to love these goods for their own sake or for what one personally gets out of them, rather than simply for what they contribute to the well-being of others. Examples include love for art, natural beauty, good food, sport and leisure, and the like. It is also good, she thinks, to devote resources—even resources that could have instead been used to safeguard or promote the well-being of others—to nurturing these loves, and to developing one's own personal talents, interests, and projects. By virtue of their inherent limitations, however, human beings cannot do these things while at the same time dedicating themselves to promoting as much good as possible for others. For people who must make choices between goods to love and projects in which to invest, the good life will involve making trade-offs between promoting the welfare of others and promoting one's own personal interests. So, on the assumption that we rationally

---

[17] Wolf 1982.

[18] Some who resist Wolf's conclusion that sainthood is not an ideal worth striving for have been inclined to challenge her *characterization* of sainthood. (See, e.g., Adams 1984.) I think that there is merit to these objections; but for purposes here, I want to stick with Wolf's understanding of sainthood, just for the sake of convenience. The question here, after all, is whether it makes sense to suppose that God would manifest the sort of devotion to human good that Wolf associates with the term "moral saint"; and to answer that question, it doesn't really matter whether she is correct in making that association.

ought to strive for a good life, we ought not to strive for moral sainthood.

Might it be the case that moral duty requires us to sacrifice a "good life" for the sake of devotion to the well-being of others? No; for in that case, what I am calling a *good life* would not genuinely be good, and it would be (contrary to what Wolf argues) rational and good to strive for moral sainthood after all. In other words, the very intuitions that tell us that it is good to pursue goods besides the well-being of others also tell us that we should not be pursuing moral sainthood.

But what about God, who is unlimited in resources and cognitive capacity? Wolf's arguments have not, to my knowledge, been cited as providing reasons for thinking that God would not be maximally devoted to the promotion of human welfare; and I think that the reason has mainly to do with divine omnipotence. One of the most widespread, even if generally unspoken, assumptions underlying the literature on the problem of evil and the problem of divine hiddenness is that, because God is all powerful, God faces no interesting or morally relevant choices between the promotion of God's own interests, projects, and so on (whatever they might be) and the promotion of human well-being. For this reason, people have tended to think that God is justified in permitting evil, suffering, and divine hiddenness only if those things serve human goods—only if, in other words, God's permission of those things is consistent with God's being maximally devoted to the promotion of human welfare.

As I see it, however, part of what it is for God to be genuinely and perfectly personal is for God to be someone with interests and desires distinct from and not necessarily oriented around those of others, projects that further those interests and desires, and a personality that is at least partly expressive of them. With regard to human beings, Wolf observes that "[the pursuit of moral sainthood] seems to require either the lack or denial of the existence of an identifiable, personal self."[19] To my mind, this is true regardless of whether the "self" in question is human or divine.

It is not that having distinct interests, projects that further those interests, and a personality expressive of them are necessary conditions on personhood. Rather, the idea is that these things comprise a central aspect of who one is, and lacking them is a deficiency that

---

[19] Wolf 1982: 424.

somehow diminishes one's personhood. If this is right, then the view that God is maximally devoted to human welfare is inconsistent with the idea that God is genuinely and perfectly personal: it implies that either God is perfect but not really or fully personal, or God is personal but importantly deficient as a person.

If the writings of contemporary philosophers of religion are any guide, many will be content with a concept of God as somehow less than perfectly personal. Although God is typically characterized as a being with personal attributes—knowledge, love, power, and so on— it is also fairly typical to find God talked about in ways that make sense only on the supposition that God is little more than a kind of machine whose programming requires it to entertain and affirm as many truths as possible while at the same time causing, allowing, or preventing worldly events in such a way as to maximize various kinds of moral and non-moral goods. Of course, nobody explicitly *says* that this is how they think of God; but (so I say, anyway) it is hard to read much contemporary philosophy of religion without getting the sense that this is in fact the picture that underlies much of it.

In contrast to this, the Christian scriptures seem to encourage us to take very seriously the idea that God is personal and, indeed, that God has a unique personality that is at least partly expressive of God's own purely *self-regarding* interests and desires. As Geller (2000) points out, the God of the Old Testament is predominantly portrayed as a God of *covenant*, which requires robust personhood; and one might think that part of why it is important that God enter into covenants with human beings is precisely that (as is typical with parties to a covenant) divine goods do not perfectly coincide with human goods, and God is interested in promoting the latter in balance with rather than to the exclusion of the former. We are told that God's ways are not our ways, that God's thoughts are not our thoughts (Isa. 55:8); and we are often reminded (and, frankly, put off by the fact) that God is interested in maximizing God's own glory (whatever exactly that means) and often in ways that seem to conflict with human interests. The scriptures do insist that God loves human beings; but the overall biblical portrait of God is one of a personal being with a unique and beautiful personality who has, in addition to an overwhelming interest in the good of human beings, a strong interest in living out the divine personality for its own sake.

Admittedly, it is at least possible that God's interest in living out God's own personality and in promoting non-anthropocentric goods would never conflict with promotion of the good for all human beings. The possibility seems remote, and I see no reason for thinking that matters have in fact turned out this way. But one might object that, so long as the possibility is there, my claim that ideal love for everyone is *inconsistent* with genuine personality is shipwrecked. For it looks as if a personal being *can* also succeed in promoting everyone else's good.

But *maximal* devotion to something is not just a matter of pursuing it when it poses no conflicts with other things one values; it is, rather, a disposition to promote that thing *regardless* of whether it conflicts with other goods one might wish to promote. So a being who is disposed to promote human welfare *only* in the eventuality that doing so does not conflict with the promotion of his or her own good falls well short of moral sainthood. Such a being is, at best, what we might call an *opportunistic saint*. Opportunistic sainthood is not supreme love, even if it superficially satisfies Wessling's characterization, since we can easily imagine a being whose love for human beings is more intensely focused upon them. So if God is merely an opportunistic saint, then God is not ideally loving toward anyone.

Consider the case, then, where God does face genuine choices between the promotion of purely human goods and the promotion of conflicting divine goods. In that case, moral sainthood would be no more rational, good, or desirable for God to pursue than for human beings to pursue. In fact, there is every reason to think that it would be irrational, bad, and undesirable for God to pursue it. For when the promotion of human goods conflicts with the promotion of divine goods—the living out of God's unique and maximally beautiful personality, the promotion of God's other, non-anthropocentric projects, and so on—there is no more reason to think that the promotion of human goods should take priority than there is for thinking that the promotion of mosquito goods should take priority over the promotion of human goods. So even if God has all the power and resources necessary to be maximally devoted to promoting the good for God's beloved, if God is *perfect* God will not be so devoted because to be so would involve a failure of rationality.

Just as there is reason to doubt that God would desire in an unlimited way the good for God's beloved, so too there is reason to doubt that God would desire in an unlimited way union with every individual beloved by God. This for two reasons.

First, it is at best unclear that we, or our personal autonomy, could survive God's *acting* on an unlimited desire for union with us.

Imagine being the child of a parent, or the spouse of a man or woman, who came as close as humanly possible to an unlimited desire for union. Being the object of such desire can hardly be said to be an unmitigated good. Can we really be sure that matters would be any different if the parent or spouse in question were God?

Here we must recall again Mark Murphy's observation that what I am calling *ideal* love does not neatly map on to our concept of *excellence* in love. Perhaps there is something about God that would allow us to endure being the object of an unlimited *divine* desire for union. But, again, whether that is so is at best unclear. If we could not endure God's acting on an unlimited desire for union with us, then God would know this and, being perfectly rational, would not have such a desire in the first place. A perfectly rational and omniscient being would have a desire for union that is limited in accord with the amount of union that we could actually endure and enjoy.

In making this argument, have I perhaps misconstrued the notion of "unlimited desire"? One might object that *unlimited desire for union* is not the same as *desire for unlimited union*. Granted, we could not endure unlimited union, and so God would not desire this; but why not think that God's *desire for appropriately limited union* might itself be *unlimited*—presumably in its intensity or in the ardor with which God is disposed to pursue it? One response might be to say that this too is a sort of desire that we could not endure. This way of thinking attributes to God what sounds like an absurdly and unsettlingly fanatical devotion to union with us. One wants divine love, to be sure; but few want to be the object of unlimitedly intense focus and longing on the part of another person.

But suppose we can endure God's unlimitedly desiring (appropriately limited) union with us. Still, there is a second reason to doubt that God would desire us in this way: namely, it is doubtful that human beings individually or together are fitting objects for an unlimited desire for union. In human relationships, we readily acknowledge that some individuals are more fitting objects for unitive desire, or certain degrees of that desire, than others. One should not, for example, desire union (even "appropriately limited" union) with one's cat to the same degree that one would desire union with a human spouse, sibling, or close friend. Even if one were capable of achieving some kind of personal union with a cat, and even if one had the capacity to pursue this in an intense way without sacrificing any aspect of one's pursuit of union with other human beings, the cat simply isn't the right sort of object for that degree of unitive desire. The reason for this has to do with the limits on the kind of union that one can have with a cat, as compared with the kind of union one can have with other sentient creatures. Personal union with other human beings is better—instrumentally and for its own sake—than whatever kind of union one can have with a cat; and a rational pattern of desire structure would reflect this fact.

For the same reason, human beings seem not to be appropriate objects for an unlimited divine desire for union. Surely God loves creatures other than human beings—cats and dolphins, for example. But presumably God desires union with such creatures to a lesser degree than God desires union with us; for the kind of union God can have with us is better than the kind of union God can have with them, and God's perfectly rational desire structure will reflect this difference in value. Likewise, however, the kind of union God can have with us is inferior to the kind of union God could have with more Godlike beings; and a perfectly rational desire structure would reflect this fact as well.

Are there more Godlike beings than us? Even if there are not, my point here still stands. Just as the last human being on earth *still* should not have *unlimited* desire for union with members of the "next best" species, so too a perfectly rational deity would not have unlimited desire for union with us simply because we happen to be the best objects available. But, in fact, the Christian doctrine of the trinity guarantees that, for each member of the trinity, there *are* more Godlike beings with whom that person can have a unitive relationship. Union with another member of the trinity will be the best of all possible kinds of union; and so it is that to which each member of the trinity will direct his or her unlimited unitive desires.

I have now argued that God would have neither an unlimited desire for our good nor an unlimited desire for union with us. I take it as evident that exactly the same reasoning, if sound, will show that, if it turns out that divine love includes both desires and the two desires can conflict with one another, God would not accord motivational predominance to that *pair* of desires. Thus, I take myself to have shown that a perfect being would not be an ideal lover of human beings, and this because maximizing either of the desires of love, or both in balance with one another, toward human beings would be neither good nor rational for a perfect being.

For those who have lingering doubts, perhaps the following consideration will serve to drive the argument home. Unlimited desire for union (even unlimited desire for *appropriately limited* union) with someone or some group, unlimited desire for their good, or unlimited love for them that includes both of these desires held in balance with one another would amount to a kind of worship. The Christian tradition has *never* maintained that human beings are appropriate objects of worship. It has never maintained that desire for the good of *any* creature, or desire for union with them, or both desires held in balance with one another are appropriately accorded motivational predominance. By contrast, it has *always* held that God is the only appropriate object of worship, and that desire for union with God, for divine goods, and for the furtherance of divine projects are precisely the sorts of desires that deserve to be accorded motivational predominance. So to suppose that God has a fundamentally different desire structure—one that locates human beings and their good at the center of all things—is, at best, absurd from a Christian point of view; and, at worst, it is blasphemous.

4.

In defending the claim that a perfect being would not be ideally loving toward human beings, I bring my response to the problem of divine hiddenness one step closer to completion.

As we saw in Chapter 2, the hiddenness problem trades on violated expectations arising out of our understanding of divine love. In Chapter 4, I argued that proper attention to divine transcendence ought to make us skeptical of positive conclusions about the nature of divine love arrived at by way of (empirically informed) philosophical reflection. This fact undercuts Schellenberg's so-called "argument from above," which starts from assumptions about the nature of God and perfect love and proceeds to the conclusion that divine hiddenness is inconsistent with the existence of a perfectly loving God.

In the present chapter I have gone a step further, arguing that even if we set aside considerations involving divine transcendence, there remain good a priori reasons for denying that God would be an ideal lover of human beings. The reason is that even a perfect being might have non-anthropocentric loves and interests that conflict with and take higher priority than promotion of the good for human beings. If this is right, then there is no incoherence in supposing that God loves human beings perfectly but nevertheless permits divine hiddenness or various other things that cause human pain and suffering for reasons that have nothing to do with the promotion of human goods. Perhaps such things are permitted instead for the realization of legitimate and worthwhile divine goods, or perhaps other goods wholly beyond our ken.

One might try to resist my conclusion by adapting a thought experiment from Jordan Wessling. As I mentioned earlier, Wessling thinks that God would manifest supreme love toward everyone. He offers two positive considerations in support of this claim. First, following a suggestion of Thomas Talbott, he says:

> maximal love, like God's other great-making properties when directed at creation, must be of universal scope and uppermost quality. Just as God's perfect knowledge ensures that he knows all true propositions infallibly, God's maximal love entails that He loves all created persons supremely. (2012: 344)

This consideration I take myself already to have addressed in Section 2: understanding divine love in the way that Talbott recommends leads to conflicts between divine love and divine goodness and rationality. Wessling's second consideration is a thought experiment. He invites us to consider two deities, Zeus and Thor, who differ in just the following way: whereas Thor supremely loves everyone but the Athenians, Zeus supremely loves absolutely everyone. Wessling then asks who, of the two, is the more perfect lover? Clearly, he thinks, it is Zeus.[20]

I think that Wessling is right to think that, as the two deities are described here, Zeus is a more perfect lover *of humanity* than Thor; but I do not think that this thought experiment shows that Zeus more closely approximates absolute perfection in love. Whatever else one says about perfect love, one at least ought to say this: perfect love might be manifested by a perfect being. But supreme love as Wessling conceives of it is pretty much the same as what I have been calling *ideal* love; and I have been arguing throughout this chapter that a perfect being would not love anyone in an ideal way. Wessling's thought experiment doesn't challenge any premise of that argument; and so I see no reason to think that it counts against my conclusions.

---

[20] Cf. Wessling 2012: 344.

I must admit, however, that I find my own conclusions discomforting. I have, as the saying goes, followed my arguments where they lead; and the view at which I have arrived seems to me to be the one that best fits the relevant data (scripture, intuition, empirical fact). But at the same time I *want* God to be maximally oriented toward the promotion of my good, and I want God to have at least a very strong desire for union with me. I do not want to hear that God might balance my interests against God's own; and I am positively disturbed to think that my own interests might well lose out in the balance. God is supposed to be my heavenly parent, after all; and at the heart of all my own twenty-first-century parental guilt is the impossible idea that parents are supposed to sacrifice absolutely everything to promote the well-being of their children. And so God must do for me.

But my discomfort at hearing that God might prioritize divine interests over my own comes from exactly the same source as the discomfort I would feel if my wife or one of my parents were to say, "I'm sorry; but your interests and mine conflict on this occasion, and today my own interests are going to win out." Those are hard words to hear; and for that reason people do not often say them to one another. In the face of them, one wants to complain that one is being treated hardly, loved poorly. But such decisions are taken all the time in healthy loving relationships, and if people did not make such choices their relationships would soon become unhealthy. The source of complaint—at least against the *abstract* claim that sometimes the other person's interests will take precedence over one's own—is ultimately selfishness. For, again, moral sainthood is neither a good nor a rational ideal, and so we have no right to demand it of anyone.

Moreover, it is worth pointing out here, precisely against the backdrop of the conclusions reached thus far, what an incredible and comforting surprise it is to learn from scripture (assuming, again, that the Christian scriptures are a source of genuine information about God's love for and dispositions toward human beings) just how *much* God loves us.[21] At the same time that the conclusions of this chapter disappoint our deeply self-oriented hopes and expectations for God, so too they dramatically underscore the beautifully comforting exclamation from the Epistle of St. John: "Behold what

---

[21] Although I do assume that scripture is a source of information about God and God's character, note again—as discussed toward the end of Chapter 4—that I do not take it to be a wholly unproblematic source.

manner of love the Father has bestowed on us, that we should be called children of God!"[22]

The gospels and the New Testament epistles tell us that, although we had no right to this—no moral claim upon God such that perfect goodness would demand this—God loved us enough to become incarnate and to die on a cross for the sake of our salvation. Whatever exactly we make, philosophically speaking, of the doctrine of the atonement, the fact that God would make that sort of sacrifice on our behalf in the absence of some obligation to do so is, in light of the conclusions of this chapter, absolutely stunning. So likewise is the claim, in the epistle to the Romans, that God causes all things to work together for the good of those who love and are called by God. Nothing in the argument of this chapter (or the book as a whole) is intended to negate this important scriptural claim.

Indeed, I want to go a step further and say that I intend my account to be consistent with the view (which I affirm, in no small part because it is plausibly implied by Romans 8:28) that part of what is involved in God's loving us is a disposition to satisfy a constraint that Marilyn McCord Adams insists must be part of any successful theodicy: namely, that God arrange for the sufferings God permits in our lives, and for the horrendous evils[23] in which we participate either as perpetrators or victims, to be *defeated* within the context of our lives. Defeating something bad is not the same as compensating a person for it, or seeing to it that its badness is outweighed. It is, rather, a matter of the bad thing's being "included in some good enough whole to which it bears a relation of organic (rather than merely additive) unity"; and an instance of evil or suffering is defeated *within the context of someone's life* if their life "is a good whole to which [that instance of evil or suffering] bears the relevant organic unity."[24]

So, on the one hand, I affirm that God is not maximally devoted to our good, and may sometimes allow our proximate good to be sacrificed; and I deny that we have any guarantee that these sacrifices will be allowed *for the sake of* our ultimate good rather than for the

---

[22] 1 John 3:1, New King James Version®. Copyright ©1982 by Thomas Nelson. Used by permission. All rights reserved.

[23] Adams characterizes horrendous evils as "evils the participation in which (that is, the doing or suffering of which) constitutes prima facie reason to doubt whether the participant's life could (given their inclusion in it) be a great good to him/her on the whole." (Adams 1990: 26).

[24] Adams 1990: 28.

sake of other and perhaps non-anthropocentric goods. But, on the other hand, I also affirm that it is part of divine love as revealed in scripture that God will, in any case, work good *for us* out of the evil and suffering in our lives, defeating their badness and guaranteeing that even lives marked by horrendous evil will be great goods, on the whole, to those who have them.[25]

At this juncture, however, one might want to ask what other projects God might have and love so much that God would sometimes prioritize them above promoting our good and pursuing union with us.[26] What sort of personality might God have such that God's pursuing union with us or promoting our good might conflict with God's living out that personality in the way that God wants to?

So a mosquito might ask about us and our projects and personalities. Tempting though it may be to ask such questions, we cannot possibly hope to find defensible answers. *Maybe* one of God's projects involves interacting with humans on certain terms that suit God's personality better than other, more humanly desirable modes of interaction. *Maybe* one of God's projects involves bringing us into a certain kind of relationship with God, or accomplishing certain earthly goals with creation.[27] *Maybe* these or similar projects inherently

---

[25] Thanks to Caroline Paddock for urging me to be explicit about the points in this paragraph and the one preceding it.

[26] Schellenberg seems to dismiss "the whole idea of God pursuing external, perhaps unknown goods for the good of creatures" out of hand on the grounds that God is the good, and so nothing "could provide for a total state of affairs as good as one in which only God exists apart from a creation in every corpuscle aflame with the presence of God" (2007: 200). If sound, the same reasoning would justify dismissing the idea of God pursuing unknown goods *not* for the sake of promoting the good of creatures, too. But I do not share the intuitions on which Schellenberg's claims in this passage seem to rest. Moreover, the biblical creation accounts in Genesis 1 and 2 seem to speak against his reasoning. God is depicted as creating all manner of different things, declaring them to be good; but, between creating the first human being and the second one, God declares that it is *not* good for the first one to be alone, thus leading God to create a second human being. None of this makes any sense, however, on the supposition that there are no further goods to be gained once one has a creation whose every corpuscle is aflame with the presence of God. Moreover, contrary to what is argued on pp. 198–201 of Schellenberg's book, I see no support whatsoever coming from *these* ideas to the conclusion that God "would make conscious awareness of the Divine available to every finite personal creature" (2007: 200). For there are many ways in which a creature, even a conscious one, might be "aflame with the presence of God" without being consciously aware of God's presence as such.

[27] Some commentators on the book of Job read the divine speeches as emphasizing that human beings are not the focal point of creation. See, e.g., Schifferdecker 2008: ch. 2 and p. 106.

involve some degree of divine hiddenness. Or maybe not. This is precisely the corner of the space of possible goods about which we can most expect to be in the dark.

Then again, perhaps we can just see that there *couldn't* be other divine loves or projects that conflict with the promotion of human goods. I see two ways of pressing this objection.

One is to suggest that this idea conflicts with God's "psychological aseity."[28] Psychological aseity is the attribute of God whereby God has intrinsically all of the resources necessary and sufficient for being maximally content. Wessling appeals to psychological aseity in order to rebut the claim that God's *creative activity* is fundamentally motivated by self-glorification. I do not affirm that claim, so much of what Wessling says in response to the objection he is concerned to address will not apply to me and my views. But his remarks can be adapted to address claims that I do affirm, and that I appeal to in order to support my conclusions. In particular, Wessling might argue as follows. Psychological aseity guarantees that God has no *self-interest* in the success of projects or the promotion of goods extrinsic to the godhead. So the idea that God has a *personality* partly characterized by non-anthropocentric loves and interests suggests either that God lacks psychological aseity or that God somehow *disinterestedly* promotes goods that might compete with the good of human beings. Both claims might seem problematic.

I have to admit that I am not particularly motivated to save psychological aseity as Wessling understands it.[29] But suppose I were so motivated. In that case, what I would want to argue—and what, in fact, I am inclined to argue in any case—is that whatever resources we have for making sense of the claim that God *disinterestedly* desires to promote the good for human beings, to pursue their salvation, and to allow them into unitive relationships with God can just as easily be marshaled to make sense of the claim that God disinterestedly desires to promote *other* conflicting goods, or to live out the divine personality in a way that happens to include some

---

[28] Wessling 2012: 345ff. Cf. also Beilby 2004: 649ff.

[29] Nor would appeal to psychological aseity help the proponent of the Schellenberg problem. That problem is built on the idea that a perfectly loving God would desire relationships with human beings. Could that desire be a disinterested one? I doubt it; for it is hard to make sense of a disinterested desire *for a relationship* with someone. It seems to me that part of what it is to desire a relationship with someone is to take some sort of special interest in them.

measure of divine hiddenness. In short, I see no reason to doubt that pretty much everything I have said so far can be recast in such a way as to avoid the suggestion that God derives any contentment from the goods, whatever they are, with which human interests are in competition.

The second way of pursuing the objection that human interests cannot plausibly compete with non-anthropocentric divine interests is to appeal to Thomas Talbott's argument for the conclusion that, in a universe governed by God, there can be no genuine conflicts of interest *at all*. Talbott acknowledges that there may well be conflicts between two people's *perceived* interests; but, he says, it "is by no means obvious that the best interest of one person could ever conflict with that of another" (2013: 313). This is partly because it is hard to imagine goods the promotion of which would conflict with someone's *best* interests. But it is also because, as he puts it, "love creates a common set of real interests" since, if X loves Y, then what is in Y's best interests is also in X's interest. So likewise, one might think, with God: if God *were* to love us maximally, our best interests would coincide with God's; hence, maximal devotion on God's part to the pursuit of our best interests would perfectly coincide with maximal devotion to the pursuit of God's own interests.

I do not find Talbott's defense of the claim that our interests cannot possibly conflict with God's at all plausible.[30] But rather than rest weight on my objection to that defense (which can be found in note 30) I want simply to observe that embracing Talbott's views will be of no help to proponents of the hiddenness argument. Suppose Talbott is right in thinking that if God were to love us maximally, then our best interests coincide with God's. Then one of three conclusions will follow: (a) God does not love us; (b) God does not always do what is in God's own best interests; or (c) sometimes, despite all appearances

[30] Suppose romantic partners X and Y are each at the same time offered once-in-a-lifetime career-advancing opportunities on opposite sides of the globe; and suppose it is true of each of them (and each knows this truth about themselves) that they will flourish as persons only if they are accompanied by the other and are not embittered by the sacrifice of a once-in-a-lifetime career-advancing opportunity. The story can be fleshed out in different ways; but it seems clear that, on one way of fleshing it out, what is in X's best interests is for Y to come to terms with making the sacrifice, and what is in Y's best interests is for X to come to terms with making the sacrifice. If Talbott's principle about love is correct, however, it follows from this that it is in each one's best interests to sacrifice *their own* opportunity. This seems highly counterintuitive at best, incoherent at worst.

to the contrary, it is in *our* best interests for divine hiddenness to occur in the ways that it does, and to produce the various negative effects that it does. This is, in effect, a crude restatement of the hiddenness problem; but Talbott's thesis about how love creates a common set of interests changes the dialectic in a significant way. For there are plenty of real and imaginable scenarios where the best interests of lovers seem to conflict; and Talbott's principle, if true, guarantees that all of these—regardless of how much evidence each party might have for thinking there is a genuine conflict, and regardless of how strongly each party might believe that the conflict is genuine—are scenarios in which at least one person is mistaken about what is in their best interests. In light of this, it seems that we should be deeply skeptical about what is in our own best interests, and this opens the door to solving the hiddenness problem by embracing option (c). I do not myself advocate that option, of course; but I do not see how those who agree with Talbott about the necessary coincidence of the best interests of lovers can justify dismissing it.

One might also be tempted to demand an answer to the question of just how far from the *idealization* of love (as characterized above) someone's behavior can depart and still count as love. For, after all, divine hiddenness causes great anguish in some, and the range of other evils permitted by God is absolutely horrendous. Grant that God might sometimes prioritize God's own interests over ours; grant that divine love will not be exactly like human love. Still, there have to be *some* boundaries on what sort of behavior can plausibly count as loving; and one might well object that permitting wars and genocides, beatings and molestations, paranoid delusions and crippling depression, all manner of violent and degenerative illnesses, not to mention earthquakes and fires and tornadoes and tsunamis is, after all is said and done, rather a distant departure from what we normally think that a person can willingly permit to be done to someone she claims to love.

I think it is true that there are boundaries on what sort of behavior can plausibly count as loving; but *identifying* the boundaries requires a level of knowledge about the range of possible reasons for divine action that I do not think we possess. It is, I think, quite reasonable to think that at least some of the behavior of an omniscient deity might be aimed at securing goods well beyond our ken. This is not to say that we can identify *no* boundaries on what sort of behavior could possibly be consistent with divine love. But I think that our grasp of the range of possible goods and evils and relations among them is insufficient for us to be warranted in thinking of any *actual* evil that it falls outside the bounds of what is consistent with divine love.[31]

Where does that leave us, then, with respect to the question whether divine behavior toward human beings deserves to be called loving? More pertinently, where does that leave us with respect to the question whether divine hiddenness should be taken as evidence that God (if God exists at all) is *not* loving toward human beings, even in an analogical way? If we cannot answer these questions by asking whether God's behavior satisfies some identifiable set of necessary conditions on love, then how *do* we answer them? In the remainder of this chapter, I try to answer that question.

5.

On the assumption that God exists and that the Christian scriptures provide reliable testimony about the character and behavior of God, answering the question whether divine behavior deserves to be called loving might seem relatively straightforward. The texts of scripture report that God enters into and faithfully keeps covenants, blesses creatures in various ways, harbors attitudes toward creatures that we normally think of as loving, manifests excessive kindness and mercy to creatures, and so on. We are given parent analogies and told that God *is* love. What more could we ask?

The trouble, of course, is that both scripture and experience also deliver up evidence that seems to undercut the portrayal of God as loving. God enters into and faithfully keeps covenants; but God is also portrayed as commanding genocide. God manifests excessive kindness and mercy to human beings, but hands Job over to be tormented by the accuser and allows Israel to be ravaged by her enemies. God is silent in the face of human suffering, apparently hard to find even when ardently sought, and apparently wholly unknown to substantial segments of the human population. How is it that God is aptly described as loving *even in the face of* such undercutting evidence? How is it that God is loving toward those who are suffering and

---

[31] For defense of this claim, see Bergmann 2008 and 2012, Howard-Snyder 2009, and Rea 2013.

toward those who are experiencing in various different ways the hiddenness of God? How is it that these people are able to participate in a positively meaningful relationship with God just by trying?

Asking these questions might seem equivalent to asking for an answer to the problem of evil, a theodicy, an answer to the question of how a perfect being could be justified in allowing people to suffer in the ways that human beings do. But in fact they are not equivalent. At the end of Section 4, I appealed to the gap between our grasp of the range of possible goods, evils, and relations among them, and God's grasp of the same to defend a broad skepticism about claims to the effect that the occurrence of some particular bad event is inconsistent with divine love. This is a version of the so-called *skeptical theist* response to the problem of evil which is, on its own, a *complete* response to that problem. But even if one solves the problem of evil by adopting skeptical theism, the question might still arise as to how it could possibly be *apt* to characterize a God who permits (say) the holocaust as loving toward the victims of the holocaust. Skeptical theism blocks the inference to the conclusion that God is not perfectly good or perfectly loving; it even blocks the inference to the conclusion that God is not perfectly loving toward those particular victims. But it does not tell us why we should not at least be in doubt about the excellence of God's love toward those victims.

The same is true in the case of divine hiddenness. Let us stipulate, for present purposes, that all divine behavior, including all that relates to divine hiddenness, is *justified*. God has perfectly good unknown (and perhaps unknowable) reasons for permitting creaturely suffering; God also has perfectly good reasons for allowing or causing the phenomena associated with divine hiddenness. Given this stipulation, God's perfect goodness is beyond question. On the plausible assumption that an imperfect lover—that is, a being who manages to love, but does so imperfectly—is also imperfect as regards goodness, God's perfect lovingness is beyond question too.

Still, we might well wonder how God's relationship with individual human beings—particularly those who suffer and those who experience God's hiddenness—is *aptly described* as loving. We might wonder what *signs* of divine love there are in the relationship. These are the "lingering questions" that I mentioned at the outset of this chapter—the questions that must be answered in order to make my solution to the hiddenness problem *satisfying*. The reason these questions linger is that there is distance between divine love and even the best human love, such that (as we have seen) it is not given a priori that a *perfectly loving being* will love all human beings equally or even at all. That God loves *us* is an article of faith, not philosophy; a dogma of revealed theology rather than natural theology. And so we must ask what it is about God's relationship to such human beings that lets us hang on to the positive analogies traditionally used to characterize divine love and to resist more negative ones.

As I explained at the end of Chapter 1, my goal will be to address what I take to be the three main sources of negatively valenced analogical characterizations of divine love: the apparent fact that experiential access to God's love and presence is restricted only to a favored few (people we might describe as "mystics"); the fact that many people have severely conflicted relationships with God, where for one reason or another God's love, concern, or very existence have been severely cast into doubt; and the fact that many people seem unable to seek or even think about God, either because they lack the concept of God or because they have undergone religious trauma that prevents them from entertaining the idea of God without suffering serious physical or psychological consequences. In Chapters 6 and 7, I argue that, contrary to what is often presupposed in discussions of divine hiddenness, experiential access to God's presence is much more widely and readily available than is typically credited in the literature on divine hiddenness. In Chapter 8, I argue that the divine authorization of lament and protest, together with the remarkable pattern of divine submission to human beings with whom God is in conflicted relationship, helps to facilitate narratives about God's behavior toward such people that will allow us to hang on to positively valenced characterizations of divine love. In Chapter 9, I argue that, contrary to appearances, lacking the traditional Christian concept of God, or being unable because of trauma or other reasons to entertain that concept, is no obstacle to seeking God, that seeking God is remarkably easy, and that anyone who can *try* to seek God is thereby able to participate in a positively meaningful relationship with God.

6

Visions and Voices

Open communication and access to presence are among our most basic expectations for love relationships. So one of the surest ways to convey *lack* of love for someone is to end all contact with them—in the slang of the contemporary dating scene, to *ghost* them.

For many people, the idea that the world, the church, or they themselves have been ghosted by God is deeply resonant. St. Teresa of Calcutta's life and vocation were profoundly shaped by intense experiences apparently of intimate contact with and communication from God. She heard the voice of Jesus address her as "My own spouse" or "My own little one"; she heard him "[reveal] His Heart to her: His pain, His love, His compassion, His thirst for those who suffer most"; she heard him call her to ministry among the poor in the slums of India.[1] But after she moved to Calcutta in response to Jesus's call, her experiences of the voice and presence of Christ waned, despite her pained longing and pleading. St. Teresa suffered greatly from the felt absence of God. Compared with many believers, however, she is among the fortunate; for at least she had *some* experiences that she took to be vivid and direct communication from God. In the eyes of many—believers included—God, if God exists at all, ghosted us sometime in the Middle Ages, or around the first or second century CE, or shortly after creation itself.

If the arguments of Chapters 3–5 are sound, we cannot rationally conclude from divine ghosting that God is not perfectly loving, or that God does not exist. But we can still wonder why it is appropriate to understand divine love on analogy with the most excellent of human loves. So, assuming God exists, it is important to ask whether

---

[1] Teresa 2007: 44.

we might simply be wrong in thinking that God has somehow *ceased communication and contact* with substantial portions of humanity.

Although the idea that we have been ghosted by God is resonant with many, it is not *at all* resonant with some. In discussing this idea with a group at my church some years ago, a woman in the audience blurted out, "What do you mean? God is talking *all the time!*" At the time, I found her remark deeply puzzling. But I have since encountered reactions like this from just about every non-academic audience to whom I have talked about the hiddenness problem, and I now think that there was something importantly true in what she was saying—not that God is constantly communicating specific propositional content to people, of course, but just that there is, in a sense to be explained, at least a kind of widespread and experientially available communication of God's love and presence.

My goal in this chapter and Chapter 7 is to explain why I think that this latter claim is true. I will do this by presenting a theory about experiences thought to be of God—*divine encounters*, as I shall call them—according to which God's presence, as well as certain kinds of divine communication, are, and always have been, experientially available to a much greater degree than is typically credited in the literature on divine hiddenness. The sorts of encounters I mainly have in view are not so much the ecstatic, visionary kinds one finds reported in the writings of mystics (though, as it happens, experiences more like these will be the primary focus of the present chapter), but rather what I take to be more common, phenomenologically low-grade sorts of encounters like sensing the majesty of God while watching waves crash on a beach or hiking down into the Grand Canyon, feeling awash in the love of God while singing hymns around a campfire, or feeling forgiven by God in the wake of confessing one's sins in prayer or hearing the Sunday morning liturgist declare, in the name of God, that the sins of the congregation are forgiven. Again, these kinds of experience, if veridical, won't count as God "talking" to us in the ordinary sense of the term; but there is, nonetheless, a perfectly good sense in which some of them are communicative.

My theory does not imply that divine encounters like these, or of any other sort, are available to just *anyone*. For example, it does not guarantee that they will be available to anyone other than those who possess some concept of God; and it seems that, if the view is true, people who have access to scripture and liturgical forms of worship will be in a much better position to experience God than those who do not. So even if my theory of divine encounters is true, it will not help to address concerns we might have about God's love for people who lack a concept of God or access to scripture and liturgy. These concerns I save for Chapter 9. But, in relation to those who do have these things, it does help. Insofar as it implies that experiences of God's presence and of communication from God are widely available, it undermines the reasons we might have for thinking that certain negatively valenced analogies—God as distant or ghosting lover, for example—are more apt than traditional positive analogies for characterizing divine love.[2]

I have no compelling argument for the conception of divine encounters that I will offer here. I endorse it, and recommend it for endorsement, because, as I hope to make clear, it accommodates a diverse range of divine encounters, it explains the effectiveness of the advice commonly given in the Christian tradition about how to have such experiences, it fits well with what we know generally about how cognition impinges upon experience and what we know more specifically about the psychology of religious experience, and it implies quite plausibly that human beings experience God in much the same way in which they experience any other person. None of this will establish that my conception of divine encounters is correct; but neither do I need to establish that for my purposes. Casting doubt on the negatively valenced analogies that I want to call into question here does not require me to prove that my theory of divine

---

[2] Charles Taliaferro seems to think that a conclusion along the lines of what I am defending here would constitute a complete solution to the hiddenness problem. Commenting on David Brown's project in *God and Enchantment of Place* (2004), which develops views about the experience of God that bear some strong affinities with my own, he writes:

> if Brown is right about the capaciousness and graciousness of God's bounteous revelation, this would constitute a direct reply to the "hiddenness of God" objection as developed by John Schellenberg. ... If Brown is right, God is more evident than Schellenberg and others grant. From Brown's point of view, our failure to see and encounter God in the world is largely due to bad theology and a failure of imagination.   (Taliaferro 2012: 110)

But Taliaferro is mistaken about this. To be sure, views like Brown's (and my own) do make some headway on the hiddenness problem; but, just as the view that I will defend in this chapter and Chapter 7 is inadequate to the task of *completely* solving the hiddenness problem, so too Brown's view is inadequate to that task as well (though I hasten to add that Brown himself never claimed that it *would* be adequate to that task).

encounters is true; it only requires me to render the theory credible. So long as I can succeed at this more modest goal, my theory can do the work that I want it to do in relation to the hiddenness argument.

1.

Spend some time in contemporary American evangelical circles and you will surely encounter people who tell you not only that they talk to God—this is just the ordinary practice of prayer—but that God talks back, or perhaps even initiates the conversation. For some people, the voice of God comes audibly, as an apparently externally generated phenomenon. Jason Lomelino, co-founder of the "Jesus Burgers" ministry in Santa Barbara, California reports having devoted his life to ministry soon after an experience wherein God apparently inquired "with an audible voice" what he was living for.[3] For others, the divine "voice" seems to come from within. One friend of mine, Stephanie, would put direct questions to God, and she often talked as if she received direct answers. I asked her once how, exactly, this went for her. Did God speak with an audible voice? Did she have some kind of vision of God? "It's like this," she said. "This one time I needed to find a friend of mine in town, but I had no idea where he was. So I asked God: 'Where is he?' After a minute, the thought came to me to go down to the coffee shop on 4th St. So I did. And there he was."

T. M. Luhrmann's *When God Talks Back* recounts a variety of similar stories about people's apparent encounters with God. God becomes present to them in some way—they hear God speak, or feel God touch their hand or shoulder, or come to be filled with a sense of being loved and forgiven. But God does not become present in quite the way that human beings with material bodies become present to one another. There is no *publicly* audible voice, even if the person herself hears one; and even if something is seen or felt, that sensation would not necessarily be had by other healthy and rational human

---

[3] Lomelino 2012: 13. Other participants in the ministry report similar experiences of God speaking audibly, sometimes asking questions, other times delivering propositional content (e.g., "I will give you this house"). Reports like this show up with some frequency in contemporary evangelical "testimonial" literature.

observers.[4] Luhrmann's interpretation of these sorts of experiences is that they result from the exercise of a learnable skill, one that lets the subjects experience natural phenomena—events within their own minds—as the voice, touch, implanted thought, or bare presence of God.[5] (Let us for now set aside the question whether this interpretation is prejudiced against the veridicality of these sorts of experiences.)

The idea that experiencing the presence of God is a learnable skill is hardly new. The medieval mystics held that the capacity to experience reliably and regularly the presence of God and communication from God is something that can be developed in a person with a great deal of practice and preparation. Many others in the Christian tradition both before and after them have held similar views. Accordingly, many manuals have been written explaining just what this practice and preparation ought to consist in.

There is variation in the advice; but, broadly speaking, there is consensus that the capacity to experience God can be developed through regular prayer, serious devotion to the cultivation of moral and spiritual virtue, and the development of various habits of mind that might reasonably be described as *seeking the presence of God, listening for God's voice, reaching out to God in love,* and the like. Authors diverge mainly in their advice about how to do these things, about how to prioritize them in relation to one another and in relation to other aspects of one's life, and about what attitudes one should take toward the experiences one will eventually have in prayer. There is general agreement, however, that devotion to prayer and other spiritual disciplines can and probably will result in occasional or maybe even frequent experiences of divine love and comfort, and occasional or maybe frequent ecstatic experiences of the presence of God. There is also general agreement that, eventually, one can come to live more or less continually with an experience as of dwelling in the presence of God, even as one goes about such mundane activities as gardening or washing dishes. Teresa of Ávila described this state as

---

[4] Philosophers seem generally to assume that vivid *sensory* experiences of God (voices, touches, etc.) are quite rare; but Luhrmann's research suggests otherwise. See Luhrmann 2012: esp. ch. 9.

[5] Luhrmann 2012: 39–40, 46–9, 73.

"spiritual marriage"; Brother Lawrence described the process leading to this state as "practicing the presence of God."[6]

Painting with broad strokes, the typical advice to those seeking greater contact with God in prayer or otherwise is to engage in certain kinds of meditative practices, along with various other spiritual disciplines. In regard to meditation, some recommend practices involving substantial imaginative engagement; others recommend contemplative practices that involve emptying one's mind or focusing one's attention on some particular object—usually a specific concept, word, sound, or mental image. The other spiritual disciplines might involve more or less tightly scheduled ritual activities (e.g., praying at scheduled times), fasting and other forms of self-deprivation, studying scripture, ritualized self-examination and confession of one's sins, cultivating greater simplicity in one's lifestyle, and so on. Of course, plenty of people report experiences of God (occasional or frequent) who do not engage in such practices; and the authors of the manuals that recommend them do not suggest otherwise. Nor, interestingly, do they typically recommend practicing spiritual disciplines *for the sake of* having interesting or comforting experiences of the divine.[7] (In fact, some caution against this.) Rather, the suggestion is only that there is a fairly reliable connection between practicing spiritual disciplines and growing in one's capacity to experience God and in one's sense of closeness to God.

The basic idea seems to be that the human mind, or some part of it, has been designed with the ability to detect God's presence, but, due to sin and vice, it is malfunctioning and badly in need of repair.[8] The spiritual disciplines contribute to this repair and, as they do, we naturally come to have a greater and more frequent sense of God's

---

[6] See especially Teresa's *Interior Castle* VII.2 (Ávila 1980: 432–8) and note on spiritual marriage (Ávila 1976: 402), and Brother Lawrence (1977).

[7] At any rate, this is true of the classic mystical manuals (e.g., the anonymously authored *Cloud of Unknowing*, St. John of the Cross's *Ascent of Mount Carmel* and *The Dark Night of the Soul*, and St. Teresa of Ávila's *Interior Castle*) as well as some contemporary manuals (e.g., the works of Richard Foster and Thomas Keating). But, of course, there are exceptions; and plenty of people, both historic and contemporary, would advise at least prayer and the cultivation of "listening" and "seeking" habits of mind for the sake of acquiring a general sense of the presence of God.

[8] This idea is explicit in Alvin Plantinga's discussion of the *sensus divinitatis* (2000: 214–16, 280–1), and can also be found in the writings of a variety of historical and contemporary mystics and theologians.

presence—unless and until God acts so as to deprive us of this sense.[9] Often, too, the suggestion seems to be that more vivid experiences of God are bestowed like gifts upon people at least partly in response to their engagement with the spiritual disciplines, their success in acquiring certain kinds of virtues, or both.[10]

The advice that can be derived from the Christian mystical tradition about how to cultivate the capacity to experience God is remarkably similar to advice given in other religious traditions about how to cultivate experience of religious realities. Moreover, there is good evidence that it *works*, at least for people with the right psychological profile, in producing the desired kinds of experiences.[11] Even so, however, the idea that experiencing God involves learnable skill might seem to raise more problems than it solves. Two in particular are worth mentioning.

---

[9] According to St. John of the Cross, one of the "dark nights of the soul" through which one must pass in the process of purification and drawing near to God involves God's deliberate action to *block* one's sense of God's presence. See, in particular, his description of the passive "night of spirit" in Book II of *The Dark Night of the Soul* (in Kavanaugh 1988), and the discussion of his nights of sense and spirit in chapter 3 of Payne 1990.

[10] Aldous Huxley gives voice to something in the neighborhood of this latter idea in his introductory remarks on the "Perennial Philosophy," which he takes to be, roughly, a universal body of knowledge about matters pertaining to "divine reality" that is conveyed in religious experience. He writes:

> The Perennial Philosophy is primarily concerned with the one, divine Reality substantial to the manifold world of things and lives and minds. But the nature of this one Reality is such that it cannot be directly and immediately apprehended except by those who have chosen to fulfil certain conditions, making themselves loving, pure in heart, and poor in spirit. Why should this be so? We do not know. It is just one of those facts which we have to accept, whether we like them or not and however implausible and unlikely they may seem. (1945: 2–3)

[11] This is attested both in the spiritual manuals themselves, and also in contemporary research on mystical experiences of various sorts. Cf. Luhrman 2011 and 2012: ch. 7, as well as Taves 2009 and 2016: ch. 11. As described in fuller detail in the texts just cited, the "right psychological profile" involves primarily a cluster of traits associated mainly with hypnotizability and the capacity for intensely focused attention on one's present experiences.

Some, of course, are inclined to think that the fact that people with these sorts of traits are more susceptible to divine encounters is evidence against the veridicality of religious experience. This is one version of the general idea that religious experiences that can be adequately explained by appeal only to natural causes ought not to be regarded as experiences of supernatural entities. Discussing this objection in detail would take me too far afield; but see my remarks on causalism in Chapter 7; Alston 1991: ch. 6; and Davis 1989: ch. 8. (Davis talks specifically about hypnotizability on pp. 199–203.)

The first is similar to one that would be faced by necromancers who thought that particular bodily regimens and meditative practices might put them in touch with the souls of the dead. We have no reason to think that we have dead-soul-detecting faculties whose performance can be enhanced by such practices; and we have no reason to think that dead souls will respond to our engagement in them. In other words: we have no reason to think that these things are at all likely to result in *causal contact* with dead souls. If we don't already have such contact, engaging in those activities won't help. So too, one might think, in the case of God. One is hard-pressed to find clearly defended—or even articulated—*reasons* (scriptural or otherwise) for thinking either that our God-detecting faculties (if we have them) are repaired by particular rituals, bodily regimens, and meditative practices, or that God can be counted on reliably to appear in response to these.

Accordingly, it is extremely tempting to adopt a skeptical interpretation of the results that people achieve through such practices, and to think that what the practices *really* accomplish is simply to cultivate certain kinds of perfectly natural mental phenomena— thoughts, emotions, perceptual imagery, or other kinds of inner experiences—which are subsequently misinterpreted as being the products of supernatural causes. As in the case of necromancy, the problem is that we are hard-pressed to find a reason to think that the practices in question put us in special causal contact with God, contact that we did not and would not have apart from our engagement in the practices.

The second problem arises out of the idea that more vivid (and, many might say, more desirable) experiences of God's presence often involve special causal contact with God, bestowed like gifts only at God's whim or in response to hard effort of some kind. The problem is that this only serves to reinforce negatively valenced analogies of divine love rather than helping us to cling to the positive ones. What human father, after all, would adopt a policy of appearing face-to-face with his children, or doling out expressions of love, only in response to years of hard effort on their part aimed at improving their moral character and cultivating various kinds of spiritual habits? Such behavior would hardly be a model even of basic human decency, much less excellence in love and parental devotion. As Schellenberg has often pointed out, understanding divine love on analogy with the best human loves leads us to the expectation that God's beloved children would *always* be able to participate in a positively meaningful relationship with God *just by trying.*[12]

Both of the problems I have just been describing depend on the assumption that coming to experience the presence of God requires *special causal contact*—roughly, contact beyond whatever everyone always and already has—with God or perhaps with some other supernatural phenomenon.[13] Both also presuppose that whatever learnable skill is involved in coming to experience God's presence, it is a skill whose exercise is aimed at increasing the likelihood of special causal contact with the supernatural. The second problem, furthermore, presupposes that the kinds of religious experience that many of us desire depend to some extent on God *responding* to human effort or the fruits thereof. These are quite natural assumptions in light of what I have said about experiencing God involving learnable skill; but I think that they are false.

According to the theory of divine encounters that I will offer in the remainder of this chapter and in Chapter 7—focusing on visions and voices in the present chapter, and other experiences of God's presence in the next—the difference between those who experience God and those who do not has, for the most part, nothing to do with differences in God's causal contact with people. Nor can the difference be attributed to a general disposition on God's part to bestow experiences of God's presence on people only in exceptional circumstances or in response to efforts in the practice of spiritual disciplines. Rather, on this account, the difference has everything to do with differences in how people cognitively engage with perfectly natural phenomena. There is indeed learnable skill involved in coming to experience God. But the skill can be acquired, for the most part, just by trying to experience the presence of God. Practicing the spiritual disciplines is one way of trying; but nothing in my account implies that this is the only way of trying, or that the function of the spiritual disciplines (or other ways of trying) is to improve our contact with or elicit a response from God. Assuming God exists, my account implies that

---

[12] Even if, as Schellenberg notes (Schellenberg 2015a: 21, 27), trying will not necessarily be easy, it is hard to see how we could *always* be in a position to participate in a positively meaningful relationship with God just by trying to do so if a long journey of preparatory work were required in order for our trying to be successful.

[13] See p. 107 for a fuller characterization of special causal contact.

God's availability to human experience is, in fact, much greater than is commonly supposed in the literature on divine hiddenness.

My account is not intended to be a general theory of religious experience, applicable across traditions. I claim only that it applies to experiences thought to be *of God*. Each of the main things I have to say about particular kinds of divine encounter has been said, more or less, by others. The novelty of my account lies mainly in the way in which it unifies some widely held claims about different kinds of divine encounter while preserving consistency with their veridicality and remaining neutral on a variety of contentious debates in the philosophy of perception and the philosophy and psychology of religious experience.

2.

What happened at Mount Sinai when Moses and the people of Israel received the Ten Commandments from God? Taking our cues from Cecil B. DeMille, we might think it was something like this: Moses spoke aloud to God, perhaps throwing himself against the side of the mount and asking, with great dramatic passion, "What have I left undone?" Then God promptly appeared, perhaps as a flame in the sky, and replied audibly, enunciating in words that anybody could hear each of the Ten Commandments, perhaps simultaneously burning them with a flaming finger into the stones that would eventually become the two tablets that Moses brought down from the mountain. But this is hardly an inevitable interpretation of the Sinai narratives.

Consider, for example, Exodus 19–20, which begins its Sinai narrative with Israel entering the wilderness and camping at the foot of the mountain, and culminates in God delivering the Ten Commandments and other laws to Moses and the people of Israel. These chapters depict God as saying quite a bit. God gives Moses instructions about how to prepare himself and the people of Israel for Moses' ascent up the mountain; God tells Moses who is allowed to come up the mountain with him and who is not; God speaks the words of the Ten Commandments; and so on.

The chapters also describe various noises accompanying the voice of God—thunder, the sound of a trumpet, the rumblings of an earthquake. It is altogether natural to read the text as implying that all of these sounds, including the voice of God, were publicly available, so that anybody present and possessed of properly functioning sense organs would have heard exactly what the text says that Moses heard. Accordingly, it is also natural to assume that the text reports the *truth* about the Sinai events only if God spoke actual sentences with a publicly audible voice. In fact, however, this very natural assumption is incorrect; and there is theological utility in maintaining an open mind about how to interpret this and other biblical texts that report encounters like this with God.

Practitioners of the method of historical biblical criticism generally rely on what we might call a *uniformity* assumption: God, if there is a God, and the world operated in biblical times in pretty much the same way that they operate now. We all rely on some version of this assumption, with different versions being determined by different ways of unpacking the vague "pretty much." When we read historical narratives, we do not typically wonder what the laws of nature were at the time when the narrated events were said to occur; we do not typically assume that miraculous events happened any more routinely than we think they do today; and we typically hold fixed most of our assumptions about how human beings across different cultures are likely to think and behave. Importantly, the strength and consequences of our uniformity assumption will be informed by our background theological commitments. Among the most relevant background commitments will be our opinions about how God acts in the world now, and about the likelihood that God might have acted very differently in the past.

Suppose we bring to the Sinai narrative a fairly strong uniformity assumption: although we acknowledge that God is providentially active in the world, we assume that the ways in which God causes worldly events, the ways in which God communicates and interacts with human beings, and the frequency with which God does such things has remained mostly fixed throughout human history. In doing so, suppose we grant that the Sinai narratives accurately report what Moses took himself to experience at Sinai, but we assume that Moses' experience of hearing God's voice was relevantly like contemporary experiences of the same sort. What then should we conclude about his experience?

It is widely believed that people nowadays who say that God has spoken to them, or that they have seen or felt God in some way, are generally reporting experiences that would not necessarily be had by just any healthy observer attending to the same (internal or external) stimuli.[14] In some cases the stimulus is an internal phenomenon that would produce in other subjects an experience as of having a hunch, intuition, spontaneous idea, dream, hallucination, or imaginatively generated perceptual image.[15] In other cases, the stimulus is an external phenomenon that would likely produce in other subjects an experience as of a perfectly natural object or event, like the thunder that reportedly accompanied Moses' reception of the Ten Commandments. This, then, is what we should expect Moses' experience to have been like as well.[16]

On this way of thinking, people who seem to hear God speak—Moses included—do not have experiences that are stimulated by an external, supernaturally originated voice that just any healthy observer in the vicinity would be able to hear. Rather, the stimulus in each case, whether internal or external, is purely natural. We might be tempted to speak of the subject as *interpreting* the natural stimulus as the voice of God; but speaking this way would be misleading, since interpretation is often, if not always, conscious and intentional.

Contemporary research on sensory[17] experiences as of supernatural phenomena (for example, visions or voices that seemingly come from supernatural beings) gives no indication that people's understanding of them depends on conscious interpretation or inference. There is good evidence that either the experience itself or the subject's immediate, non-inferential understanding of it is influenced by her

---

[14] Cf. Luhrmann 2011, Taves 2009 and 2016: pt. 2, and references therein.

[15] I take it that experiencing some stimulus *as a hallucination of a divine voice* is both possible and different from experiencing some stimulus *as a divine voice*. But, of course, this is not to say that all, or even most, hallucinations are experienced as hallucinations.

[16] This idea is suggested by Tanya Luhrmann (2011: 75; 2012: 249).

[17] For purposes here, sensory religious experiences are just ones that include sensory phenomenology. Thus, on my usage, the category of sensory experiences is at least roughly co-extensive with Caroline Franks Davis's category of "quasi-sensory experiences." (Davis 1989: 35–9) On her characterization, quasi-sensory experiences are "religious experiences in which the primary element is a physical sensation or whose alleged percept is of a type normally apprehended by one of the five sense modalities" (1989: 35). Note that such experiences can be veridical as religious experiences even if the sensory phenomenology corresponds to nothing in external reality. St. Peter's vision, reported in Acts 10: 9–16, of "something like a large sheet" filled with various kinds of animals coming down from heaven before him seems to be of this sort: there is no reason to suppose that the experience is veridical *as* a divine encounter only if there was an actual tablecloth that just anyone nearby could see and touch. (Cf. Davis 1989: 39.)

cognitive states. This claim is partly supported by evidence that the very ability to have such experiences depends both on the subject's background beliefs and on measurable psychological traits that can be cultivated or modified by appropriate training.[18] But none of this implies that taking oneself to be seeing, hearing, or in some other way experiencing God depends on inference or conscious interpretation. Instead, such judgments tend automatically to accompany the relevant experiences.

If this is right, then what happens in divine encounters like those I have been discussing is relevantly similar to what happens in more ordinary cases where observers with different background beliefs, desires, fears, or other cognitive states report different experiences in the presence of the same natural stimuli. A trained ultrasound technician will experience blotches on her screen as the limbs of an infant, whereas others may see only blotches.[19] An anxious person may experience noises in the house as the sound of an intruder's footsteps, whereas someone else may hear only the house settling. Someone who has learned to read Russian will experience certain kinds of marks on paper as letters of the Cyrillic alphabet whereas others may see only squiggles.[20] And so on. In each of these cases, and plausibly also in cases where people seem to hear the voice of God, there is no interpretive act; there is simply "experiencing as."[21]

We use "experiencing as" language when we want to differentiate between the stimulus for an experience—vibrations in the air, blotches on a screen—and the *phenomenal character* and *representational content* either of the experience itself or of certain beliefs or judgments that spontaneously arise in response to our experience. Sometimes when we experience x as y (where 'y' is not simply another name for the stimulus), we do so just by directing our attention to particular features of the stimulus. This is a fairly common

[18] See Taves 2009 and Luhrmann 2012: ch. 9. Both mention that the relevant psychological traits seem to be reliably indicated by the Tellegen Absorption Scale.

[19] This is not to deny that those who "see only blotches" see blotches that, unbeknownst to them, in fact image the limbs and other body parts of an infant. Rather, it is simply to deny that the limbs and such are represented in the content of their experience.

[20] The "Cyrillic alphabet" example comes from Siegel 2006; the "ultrasound" example comes from Stokes 2014.

[21] On the idea of *experiencing as* (and, specifically, *seeing* as), cf. Hanson 2002. For an early application of this notion to religious experience (which I would not endorse in all its details), see Hick 1968.

explanation of what happens when we experience duck-rabbit or vase-lady drawings first as a duck or vase and next as a rabbit or lady.[22] But sometimes our experiencing x as y seems not to be the result of mere attention effects, but the result of cognitive processing of the stimulus (if the stimulus is a mental phenomenon) or of its effects upon our sensory apparatus.

Consider again the ultrasound, intruder, and Cyrillic alphabet cases. In each case, it looks as if we have subjects with different cognitive states not only *reporting* different experiences but spontaneously *taking themselves* to have the experiences they report—rather than, say, reflecting on an experience they share in common and coming to different interpretations of it. Moreover, the cognitive differences—i.e., the various background beliefs, emotions, and other attitudes and dispositions like doubt, fear, faith, openness, curiosity, hope, desire, and so on—seem to explain the other differences. It is precisely because of cognitive changes conferred by training that the ultrasound technician spontaneously takes herself to see the limbs of a baby, for example; and similarly for the other cases.

It is an interesting question whether cognition not only shapes how one understands one's perceptual experiences but, furthermore, sometimes shapes the experience itself. If it does, then perception is *cognitively penetrable*, at least on the most common definitions of cognitive penetrability.[23] If perception is cognitively penetrable, observers who process the same stimulus in different ways might not only report and *take themselves* to have different experiences; they might *actually have* different perceptual experiences. They can have different experiences because experiences are distinguished at least in

---

[22] It is a common explanation, but there are other options. Cf. MacPherson 2012: 35ff.

[23] For purposes here, let us assume that the following definition is adequate:

(CP) [W]ith certain conditions fixed—namely, what is perceived [i.e., what I am calling the "stimulus"], the perceiving conditions, the state of the sensory organ, (and perhaps the attentional focus of the subject)—it is possible for two subjects (or one subject at different times) to have perceptual experiences with different contents, on account of the differing content of the states of their cognitive systems. (MacPherson 2015: 339–40)

Note that this definition is crafted so as to remain neutral on the question whether what I am calling attentional effects might suffice for cognitive penetration—this is the point of the parenthetical condition in the definition. For purposes here, I am not neutral on this question. I want to say that differences in experience that result from mere attentional effects are *not* the result of cognitive penetration.

part by their phenomenal character and representational content, both of which can be shaped in different ways by cognition (on the assumption that perception is cognitively penetrable). So the ultrasound technician may *see* the limbs of a baby whereas I do not, even though we are both looking at the same screen. The anxious person may actually *hear* the intruder (if there really is one), whereas another person only *seems to hear* the house settling.

In saying that the ultrasound technician and I see different things, or that the anxious person and her companion hear different things, I do not mean to suggest that there is for each person a different *object* of experience. Terms like "see" and "hear," as well as more general terms like "experience" and "perceive," are ambiguous in a way that is important to attend to here. Saying that x hears an intruder, for example, might mean only that an intruder is among the objects of x's experience—it is among the things that the experience is about, even if the experience does not represent the relevant sounds as sounds of an intruder.[24] In that sense, the anxious person and her companion perceive the same thing—an intruder—even though (if cognitive penetration occurs) they have different experiences (one having an experience as of an intruder, and the other not). But saying that x hears an intruder might instead mean that an intruder is among the objects of her experience *and* is part of the representational content of that experience—i.e., the experience is about an intruder, and an intruder is represented as such to the subject in the experience.[25] It is in this latter sense that the ultrasound technician and I *see* different things, and the anxious person and her companion *hear* different things; and this will typically be the sense in

---

[24] Note, too, that the object of an experience is not necessarily its stimulus. This is clearest in the case of indirect perception: the ultrasound technician sees baby limbs; but the stimulus for the experience is the light emitted by the ultrasound monitor. In that case, the light, too, is perceived as such; but we should not conclude from this that the stimulus of an experience is always included in its representational content.

[25] Sometimes, too, people say things like "x hears an intruder" when there is no intruder, but x has an experience whose representational content nonetheless includes an intruder. For example, the following remark is hardly a linguistic abomination: "I heard an intruder last night, but when I got up this morning I discovered that it was only some branches falling on the roof." Still, for purposes here, I want to leave this sort of usage aside. In the example just given, I would want to say that, although it is not an abomination, the remark is imprecise shorthand for a more accurate claim like "I *thought* I heard an intruder last night, but in fact what I heard was only branches falling on the roof."

which I am using terms like "see," "hear," and so on in the remainder of this discussion.

It is a matter of controversy whether perception is in fact cognitively penetrable. If it is, then perception-like divine encounters can be understood in terms of cognitive penetration. But the claims that I most want to make about these sorts of experiences—that they involve purely natural stimuli, and that cognition makes a difference as to whether the subject takes herself to be having a divine encounter—do not depend on the cognitive penetrability of perception. This for two reasons.

First, it is not clear that all of the divine encounters I will be discussing strictly count as *perceptual*. Stephanie's inner experience of the voice of God, for example, would typically not be classified as such, since it lacks an external stimulus.[26] Second, nothing in my own discussion precludes alternative interpretations of the various kinds of "experiencing as" phenomena that are commonly cited in support of the cognitive penetrability of perception. Perhaps, for example, experiential differences between me and a trained ultrasound technician can be explained by appeal to mere judgmental effects—differences, shaped by cognition, not in the character and content of the experiences themselves but in our automatic and immediate responses to certain kinds of experiences.[27] Perhaps similar explanations can be offered for the other cases I have cited, and for perception-like divine encounters as well. Nothing in my discussion rules this out.

Accordingly, I will avoid speaking in terms of cognitive *penetration* (except when discussing views that are specifically concerned with it), and will instead speak, where necessary, of cognitive *contributions* to experience, or of *cognitively impacted* experiences, with the understanding that this way of talking is meant to be neutral on the question whether cognition affects the character or content of the experience itself or instead only affects our spontaneous responses to experience.[28]

---

[26] We could, of course, define "perception" so as to accommodate such experiences, at least when they are veridical. Perhaps we could also raise questions about what it means for a stimulus to be "external." (Here and, I think, typically "external" means something like "non-mental" or "outside the mind of the experiencer.") But I see no advantage here to entering into controversies about how to define these terms.

[27] Cf. Machery 2015.

[28] Cf. Caroline Franks Davis's discussion of "incorporated interpretations" (Davis 1989: 149–55, 159–65). It is not clear to me that the incorporation of interpretation is

Return, then, to divine encounters where the subject takes herself to be receiving direct communication from God. On the view I am offering, these are cognitively impacted experiences whose stimuli (whether internal or external) are purely natural phenomena. The ability to experience natural phenomena in this way is, furthermore, a kind of skill—one that may not have been consciously or intentionally developed by the subject but is, nonetheless, partly the product of socialization, training, and various other learned ways of experiencing and engaging with the world around her. As I have already noted, this way of thinking about divine encounters fits well with the evidence from research on the psychology of religious visions. As shall become clear later, it also fits well with the main (competing) theories about the nature of religious experience more generally.[29]

Moreover, it is important to recognize that this characterization of divine encounters is fully consistent with the view that at least some of them are experiences *of God*, and even (e.g.) of *God's voice*; and so there is no reason to think that, in general, it casts doubt on experiencers' own characterizations of their experiences. So, for example, it is consistent with what I am saying that God really did ask Jason Lomelino what he was living for, that God really did tell Stephanie to find her friend at the coffee shop on 4th street, and that Moses (and perhaps also the Israelites) really did hear God speak at Mount Sinai.[30] So long as the natural events stimulating these experiences

---

exactly the same phenomenon as what I am calling cognitive impact; but it is, at any rate, quite similar.

[29] My account bears some affinities with Adam Green's "shared attention" model of religious experience (Green 2009). But whereas Green largely ignores the role played by cognitive impact and is instead concerned to emphasize the role played by *shared attention* in constituting these experiences as divine encounters, I have wanted to emphasize the former, taking the latter to be a trivial consequence of the supposition that, for veridical divine encounters (a) the subjects in question are disposed to experience the relevant natural stimulus as a divine encounter, and (b) God intends for them to experience the stimulus in the ways that God does. It is worth noting, too, that not just any kind of attention-sharing is going to produce an experience of God. Even as I write this paragraph, for example, I am convinced that both God and I are attending to the words I write as I write them; but I am, at present, having no experience of God. If it is said that this falls short of shared attention precisely because, though I believe (and, I would say, *know*) that God and I are attending to the same thing, I am not in the relevant sense "aware" that God is attending to what I am, then I reply that the notion of shared attention with God already builds in a presupposition of *divine encounter* and so cannot be used to elucidate the latter notion.

[30] I say "perhaps also the Israelites" because there are some exegetical reasons for denying that the people of Israel heard anything but thunder. See note 34 for more on this.

were at least partly explained by God's intention that the subjects experience them in the ways that they did, it is appropriate to say that God communicated with them. Perhaps God communicated with Stephanie by providentially arranging for perfectly natural brain events to raise her own latent knowledge of her friend's whereabouts to salience; perhaps instead God's activity resulted in her brain's realizing a brand new thought whose content included previously unknown information. Perhaps God also providentially arranged for perfectly natural events to occur in Jason Lomelino's brain producing what Tanya Luhrmann calls a *sensory override*—an experience that is relevantly like a hallucination in that there is no external stimulus, but that differs from a hallucination in being non-pathological. So long as God is intentionally causally involved in these encounters, it seems appropriate to speak of the experiences as veridical.

Although I do not deny that it is correct to say that God has communicated with people like Stephanie and Jason Lomelino, I do deny that, in saying this, we must believe that God entered into some kind of special causal contact with them. For purposes here, I take it that someone's experience involves special causal contact with God if, and only if, God or some supernatural phenomenon involving God or God's activity is either the immediate stimulus for their experience or in some other way its direct cause, so that the occurrence of the experience, its character, its content, or some combination of these can be adequately explained only by reference to God or the occurrence of some supernatural phenomenon. There is no reason why the providential acts that might explain Stephanie's and Jason Lomelino's experiences cannot be realized in perfectly natural events that are adequately explainable by appeal to natural causes operating in accord with the laws of nature. Of course, if God is causally involved in the occurrence of some natural event, no perfectly natural explanation will be *complete*; but the same will be true for a great many other providential happenings that, except when seen through the lens of faith, have perfectly adequate natural explanations.[31] My point, then, is emphatically not to deny either the veridicality of these experiences or God's causal involvement in producing them, but just the supposition that such experiences, when veridical, involve special causal contact with God in the sense just described.

---

[31] Cf. the understanding of miraculous phenomena generally that is laid out in Holland 1965.

3.

What happened at Mount Sinai? If we bring to the text a strong uniformity assumption and relatively few constraining theological assumptions, then we can sensibly read Exodus 19–20 as reporting cognitively impacted experiences involving natural stimuli. We should expect, then, that whatever the relevant stimuli were, not just anyone undergoing those stimuli would have taken themselves to be having experiences whose content included a divine voice delivering instructions, commandments, and the like. But this is not to deny that Moses himself did; nor is it to deny that the nearby people of Israel did as well.

Moreover, it is important to see that we do not *have* to bring a sparse or non-traditional set of theological assumptions to the text in order to read Exodus 19–20 as reporting cognitively impacted experiences. As I have already explained, the fact that cognitive processing is involved in taking oneself to have an experience of God's voice is perfectly consistent with God's having genuinely *spoken* to one in that experience; and it is also consistent with receiving previously unknown propositional content in the experience. So too, then, one who believes that God genuinely said to Moses and the people of Israel all of the things that Exodus 19–20 report God to have said might, without incoherence, *also* believe that God said those things by way of cognitively impacted experiences involving natural stimuli rather than by way of publicly available divine vocalizations that just any nearby healthy observer would have heard and understood as Moses and the Israelites did.[32]

On this interpretation, the fuller story about what happened at Sinai would, presumably, be that certain vibrations of the air stimulated the sensory faculties of both Moses and the people of Israel; and, whereas some might genuinely have *heard thunder* as a result of that stimulation, Moses and Israel *heard the voice of God*.

Indeed, in this case (though maybe not in every case) we don't even need to say that either Moses or the hearers of thunder were misperceiving. Perhaps the stimulus *was* what we ordinarily call "thunder"; but perhaps too, given God's providential intentions, it was correct to

---

[32] But, again, on what Israel heard see note 34 below.

cognize it as divine communication of instructions and the Ten Commandments.[33] Such a reading might be motivated by commitment to a strong uniformity assumption. But it might also be motivated independently by a general theory about divine revelation, or by a general theory about divine encounters.[34]

In presenting the ideas of this chapter at conferences and other venues, I have sometimes encountered the objection that it is hard to see how *new information* (like the Ten Commandments and other laws given at Sinai) could be conveyed without special causal contact. But I fail to see the problem. Moses' *causal* contact with God, on the view I am offering here, was the same as what the rest of us enjoy—namely, contact with God as the sustainer of all things. (Likewise for the Israelites; likewise too for anyone else, like Stephanie, taking themselves to be getting new information from God.) His experiences, like all others, were stimulated by natural phenomena providentially ordered by God. There is no reason to doubt that someone relevantly like Moses could have had an experience as of a flash of inspiration wherein the Ten Commandments and other laws presented themselves as generally good ideas. Nor is there in principle reason—apart from the sheer improbability of the event—for

[33] Note, however, that if God was indeed communicating to Moses, one who perceived *an absence of communicative content* would be misperceiving. There is a difference between perceiving noise while failing to perceive communicative content and perceiving noise *as devoid of communicative content*.

[34] Sommer (1999), for example, observes that the text is ambiguous in what it reports about the sounds that were heard by Moses and by the people of Israel, particularly at Exodus 19:19. The crucial word in that verse is the Hebrew *qol*, which some translations render as "thunder" and others as "voice" (both legitimate, says Sommer). According to Sommer, other biblical texts are similarly ambiguous on what Israel heard, and one of the options that emerges in later commentary on the Sinai narratives is that the people of Israel in fact heard *nothing*. One particular development of this "minimalist" interpretation grounds it in a general theory about divine revelation. Taking cues from 1 Kings 19:11–13, wherein it is said that God was not in the wind, the earthquake, or the fire that passed before Elijah, but in (as the New Revised Standard Version translates it) a "sound of sheer silence," Menachem Mendel of Rymanover suggests that what Israel hears at Sinai is "a sound (*qol*) of thin utter silence" (Sommer 1999: 442). Thus, "God has a voice, but it is inaudible" (1999: 442–3). Associated with and partly motivating this reading is a theory of revelation according to which all divine revelation is filtered through human interpretation. The words of God, according to this theory, are not given to human beings by way of anything analogous to audible vocal dictation; rather, human beings arrive at those words by way of a process of interpretation. Again, God's *voice* is silent; what is interpreted are, presumably, whatever perfectly mundane internal or external experiences one takes at any given moment to be the conveyors of divine revelation.

doubting that people relevantly like the Israelites could have had a kind of simultaneous or collective flash of inspiration with the same content. On the view I am offering, the crucial difference between (veridical) divine encounters in which new information is seemingly conveyed and other, more mundane sorts of (veridical) experiences lies not at the level of direct stimulus or causal contact but only at the level of cognitive processing and divine intentionality.[35]

My point, then, is that the question whether God spoke openly to Moses and the people of Israel with a publicly audible voice is settled neither by the text alone nor by the text plus the bare supposition that the text tells the sober truth about what happened at Sinai. Rather, it is settled (if at all) by the text plus a variety of background assumptions and other evidence, some of which may well be or depend upon systematic theological considerations. Furthermore, it seems that the same could plausibly be said for all of the other narratives in scripture that seem to depict God as speaking or appearing in ways that would be audible or visible to any bystander possessed of properly functioning sensory faculties.

Obviously there will be some variation in which systematic theological considerations are relevant to the interpretation of any given narrative. But surely one consideration relevant to all of them is the fact that there is no reason (theological or otherwise) to think that either God's love and concern for human beings, or general human needs for particular kinds of interaction with God, have changed over time. Thus, absent defeating considerations, there seems to be some presumption in favor of interpreting narratives like Exodus 19–20 in accord with a fairly strong uniformity assumption. And so there seems to be some presumption in favor of interpreting them as reporting cognitively impacted experiences involving natural stimuli.[36]

---

[35] It has also been objected that my account makes it too easy to have divine encounters: with the right cognitive contributions, it seems that *any* natural stimulus *can* be experienced as a divine encounter. To my mind, however, this is a feature and not a bug.

[36] Even narratives that report post-mortem appearances of the resurrected physical body of Jesus can be understood in this way if we assume (as seems plausible) that the resurrected body of Jesus is a natural, even if unusual, object. We might suppose that some cognitive impact is involved in the perception of that body as the body *of Jesus*, or *of a divine being*; but that is compatible with the claim that in these cases—unlike, say, the case of the divine voice at Mount Sinai—something physical would have been perceivable by just any bystander possessed of properly functioning sensory faculties.

If that is right, then there is no scriptural mandate for believing that, apart from the incarnation, God has ever appeared or spoken in explicit, *publicly available* ways to human beings.[37] Indeed, independently of the foregoing considerations, there is positive scriptural warrant for believing that God has never done so. The idea recurs multiple times in the Old Testament that no one can "see God and live" (Gen. 32:30; Exod. 33:20). We might note, too, that even though a visual term is used, it is implausible to think that the idea here being expressed is essentially connected to vision. Do we *really* want to say that, although it is perilous to enter the direct presence of God with eyes open, it is perfectly safe to do so with eyes shut? More plausibly, the idea is that human beings simply aren't constructed to endure a full-blown direct sensory presentation of God (visually, aurally, etc.). But then it is a serious interpretive challenge to figure out how to square this claim with biblical accounts wherein people *do* seem to encounter God directly in perception. The Sinai narratives are among those accounts, as is the vision wherein Isaiah received his calling (Isa. 6), Moses' view of the divine glory and his hearing of the divine name (Exod. 33), and others. Appealing to cognitive impact affords one strategy for bringing these passages into harmony with the general principle that God cannot be directly perceived. Again, this is not to deny that God has appeared or spoken in any meaningful sense of these terms—far from it. Rather, it is simply to suggest that one viable interpretation of the scriptures is that all such appearances involve natural rather than supernatural stimuli.

Suppose we grant all that I have been arguing for in this section. How is this characterization of what most of us would regard as *dramatic* and *vivid* experiences of God at all relevant to the question whether experience of God's presence is *ubiquitously* available, such that there is some truth in the remark that "God is communicating [or at least experientially available] all the time"? And how do possession of a concept of God and access to scripture and liturgical modes of worship help us to receive such communication? The short answer is that, on my view, experiencing the presence of God is always going to involve cognitive contributions to the experience of purely natural stimuli; and *anyone* whose mind can make the relevant

[37] Note that "publicly available" is supposed to capture the idea that anyone with properly functioning sensory faculties but without the relevant (or competing) cognitive processing would have perceived a voice.

cognitive contributions can experience at least the presence of God, and perhaps even communication from God. Moreover, the relevant cognitive contributions are more likely to occur as one learns to view the world as an arena of ongoing divine activity; possessing a concept of God is necessary for viewing the world in this way, and immersion in scripture and participation in liturgical forms can significantly help one to view the world in this way; and, to the extent that it is *correct* to view the world as an arena of ongoing divine activity, one will thereby be in a position to have veridical experiences of God's presence and, indeed, of communication from God.[38] I will develop this view in more detail in Chapter 7.

---

[38] Though I don't mean to suggest that having a concept of God is *necessary* for having what I am calling a divine encounter. Cf. Davis 1989: 161–3 for discussion of senses of the presence of God that occur in people who lack a concept of God and are only retroactively recognized as such.

7

Divine Presence in a Material World

In Chapter 6, my main focus was on divine encounters that have some kind of sensory character—visions and voices primarily, but the account I sketched obviously applies equally to encounters that have olfactory, tactile, or gustatory character as well. In the present chapter, I want to cast my net more widely, showing how the view I advocate covers other kinds of divine encounter and, in so doing, locating the account in relation to a few important decision points in the literature on religious experience.

I will begin in Section 1 by first identifying the four decision points on which I want to focus and then explaining where my view falls in relation to the first of them. The next three sections focus on each of the remaining three. What will emerge over the course of that discussion is a clearer picture of what is and is not unique about my view, and of what might be some of the advantages of accepting it. In the final section, I offer some reasons for thinking that the view of divine encounters that I favor is the most plausible account of how creatures like us might experience divine presence in a material world.

1.

The first decision point—in order of discussion, if not necessarily importance—concerns the question of paradigms. William James maintained that "personal religious experience has its root and centre in mystical states of consciousness" (1902: 370), and many have followed him in this thought, or something close to it. In order to explain the "something close to it" qualification, and the significance of this particular decision point, I must first offer brief characterizations of mystical states and a few other types of religious experience.

Mystical states are variously defined and distinguished from other types of religious experience in the literature. It does not much matter for my purposes exactly how this territory is divided; but the discussion will proceed more smoothly if we take for granted some classificatory scheme or other. For purposes here I will adopt William Wainwright's taxonomy,[1] making one modification with an eye to including certain kinds of religious experience that he seems to leave aside.

Wainwright explicitly recognizes four categories of religious experience: (a) ordinary religious feelings and sentiments, (b) visions, voices, and occult phenomena (e.g., telepathy, clairvoyance, and precognition), (c) mystical experiences, and (d) numinous experiences. He does not claim that this taxonomy exhausts the category of religious experience; he gives it only to distinguish mystical experiences from other kinds of religious experience with which he thinks they should not be confused.

His characterizations of experiences in the first two categories are exactly as you might expect from their labels. Examples of the first include, e.g., a sense of one's own dependence; a feeling of sinfulness; or feelings of love, awe, trust, or devotion directed toward God or some other religiously significant object.[2] Examples of the second are of a piece with the sorts of examples discussed in Chapter 6. Wainwright stresses that religious sentiments and affections are not necessarily *mere* feelings—they might also be "feelingful convictions" with genuine cognitive content. They differ from mystical states primarily in *not* being "like ordinary perceptual experiences," which apparently amounts to not involving "an intuitive sense of objective presence or reality."[3] Visions, voices, and occult phenomena, by contrast, typically are perception-like; but they differ from experiences in the latter two categories primarily in the fact that, unlike the latter types of experience, they typically have specific empirical content, and are typically *obviously* culturally conditioned.[4]

---

[1] Wainwright 1981: ch. 1.   [2] Wainwright 1981: 1–2.
[3] Wainwright 1981: 3.
[4] Wainwright 1981: 6–7. Obviously this characterization helps us draw distinctions at the level of *types*; but the "typically" qualifiers make it hard to know how to classify particular token-experiences that have (say) both visionary quality *and* the defining characteristics of mystical experiences without having specific empirical content or

Mystical experiences, he says, are unitary states (that is, they involve some kind of sense of unity) that are noetic (or perception-like), but lacking in *specific* empirical content.[5] Numinous experiences differ from these primarily in that they are *not* unitary, and they do not *necessarily* lack specific empirical content. In characterizing the relationship between mystical and numinous experiences, he writes:

> A sense of unity is at the heart of mystical experience. Distances are annihilated, and distinctions overcome. If the experience has an object, the mystic experiences identity or union with that object. By contrast, a sense of absolute otherness, or distance, or difference is built into the very fabric of numinous experience. The numinous object is fascinating and wonderful, but it is also awful, majestic and overpowering; in its presence one feels empty, stripped of power and value.[6]

As he goes on to note, Rudolf Otto, whose classic *Idea of the Holy* is the foundational twentieth-century treatment of numinous experience, took mystical experience to be a species of numinous experience.[7] But Wainwright himself thinks that the differences between unitary and non-unitary experiences are striking enough to justify classifying the two separately.

In addition to the four categories of religious experience that Wainwright recognizes, I would want to add (at least) a fifth, whose members we might describe as *garden-variety divine encounters*—i.e., divine encounters that are not aptly described as visions, voices, or occult phenomena, are more than mere religious affections or

---

being obviously culturally conditioned. Matters are complicated further by the fact that Wainwright allows that numinous and mystical experiences *can* be culturally conditioned (1981: 22ff). I am also unsure how to unpack the idea of "specific empirical content." For example, in commenting on Stace's (1960) influential typology of mystical experiences, Wainwright says that "the sense of transfiguration" has "an equal right to be regarded as essential (or at least typical)" of a certain kind of mystical experience, and then characterizes this as follows: "Natural objects become 'transparent, luminous, visionary'" (1981: 10). This *sounds* to me like a visionary experience with specific, falsifiable, empirical content: namely, that things nearby have become *transparent* and *luminous*. Yet Wainwright takes the *lack* of specific empirical content to be partly definitive of mystical experience.

[5] Wainwright: 1981: 2. Wainwright does not define "noetic"; but he does characterize noetic states as perception-like. This, together with remarks quoted in note 4, lead me to think that he understands noetic experiences to be ones that involve an intuitive sense of objective presence or reality.

[6] Wainwright 1981: 5.   [7] Otto 1958.

sentiments, but do not rise to the level of being numinous or mystical experiences.[8] That there are such things seems obvious; and I see no good reason for trying to force-fit them into Wainwright's other categories.

For example, it is not uncommon for people to report having a sense of God's presence in the midst of a church service, or around a campfire singing hymns or praise songs; nor is it uncommon for people to experience the love and forgiveness of Christ in the Lord's Supper, or at various other points in a Christian liturgy. Although some of these experiences might be describable as mere "feelingful convictions," a type of experience Wainwright locates in the category of religious affection or sentiment, some are described in terms which make them sound like "intuitive senses of objective presence or reality," which would exclude them from that first category. And yet it does not seem that such experiences generally rise to the level of being mystical or numinous.

Similarly, people often report apparently non-mystical, non-numinous experiences of God's presence, love, majesty, and the like in nature—out in the woods, on the beach, climbing a mountain, and so on. People sometimes experience God speaking to them through the scriptures, or through a sermon, or through the words of a friend. Jesus himself said that when we feed the hungry or visit the sick, we do as much *for him*; and so it stands to reason that these acts too might be vehicles for genuinely experiencing the presence of Christ. The apostle Paul characterizes the church as the *body of Christ*; and so one might reasonably think that the presence, love, forgiveness, and so on of Christ can be experienced through the presence, love, forgiveness, and so on of other believers. Christians are told that the Holy Spirit dwells within them, that their bodies are temples of the

---

[8] Admittedly, Jerome Gellman speaks of "garden-variety mysticism" (2001: 84f.). Similarly, Caroline Franks Davis notes that numinous experiences can be "mild," and cites as examples "a general sense of 'sacredness' in the world, a feeling of happy dependence upon or devotion to an 'other', or a gentle yearning for something, one knows not what" (1989: 53). But these kinds of experiences do not seem to me to quite fit Wainwright's characterization of mystical or numinous experiences, which is part of why I'm looking to modify his taxonomy. Ultimately, though, what matters to me is *not* the question whether garden-variety divine encounters can, under some plausible characterization of the mystical or numinous, count as such, but rather simply this: that there are such experiences; that, for good reasons or bad, they are sidelined or altogether ignored in some important typologies of religious experience (like Wainwright's); and that my account is meant to cover them.

Holy Spirit, and that the Holy Spirit will speak to their hearts; and people often report experiential awareness of these things, too.

It may be tempting to insist that some of these types of experience (e.g., seeming to experience the presence of Christ in the homeless person to whom you are serving soup at the shelter) are not genuine divine encounters; and it may be tempting to try to force the rest into Wainwright's other categories. But I see no particularly compelling reason to give in to these temptations. The experiences just described are obviously not aptly cast into the category of visions, voices, and occult phenomena; and there is no reason to think that *all* of them would have to be mere feelingful convictions rather than intuitive senses of objective presence. Nor does there seem to be reason to insist that those that are not mere feelingful convictions display the defining characteristics of experiences in Wainwright's other categories. As I see it, experiences like these can easily resemble experiences in the first category by their *ordinariness*, while at the same time resembling numinous experiences in their noetic quality.

Throughout much of the twentieth century, there has been a strong tendency to focus on mystical experiences, numinous experiences, visions, voices, occult phenomena, or some combination of these as paradigms for the study of religious experience, and largely to neglect what I am calling miscellaneous other divine encounters. Let us call this methodological tendency *sensationalism*—so named because it involves a tendency to favor, for one reason or another, certain kinds of sensational divine encounter over mundane and sometimes highly ambiguous ones as paradigms. There are, to be sure, some advantages to be gained by limiting one's focus in this way. There are also pitfalls.[9] In any case, my own ambitions require expansion rather than narrowing of focus, since I am concerned mainly to sketch an account of divine encounters that encompasses both sensational and garden-variety ones, explaining how all of them are more widely and readily available than is usually thought. Accordingly, I take a non-sensationalist approach, following philosophers and theologians like David Brown, Mark Wynn, and Sameer Yadav who, for various reasons, focus on a broader class of paradigms than has been typical in the twentieth-century literature on religious experience.[10]

---

[9] For discussion of advantages, pitfalls, or both of narrowing one's focus to sensational experiences of various sorts, see Alston 1991: 28, Coakley 2009, Gellman 2001: ch. 6, and Jantzen 1989.

[10] Brown 2004; Wynn 2009, 2013; Yadav 2015.

One of the main reasons why people have found it fruitful to restrict their theoretical attention to sensational mystical experiences is that it makes certain kinds of inquiry into the cognitive significance of religious experience more tractable. Like Wainwright, many have recognized important similarities between mystical, numinous, and certain other kinds of religious experiences on the one hand, and perceptual experiences on the other hand; and so many have sought to exploit these similarities in defending the cognitive significance of religious experience. Doing so is made much easier if one can identify a class of paradigms that resemble perceptual experiences in being vivid and representational—hence the tendency to focus on sensational experiences. The task is also made easier if one can identify paradigms that, like perceptual experiences, can be classified with reference to shared phenomenal and representational characteristics that are not bound to particular cultures or religious traditions.

Sensationalism, then, is connected with two other theses, specifiable to whatever class of paradigms one has selected for theoretical attention, that have become important decision points in the literature:

Perceptualism: religious experience, in the paradigm instance, is relevantly analogous to perceptual experience.

Perennialism: the paradigmatic religious experiences, or an important subclass of those, share significant phenomenal or representational characteristics in common that transcend cultures and religious traditions.[11]

Both of these claims, specified at least to mystical and numinous experiences, have enjoyed broad acceptance over the past century;

---

[11] Bush (2014: 39) notes that perennialism owes its name to Aldous Huxley's *The Perennial Philosophy* (1945); but there is probably no single thesis (including the one I have offered) that precisely captures what all perennialists are supposed to agree upon. As Kukla (2005: 111) points out, what *exactly* perennialism amounts to is underspecified in the literature. It is often characterized as the view that religious experiences have "core characteristics" that are the same across religions and cultures. (Cf. Alston 1991: 39 n. 29; Bush 2014: 39, 134ff.) But as both Kukla and my friend Reader 2 note, this characterization is trivialized by the fact that, at some level of generality, *all* experiences share common characteristics. My own characterization of perennialism is most significantly informed by the (rather different) characterizations offered in Alston 1991, Bush 2014, Forman 1990, Huxley 1945, and Wainwright 1981.

but, at the same time, each is controversial and has been subjected to trenchant critique.

Perceptualism is also connected with a third thesis that is natural to affirm in light of the analogy between religious and perceptual experience but, so far as I can tell, tends more to be affirmed as a constraint on a successful epistemology of religious experience by those who *deny* the evidential value of religious experience than by those defending perceptualism:

> *Causalism*: paradigmatic religious experiences, or an important subclass of those, typically result, at least in part, from special causal contact with God or some other religiously significant phenomenon.[12]

The idea, roughly, is that if religious experiences can be adequately explained *without* reference to supernatural causes, that is reason to believe they are something other than perception-like experiences of supernatural entities or phenomena.[13] This thesis too, then, has become an important decision point in the literature.

For my part, I endorse perceptualism, but without the sensationalist focus; I am neutral on perennialism; and, as I have already made clear, I reject causalism. I will discuss perennialism briefly in Section 2, and then, in Section 3, I will discuss perceptualism and make some further remarks about causalism.

2.

Critics of perennialism deny the Jamesian view that paradigmatic religious experiences share important phenomenal or representational characteristics in common that are universal across cultures and religious traditions. Instead, they typically endorse *constructivism*,[14] the view that the character, content, or both of all religious experiences is shaped in significant ways by the background beliefs,

---

[12] See Chapter 6, p. 107 for my characterization of special causal contact.

[13] Cf. D'Aquili and Newberg 1998; Fales 1996, 2003; Jordan 1994; and Schellenberg 2007: 184–5, 188. These sorts of naturalistic challenges to the cognitive value of mysticism are addressed by Alston and Davis in the sources cited in note 29, as well as in Gellman 2001: chs. 4 and 5, and Wainwright 1981: 69–73.

[14] Term due to Forman (1990: 110).

desires, or other cognitive states of the experiencer. Although they do not use the language of cognitive penetration, and despite the fact that they defend their views in different ways, constructivists like Steven Katz, Wayne Proudfoot, and Stephen Bush share in common the view that cognitive penetration is ubiquitous.[15] As Bush puts it, "concepts are necessarily involved" in our experience in such a way as to somehow "mediate," "shape," or be "essential constituents" of them.[16] This is a strong thesis. It is clearly meant to imply that *religious* experience always involves cognitive penetration; and if we take it at face value, it actually implies the much stronger (and almost certainly false) thesis that experience of any sort—religious or otherwise, human or otherwise—is simply impossible in the absence of cognitive penetration.

There is quite a lot of evidence that cognition impacts religious experience, and this seems to be the primary motivation for constructivism. But constructivists, in making their arguments, have tended simply to assume that cognitive impact implies cognitive penetration; and perennialists have seemingly been happy to go along with the assumption.[17] So the debate has tended to focus on whether *all* experience is cognitively impacted, or whether there might be some type or component of religious experience that is

[15] Katz, for example, insists that there are "NO *pure (i.e., unmediated) experiences*," that "the experience itself as well as the form in which it is reported is shaped by the concepts which the mystic brings to, and which shape, his experience," and that complex "pre-experiential" patterns of tradition-dependent belief "affect the actual experience" of mystics within a given tradition (Katz 1978: 26, 34–5; emphasis in original). Proudfoot writes that mystical religious experience "is shaped by a complex pattern of concepts, commitments, and expectations which the mystic brings to it. These beliefs and attitudes are formative of, rather than consequent upon, the experience" (Proudfoot 1987: 121). Bush says that he agrees with Katz and Proudfoot that "concepts are necessarily involved in experiences"; he talks of experience having a "conceptual aspect"; and he endorses a theory of concepts which implies that subjects with different culturally conditioned capacities to report their experiences can thereby differ in how they experience a stimulus (Bush 2014: 145–8). Cf. also Hick 1968.

[16] Bush 2014: 148, emphasis in original; see also the discussion of Katz and Proudfoot, especially at Bush 2014: 134–5 for the language of mediating, shaping, and essential constituency used in characterizing the role of concepts in experience.

[17] I say this because: (a) constructivists, in making their arguments, typically point to evidence of cognitive impact without considering questions about the locus of impact, and (b) perennialists, in trying to rebut those arguments, tend to focus their attention on *reports* of religious experiences that present those experiences as devoid of conceptual content. The result has been that, as André Kukla notes, "most of the debate . . . consists in a battle of quotations" (Kukla 2005: 121).

free from cognitive impact—for example, something like what Robert Forman calls a state of "pure consciousness."[18] What seems not to have been recognized is that one can admit that cognition generally contributes to religious experience without making any commitment as to the locus of cognitive impact.[19]

Even those, like Alston and Wainwright, who have explicitly declared neutrality on the debate seem to have done so for reasons other than seeing a neglected middle ground. Alston, for example, remains neutral because he is not so much concerned with the question whether the character or content of religious experience is impacted by cognition as with the question whether cognition somehow makes a difference as to the nature of the *object* of experience. (He insists it does not).[20] Wainwright remains neutral because, although he is concerned with the question whether there is a core set of characteristics shared by all mystical experiences, he rightly notes that this may be so even if mystical experience is, in general, shaped in significant ways by the cognitive states of the experiencer.

My own view, however, is crafted to leave room for the neglected third possibility. My central thesis is simply that all divine encounters—including apparent perceptions of external voices or visions, communications from God occurring wholly within the subject's own mind, and general senses (vague or vivid) of divine love, forgiveness, comfort, presence, and the like—involve entirely natural stimuli and require no special causal contact with God, and that cognition enters in as part of the explanation for why the stimuli are *experienced as* divine encounters. Accordingly, my view has the advantage of being neutral on the debate between perennialists and constructivists precisely by virtue of its corresponding neutrality on an important debate in the philosophy of perception.

---

[18] Forman 1990: 8, 21ff.; Bush 2014: 145ff.

[19] This is not, however, the only thing that has gone unrecognized in the debate. For a fuller (and, in my view, mostly sound) critique of the arguments on both sides of the debate, see Kukla 2005: 110–24.

[20] Alston 1991: 38–9, and esp. n. 29. As he puts it, "the subject's conceptual scheme and belief tendencies can affect the *way* something appears to her," but it cannot "affect *what it is* that appears to her" (1991: 39 n. 29; emphasis in original). Note, too, that the phrase "what it is that appears to her" is ambiguous in the way that "x sees ___" is ambiguous. (See Chapter 6 of this book, p. 104, for discussion.) In Alston's usage, "what it is that appears to her" refers just to the object(s) of the experience, and not to the experience's representational content. (See also Alston's discussion of direct vs. indirect perception, 1991: 20ff.).

3.

I turn now to the relationship between my view and perceptualism. The idea that there are connections to be drawn between experience of the presence of God and perception has a long history in the tradition. The idea that human beings have one or more *spiritual senses*—a capacity or group of capacities analogous to the familiar physical senses—has been particularly prominent. Some authors posit spiritual senses analogous to each of the familiar five—spiritual taste, spiritual touch, spiritual vision, and so on. Others posit a single spiritual sense—e.g., John Calvin's *sensus divinitatis*.[21]

It is sometimes difficult to discern how much of the talk about spiritual senses is supposed to be metaphorical and how much is supposed to be literal. It is also sometimes difficult to know where exactly to locate our alleged spiritual senses. We have a pretty good understanding of human vision, audition, and olfaction, for example; we know which organs are associated with the relevant sensory experiences, we know how those organs connect with our brains, we know which parts of the brain are associated with those experiences, and so on. By contrast, we know none of this with respect to the *sensus divinitatis*, or the "organs" of spiritual vision, audition, and the like, if there are such things. Nor have those who have believed in such things tended to encourage investigation along these lines. Even so, the idea that there is *something* perception-like about the experience of God has retained significant appeal throughout the history of the church.

Over the past century or so, perceptualists have tended to develop their theories within a sensationalist framework—in some cases because they think that certain kinds of sensational religious experience are most deserving of theoretical attention, and in other cases because doing so helps to make their theoretical task more tractable. Perhaps in part because of the connections between sensationalism and perceptualist projects, anti-sensationalists like Grace Jantzen, Sarah Coakley, and Mark Wynn have expressed opposition to an unqualified perceptualism.[22] Causalism, as I have noted, is also natural to affirm in connection with perceptualism; and, although it seems not to be typically affirmed by those defending the cognitive

---

[21] On the *sensus divinitatis*, see Plantinga 2000: 172ff.
[22] Cf. Coakley 2009; Jantzen 1988, 1989; and Wynn 2009.

value of religious experience, it is typically also (when considered) not denied.[23]

As I have already indicated, although I embrace perceptualism, I reject causalism and count myself among the anti-sensationalists. In part because of this, my view has advantages over its competitors that are of particular significance in relation to the hiddenness problem. I will explain why in the course of highlighting some salient points of agreement and contrast between my view and a few of the most important competing or neighboring views, with particular attention to the views of William Alston and Mark Wynn.

I will begin with Alston, whose account of Christian mystical experience is one of the most important perceptualist theories of religious experience developed within the last century. For Alston, a "mystical experience" is roughly what I am calling a divine encounter—namely, any experience that the subject takes to be an experience of God. His goal in *Perceiving God*, his most thorough and influential work on religious experience, is to show that mystical experiences play a role with respect to beliefs about God that is strongly analogous to the role played by sense perception with respect to beliefs about the external world. Accordingly, he needs to focus on mystical experiences that strongly resemble sensory experiences; but, to avoid begging questions, he also needs to excise from the class of paradigms all experiences—like visions and voices—that are themselves sensory. So, although he recognizes a wide range of paradigms, his working class of paradigm religious experiences is narrower even than James's, including just those mystical experiences that are non-sensory but otherwise relevantly like sense experiences (as he understands them) in being both focal and direct.[24]

Focal experiences are ones that attract the subject's attention so strongly as to blot out everything else. Because he restricts his theoretical efforts to focal experiences thus characterized, it seems fair to count him among those working within a sensationalist framework. Direct awareness is awareness that is mediated by nothing except perhaps one's own mental states. This is not to say that there is no

---

[23] Cf., e.g., Alston 1991: esp. 66–8 and 228–34; Davis 1989: ch. 8, esp. 226–8; Gellman 2001: esp. 95–102; and Wainwright 1981: 175–6, 184. Of these philosophers, Gellman seems to come closest to affirming causalism (at 2001: 99–101).

[24] Alston 1991: ch. 1.

causal mediation between the object of our awareness and our sensory faculties. Rather, it is just to say that we are not aware of the thing in question *through our awareness of something else* (except, again, perhaps our own mental states). For example, suppose my awareness of a table is mediated by nothing other than my own visual and tactile sensations of it. Then my awareness is direct. By contrast, suppose a scientist becomes aware of the presence of a subatomic particle by perceiving its vapor trail. Insofar as the *vapor trail* is part of the representational content of the experience, and the scientist's awareness of the particle comes *through* her perception of the vapor trail, the scientist's awareness of the particle is indirect.[25]

I agree with Alston that experiences within the class of paradigms that he has circumscribed would play the sort of justificatory role that he thinks mystical experiences play. Moreover, insofar as I allow that among the possible natural stimuli for a divine encounter are a person's own mental states—e.g., Stephanie's thought, construed by her as the voice of God, that her friend is at the coffee shop on 4th street—and insofar as Alston is willing to count awarenesses mediated by a person's own mental states as "direct," it appears that my account is consistent with the claim that Alston's class of paradigms is non-empty.[26] Furthermore, Alston seems to have no objection to the view that at least some important kinds of divine encounter are as I say that *all* divine encounters are: namely, cognitively impacted

[25] Alston 1991: 20–4. Alston distinguishes two kinds of indirect awareness: indirect perceptual recognition, wherein someone is indirectly aware of something but the thing in question does not appear in her experience, and indirect perception, wherein someone is indirectly aware of something and the thing does appear in her experience. The particle case would be one of indirect perceptual recognition: nothing resembling the particle itself appears in the scientist's visual field. His example of indirect perception is seeing someone on television (1991: 21).

[26] As I see it, Stephanie's experience is quite like some of Alston's paradigms. Consider, for example, the following (chosen more for the sake of brevity than for any significant differences between this and the other paradigm cases that Alston offers):

> I attended service at a church in Uppsala. During both the Confession of Sin and the Prayer of Thanksgiving which followed Communion, I had a strong consciousness of the Holy Spirit as a person, and an equally strong consciousness of the existence of God, that God was present, that the Holy Spirit was in all those who took part in the service. The only thing of importance was God, and my realization that He looked upon me and let His mercy flood over me, forgiving me for my mistakes and giving me the strength to live a better life.
> (Anonymous report in Unger 1976: 114; quoted in Alston 1991: 14.)

experiences whose stimuli are perfectly natural phenomena.[27] To the extent that we disagree, then, it is on just the following points: whereas my account denies causalism, and furthermore maintains that *all* divine encounters are cognitively impacted experiences involving purely natural phenomena, Alston leaves those questions open. Although this difference might seem small, I think that it is important in the present context.

As I noted in Chapter 6, the hiddenness problem gains traction from the idea that experiencing God's presence requires some kind of special causal contact with God. Alston himself associates the idea that experiential awareness of God's presence is ubiquitous with what sounds to me like a rejection of causalism.[28] Closing off this possibility therefore helps to mitigate the hiddenness problem.[29] The hiddenness problem also gains traction from the idea that experience of God requires or at least often comes as a special divine response to hard effort at the cultivation of virtue or certain kinds of spiritual habits. Positing an important role for cognitive penetration, however, goes a long way toward explaining why practicing certain kinds of spiritual disciplines might be relevant to acquiring the skill of experiencing God—in short, it fosters the right kind of cognition—in a way that mitigates this concern.

As noted earlier, my account also diverges from Alston's as regards sensationalism. Again, this has more to do with differences in our

---

[27] Cf. Alston 1991: 28, 37ff., and 66-8. Thanks to Reader 2 for saving me from some serious blunders in my interpretation of Alston, both here and on a few lesser points in this chapter.

[28] He cites John Baillie (1939) as offering "a powerful presentation of the position that all (or most) of us are experientially aware of God all (or most) of the time," and as defending at length a view that he (Alston) contrasts with one according to which religious experience involves "some divine activity over and above that which is directed to everything else in creation," namely the view that "God satisfies the causal condition for being *perceivable* in a certain experience just by keeping that experience in existence" (Alston 1991: 11 n. 3, and 65).

[29] So far as I can tell, the most significant disadvantage that might come from rejecting causalism is that it plays into the hands of critics who think that causalism would have to be true if there are veridical, perception-like divine encounters. As Alston himself points out, however, neutrality has the same potential disadvantage; so my own account is no worse off than his on that score. It would be too much of a digression to try to respond to the critics; but, in any case, the response I'd favor would be along the same lines as those offered by Alston (1991: 228-34, 2003a: 140-2, and 2003b: 161) and Davis (1989: ch. 8, esp. 223-8). Note, too, that the "non-crude interventionist" view briefly sketched by Davis (1989: 226-8) bears significant similarities to the account I have offered here.

goals than with any substantive disagreement. Alston does not deny, for example, that what he would call "non-focal" experiences are also worthy of theoretical attention. Nevertheless, this difference, too, is important in the present context. For the hiddenness problem also gains traction from the idea that the only *real* or *religiously important* or *genuinely meaningful* experiences of God are the sensational ones. This idea is encouraged by the sensationalist focus of so much of the literature (both popular and scholarly) on religious experience, and it plausibly contributes to the devaluing of garden-variety divine encounters and to increased longing for and suffering in the absence of more sensational ones. This plays into the hiddenness problem because sensational divine encounters are (anecdotally, anyway) much rarer than garden-variety ones.

Many believers report non-sensational divine encounters—experiences like feeling God's power and majesty through perceptions of the sea or of the night sky; feeling God's forgiveness when the Sunday morning liturgist declares, in the name of Christ, that the congregants' sins are forgiven; experiencing Christ's presence in the singing of hymns, the veneration of icons, participation in the Lord's Supper, or in fellowship with other believers; and so on. On my account, these sorts of experiences do not involve any less contact with God than more sensational ones, nor do they necessarily involve any less of a response from God to our prayers or other kinds of efforts than more sensational ones. As a result, it is harder to see why the sensational ones should be valued more. On my account, the preference for sensational encounters over garden-variety ones starts to look more akin to a preference for loud music over soft, or for spicy curries over mild.

In contrast to Alston (and others), and more in keeping with the aims of my own project, Mark Wynn argues for a "broadening of the concept" of religious experience to include experiences that are not focally *of God* or any other supernatural object, as well as experiences wherein the sense of the presence of God is mediated by the activities of the body within and the emotional responses elicited by a particular physical context or environment.[30] Experiences of the first sort will not be divine encounters; and Wynn seems to deny that they are, in general, well understood on analogy with perception.[31]

---

[30] Wynn 2009. See also Wynn 2013: esp. chs. 1–3.　　　[31] Wynn 2009: 149.

But experiences of the latter sort *are* divine encounters, and here it seems that Wynn does want to allow that the experiences in question are analogous to certain kinds of (indirect) perception or perceptual recognition.

The sorts of divine encounters that Wynn discusses are not, as he puts it, fundamentally "of God as the efficient cause of certain events characterized in neutral or meaning-independent terms," but are instead "senses of God" that are "realized in some recognition of the existential meaning which attaches to a material context."[32] The examples he focuses on involve the "sylvan experiences" of Wendell Berry on the trails of the Red River Gorge in Kentucky and of Erazim Kohák in the woods near his home in New Hampshire. Although he does not say as much, these examples are naturally understood as involving cognitively impacted experiences.

Kohák, for example, observes that the woods can be experienced in much the same way in which you might experience someone else's kitchen. You walk into a kitchen that is not your own, and, as Kohák has it, you experience that place *as belonging to someone else*—as a "sphere of someone's mineness," so to speak.[33] The experience arises out of the presence of a certain kind of order—order that is alien in the sense that it is not the order *you* would impose, but order that is nonetheless readily discernible as such. Likewise, he thinks, with the woods: they too can be encountered as a sphere of mineness, only "this 'mineness' is not that of human beings or of the creatures that inhabit the woods, but of God."[34] Encountering the woods and their order in this way is importantly *different* from encountering the order of the woods in the usual design-argument sort of way, i.e., as a basis for inference to God's existence, or as a background presupposed in the non-inferential recognition of God's activity as efficient cause, or as a neutral backdrop to the presentation of God to a believer in some kind of supra-sensory experience. It is to experience the woods simply as having the property of *belonging to someone else*, or of *belonging to God*.[35]

---

[32] Wynn 2009: 149–50.

[33] Kohák 1984: 198, quoted (along with surrounding context) and discussed in Wynn 2009: 159ff.

[34] Wynn 2009: 159.

[35] Wynn 2009: 159–60. There are obvious affinities with this view and the view, which Del Ratzsch (2003) attributes to Thomas Reid, that design in nature is recognized perceptually rather than by way of inference.

Similarly, in discussing Wendell Berry's sylvan experiences, Wynn talks as if one's awareness of the "storied history" of a place like the Red River Gorge partly determines both the phenomenal character and the representational content of what one experiences in that place. So, for example, he talks about how Berry is overcome by a sense of loneliness and melancholy, partly as a result of his awareness of the history of the place. Moreover, as Wynn has it, it is not as if the sense of loneliness and melancholy is merely *caused* by his perceptual experience as accompanied by his awareness of the relevant history. Rather, as Wynn puts it, "his sadness is in part a visceral registering of the past of this place."[36]

Berry also describes feeling a sense of unsettledness in the woods, and of disconnection from his ordinary familiar environs; and these feelings, in turn, contribute to a general sense of his own insignificance, which also is a source of sadness. And yet, over time, the sense of unfamiliarity fades and he comes to feel a kind of oneness with the woods. In these feelings, partly evoked by the material environment and partly by his awareness of the relevant history of the place, two important truths are also conveyed: "human beings stand in an extended natural environment which accords no special significance to their activities . . . and yet it is also true that we can feel at home in 'wild' nature" (Wynn 2009: 152). Wynn's view seems to be that these truths are not conclusions Berry arrives at as a result of reflecting on the contents of his experiences, but rather they are *among* the representational contents of his experiences. In other words, Berry has an experience that represents him as insignificant in relation to his external environment and yet also as being capable of feeling at home in that raw and untamed environment.

As Wynn has it, the important truths just mentioned involve an appreciation of what Wynn calls the "existential meanings" that are "stored up in" and presented by Berry's material context. This way of talking fits with a broader strand of thought in contemporary philosophy and theology that bucks against the modern conception of the material world as "disenchanted," or entirely free of properties that fall outside the scope of what is investigated by the natural sciences. John McDowell and David Brown, for example, have in different ways defended views according to which the natural world and its

---

[36] Wynn 2009: 151.

objects are laden with meaning and value that can be apprehended perceptually in a way similar to that in which Wynn's "senses of God" are apprehended.[37] Sameer Yadav, in turn, sets McDowell's view in dialogue with Gregory of Nyssa to develop a full-blown theory of religious experience and the spiritual senses.[38] On Yadav's view (which he takes to be an elaboration of Gregory of Nyssa's view), the spiritual senses are capacities acquired through training for perceiving divine intentions and activities indirectly in a way precisely analogous to the way in which a scientist might perceive the movements of fundamental particles by way of their vapor trails.

All of these views share two important features in common with my own. First, they expand the class of paradigmatic religious experiences in a way that includes the sorts of divine encounters that I said were excluded from Alston's class of paradigms. Second, they imply that background cognitive states, such as those that comprise one's moral character and system of values or one's awareness of the storied history of a place, can contribute to making one's experiencing of a particular material context into a divine encounter.

At the same time, however, each is also heavy-laden with commitments in both metaphysics and the philosophy of perception. Wynn is superficially committed to the puzzling view that meanings can somehow be "stored up" in material places; Yadav, following McDowell, is committed to pervasive cognitive penetration in human experience; and all but Wynn are committed to views according to which normative and paradigmatically supernatural properties are pervasively distributed throughout the natural world.

These commitments are clearly vital for the various larger projects in which each of these different authors are engaged; perhaps they are also defensible. But one of the most important take-away lessons of the present chapter is that *none* of these commitments is strictly required for the explanatory work that I aim to do—namely, that of showing how coming to be able to experience pervasive divine communication in the material world might require a certain kind of skill that will be in principle learnable by anyone who has the concept of God, and especially by those who have access to the scriptures and the liturgies of the church.

---

[37] Cf. McDowell 1996 and Brown 2004. See also Dalferth 2001 and 2006 for a closely related view.

[38] Yadav 2015.

On the view that I advocate, all divine encounters have purely natural stimuli; whether the stimulus for a divine encounter is *experienced as* a divine encounter depends importantly upon the subject's cognitive states; and it is precisely the differences in people's cognitive states that explain why some have the ability to encounter God in natural phenomena whereas others do not. Appeal to the cognitive penetrability of perception affords a helpful explanation for how these core claims might be true when the experiences in question are perceptual. But, as I have already explained, such appeal is not necessary; nor, importantly, does my view carry the stronger commitment to *pervasive* cognitive penetration that, for example, Yadav's view embodies.

Likewise, the view that I advocate is committed neither to the overlay of normative and supernatural properties posited by those with views like Brown and Yadav; nor is it committed to the idea, apparently advocated by Ingolf Dalferth, that the experience of God is mediated by some *very particular* natural phenomenon, namely, our awareness of our own contingency and fragility, and the accompanying sense of the difference between existing and not existing.[39] Instead, I can dispense with the overlay of normative and supernatural properties, and I can also allow that a great many natural stimuli mediate exactly the same sense of the presence of God.

4.

In earlier work, I characterized religious experience as follows: a *religious experience* is an apparent direct awareness of either (a) the existence, character, or behavior of a divine mind; or (b) the fact that one of one's own mental states or a testimonial report communicated by others has been divinely inspired.[40] Although I did not say as much, I also thought of externally stimulated religious experiences—as I thought of it, the experiences referenced in (a) rather than (b)—in broadly causalist terms. The idea underlying both my definition and my causalism was that religious experiences are *of God*; and since God is an immaterial, non-natural, minded entity, experiences of God ought to involve either something mental or something external but clearly supernatural as the stimulus. On this way of thinking,

---

[39] See Dalferth 2006: 134.   [40] Rea 2002: 68.

experiencing the physical world simply isn't a way of *genuinely* experiencing God, and this primarily because God is not a physical thing. This way of thinking, however, as well as the definition it gave rise to, now strikes me as deeply misguided; and I want to close this chapter by explaining part of the reason why. In doing so, I take myself also to be explaining why I think that the view of divine encounters that I have sketched in this chapter is the most plausible account of how creatures like us would *have* to experience the divine presence in a material world.

Consider the problem of other minds—roughly, the question of how we detect the presence of genuine mentality in or associated with another physical body. We can detect bodies by way of sense perception; but other people's souls, if there are such things, or distinctively mental properties (e.g., pains, pleasures, and other qualitative states), are not available to us by way of sense perception. So how do we detect them?

In the contemporary literature on this problem, there are four main responses. Some say that we employ analogical reasoning; some say that we employ inductive reasoning; some say that we employ inference to the best explanation; and some say that the belief that certain other bodies are inhabited by minds is one that need not be based on any kind of inference from other beliefs, but is justifiably held (presumably) just on the basis of our experience of that body.

I don't want to try to adjudicate between these responses; rather, I simply want to highlight a thesis that they all seem to presuppose:

> We have no special causal contact with other people's minds or their mental states. Rather, the stimulus for whatever experience we might have of their mind or mental states is something non-mental, and if the experience *seems* to be of something mental, that is the result of background reasoning of some sort (for example, inference to the best explanation, or analogical reasoning) or our own prior, basic belief that other bodies are (typically) inhabited by other minds.

Absent this assumption, the problem of other minds would be easy to solve. We could simply point to our special causal contact with other minds, as evidenced by the inadequacy of purely physical explanations for some of our experiences, as our evidence for other minds.[41] The problem of other minds is serious only on the assumption that

---

[41] For purposes here I will assume that "mental" contrasts with "physical," though I do not actually endorse the reductionism that this assumption might convey.

we have no such contact, so that every physical event we are aware of is at least adequately explained, even if not fully accurately explained, without appeal to other people's minds.

As I see it, then, reflection on the problem of other minds reveals that the only way we manage to experience the presence of other human minds within the material world is by way of *cognitively impacted experiences whose stimuli are natural, physical phenomena.* This, then, is how we experience the presence of other human *persons* as such, and this regardless of whether they are material or immaterial. A natural further conclusion, then, is that what it would be for creatures like us to experience the presence of an immaterial divine person within the material world would likewise be for us to have a cognitively impacted experience whose stimulus was some natural physical phenomenon. So, in other words, reflection on the problem of other minds points to the conclusion that we would experience God's presence in much the same way as we experience the presence of created persons—especially if created persons are immaterial, but also even if they are not.

In *Being and Nothingness*, Jean-Paul Sartre gave consideration to the problem of other minds and argued that, in fact, the presence of other human minds is given in experience. Importantly, however, he did not seem to think that we have any *direct* awareness of other minds. Rather, we experience the presence of another mind through our experience of our own reactions to the "look" of the other person.

Sartre focuses primarily on shame, and argues that it is precisely that sort of experience—one in which we recognize *ourselves as objects of someone else's perception*—that conveys to us the existence of the Other *as* another person (as opposed to merely a body, or non-personal object). So, he writes: "It is in and through the revelation of my being-as-object for the other that I must be able to apprehend the presence of his being-as-subject."[42] But the "revelation" he describes here is one that comes simply through the *shame* that one experiences upon (say) being caught making a vulgar gesture or looking through someone else's keyhole.[43] On such occasions, in other words, the experience of shame has as part of its representational content the fact that *there exists another subject for whom I am an object of perception.*

Sartre's understanding of shame as occasioned by the "look of the Other" makes it out to be a paradigm case of a cognitively impacted

---

[42] Sartre 1956: 344–5.   [43] Sartre 1956: 302, 347–8.

experience. It is precisely because of relevant background cognition that Sartre takes his experience of the look of the Other on this particular occasion to be one that represents the presence of another person. My claim is that the presence of God is experienced in much the same way. With the right background cognition, the presence of God is as perceivable in natural circumstances as the presence of another person is perceivable to Sartre in cases where the look of that person is prone to induce shame or similar emotions.

In sum, then, I think that reflection on the problem of other minds and on the way in which we apprehend the presence of other persons supports the account of divine encounters that I have been describing here; and (especially given the sorts of dualistic assumptions that have characterized much of the Christian tradition) my view also has the advantage of making experiences of God's presence to be entirely of a piece with our experience of the presence of created persons. Just as experiences of other human minds are cognitively impacted experiences of purely natural stimuli, so too experience of God is cognitively impacted experience of purely natural stimuli. Moreover, an interesting consequence of this conclusion is that someone who demands experiential evidence of God's existence as a condition on believing in God will be in roughly the same position as a solipsist—a skeptic about other minds—who demands experiential evidence of other minds as a *condition* on believing in them. Absent some reorientation of their way of *looking at the world*, there will be no way to dislodge them from their skepticism.

On the account that I am offering, the most notable difference between experiencing the presence of God and experiencing the presence of another (immaterial, human) person is that the latter sort of experience comes more or less naturally, whereas the experience of the presence of God involves, for most of us, the acquisition of a skill. According to scripture, divine presence is available all around us, in a variety of different ways. The heavens "proclaim" the glory of God; the church is (in some sense) the body of Christ; the Holy Spirit dwells in individual believers; the elements of the Eucharist are (in another sense) the body and blood of Christ; and so on. But we have to *learn* to see these phenomena as loci of God's presence.

Again, however, this is not a skill that must be acquired intentionally, like the ability to skate backward. It is a skill that *can* be cultivated intentionally, but often enough it seems to develop more or less naturally through intersecting processes of socialization, acquisition of religious faith and certain kinds of doctrinal beliefs, and immersion in scripture, religious community, and various kinds of liturgical practice. Toward the beginning of Chapter 6, I indicated that my account implies that people who have access to scripture and liturgical forms of worship will be better positioned to experience God than people who do not; and by now it should be clear why. Both scripture and liturgy contribute to the cultivation of the kinds of cognitive states—beliefs, attitudes, desires, and the like—that, on my account, facilitate experiences of the presence of God. In earlier work, I said that scripture and liturgy can *mediate* the presence of God.[44] I still believe what I wrote there, but I would now try to understand the relevant mediation in terms of cognitive impact. Over the past decade an increasing number of philosophers have begun to call attention to and explore the impact that both narrative and ritual can have on our beliefs, desires, attitudes, understanding (both tacit and explicit) of our circumstances, and other aspects of the "lens" through which we look at the world. In much of this work we also find claims to the effect that attention to biblical narratives, as well as participation in liturgical forms worship, can facilitate various kinds of religious experience.[45] In light of the present account of divine encounters, it is easy to see why this might be so.

Furthermore, as I noted earlier, the advice from mystics in the Christian tradition on how to experience the presence of God is surprisingly uniform; and, in broad outline, this advice is of a piece with advice in other religious traditions about how to cultivate experiences of religious realities.[46] As I also noted, there is both anecdotal and scientific evidence that the advice works, by and large, for a significant proportion of the population. People who have the relevant measurable traits and who cultivate the right kinds of spiritual habits will be more likely to have religious experiences of various kinds.[47] People who, in addition, have the concept of

---

[44] Rea 2009a, 2011a.

[45] Cf. Stump 2012, the essays in Cuneo 2016, and Timpe 2014. The idea that God's presence is mediated through liturgical acts is also a theme in the literature on sacramental theology. See, e.g., Lawler 1987: ch. 2, and Vorgrimler 1992: 68–73.

[46] Cf. e.g., Wainwright 1981: 89; Luhrmann 2012: ch. 6.

[47] Note that I do not expect that there is any necessary connection between having the "right measurable traits" and "cultivating the right spiritual habits" and being a virtuous person. It is sometimes suggested that God requires a certain degree of virtue or purity from a person before providing her with experiences of the divine presence.

God, will be more likely to have what I am calling "divine encounters" (if they are trying to do so).

If all that I have said so far is correct, then it seems likely that quite a lot of people who have the concept of God, and especially those who have access to scripture and liturgical forms of worship, will be able to have divine encounters just by trying.[48] Some ways of trying will be more effective than others; and, as Schellenberg notes, there is no reason to think that trying will be easy. There is also no reason to think that most people will be able to have exactly the kinds of encounters they *want* to have. But insofar as my account implies that simply looking at one's circumstances through a certain kind of theistic lens can suffice to provide a person with an apparent awareness of God's presence, it seems quite plausible to think that, if the account is correct, that sort of experience is widely and readily available to people who have the relevant lens and who persist in trying to have that sort of experience. And, on the assumption—which I endorse—that God is always and everywhere *intending* that people experience as much of God's love and presence as they are able given their psychological profile, background cognition, and so on, there is a clear sense in which all that I have been saying in this chapter implies that God is constantly communicating, and that any experience of God's love or presence that a person manages to have will be veridical (at least as regards God's love for them, and God's presence, if nothing else).

One might wonder how, if experience of God's presence and love is available in the ways I say it is, the capacity to have such experiences could be *lost*, as it so often seems to be. Consider again St. Teresa of Calcutta, for example. Do we want to say that she *forgot* how to experience the love and presence of God, or that she ceased trying? Clearly not. But then how can we explain the fact that, after a period in her life of frequent and vivid divine encounters, she found

(For example, Alston (1991: 144, 198–9) comments on the broad acceptance of this idea within the Christian tradition, and possible scriptural support for it, though does not himself quite seem to endorse it; and Huxley (1945: 2–3) affirms it.) But I see no evidence that people who have divine encounters (sensational or otherwise) are, as a rule, more virtuous or sincere or "pure in heart" than people who do not. It is partly for this reason that I prefer an account of such experiences according to which they are not a sign of special divine favor.

[48] Again, however, I do not mean to suggest that having a concept of God is *necessary* for having a divine encounter. Cf. Chapter 6, note 37.

herself suddenly, agonizingly, and persistently unable to have them any longer?[49]

There is, of course, no way of knowing for sure what was going on in her case, or anyone else's for that matter. But, at a certain level of generality, this phenomenon is easy to explain on my account, and in a way that gives it a further advantage over competitors. Those who endorse causalism will have a hard time avoiding the conclusion that God has, for one reason or another, *withdrawn* from such people. This is precisely the conclusion that St. Teresa reached about her own case; and it is precisely the sort of conclusion that contributes to making the phenomenon of divine hiddenness so agonizing for people. On my account, however, the most likely explanation is simply that relevant changes in the person's background cognition are the problem. The person has, so to speak, lost or suffered some kind of occlusion of the relevant "lens" that facilitated her experience of the presence of God. Some might be quick to cite sin, doubt, or some kind of loss of love for or allegiance to God as the likely cause of this; but it seems obvious that other, less "blaming" explanations are also possible. For example, I think that persistent or empathetic engagement with the sufferings of other people, and perhaps simply the persistent observation of such suffering, can make it hard to look at the world as an ongoing arena of loving divine activity and can, accordingly, also make it hard to experience God's love and presence. No doubt other explanations are possible as well.

That said, however, it must be acknowledged that the problem of hiddenness now bubbles again to the surface. For, although my account implies that experience of God's presence is much more widely and readily available than is commonly acknowledged, it does not imply that it is *universally* available to just anyone who might want it. What is God doing for those too overwhelmed by suffering (their own or others), or too angry with God, or too doubtful of God's existence to view their circumstances in ways that would let them experience God's love and presence? What is God doing for the people who lack access to scripture, liturgy, or to the very concept of God? What about people who, for one reason or another, simply lack the capacity for experiential awareness of God? It is the goal of Chapters 8 and 9 to address questions like these.

---

[49] Thanks to Charity Anderson for pressing this objection.

8

A God to Contend With

Conflict and suffering are woven into all human relationships, including the most intimate and loving. As a relationship starts to become intensely conflicted, however—as it becomes increasingly fraught with negative emotion and unhealthy patterns of engagement—questions arise about whether it still can be positively meaningful. Accordingly, questions also arise about whether it still counts as loving. To knowingly and willingly *allow* a relationship to become so conflicted that it is no longer positively meaningful for the other party is a paradigmatic failure of love.

My concern in this chapter is with people whose relationships with God are intensely conflicted—for example, people who are angry with or severely distrustful of God; people who, from their own personal experiences or from reflecting on the experiences of others, have come to see God as neglectful, abusive, or in other ways cruel;[1] people so bewildered by God's silence in the face of human suffering that they have been pushed from faith to unfaith, or to a stance of protest against God, or to a concept of God as impotent[2] or unconcerned with human affairs.[3]

Human lovers, insofar as they excel at loving, avoid letting their love relationships become intensely conflicted; they tend to pursue resolution and reconciliation when conflict arises. Accordingly, in relationships where intense conflict is present or looming on the horizon, persistent deliberate withdrawal, hiding, and silence typically indicate a failure to love (except, of course, when these things are required for one's own self-protection). For this reason, divine hiddenness calls into

---

[1] Blumenthal 1993: esp. 247ff.; Brueggemann 2012: ch. 10. Cf. also O'Connor 2002: ch. 9.
[2] O'Connor 2002: 122.   [3] Milazzo 1991: 163–8.

question the aptness of characterizing God as loving toward those for whom the divine–human relationship is intensely conflicted. As I have explained in earlier chapters, the problem is not that divine hiddenness violates a manifestly necessary condition on divine love; it doesn't. Rather, the problem is simply that the deviation from what we normally take to be excellence in love is, in this case, so sharp that certain counter-analogies become salient. Why, under these circumstances, is it apt to characterize God on analogy with the most excellent of human lovers? Why is it not more apt to think of God on analogy with a cruelly indifferent sovereign, or a parent who plays favorites and is willingly, even harmfully, neglectful of his disfavored children?

Within the Christian tradition, these questions are partly answered by appeal to God's creative and sustaining activity—God's general goodness to all of creation—as well as to the life, death, and resurrection of Jesus. These indicators of divine love, to the extent that one believes in them, are undeniably significant. But in the present context, appeal to them alone is not sufficient to address the problem.

God's creative and sustaining activity points to a kind of original love for all of creation; the incarnation and atoning work of Christ point to God's dramatically loving willingness to supply a path by which *God's grievances against human beings* might be addressed. But for those whose relationships with God are intensely conflicted, the problem is not that they fail entirely to benefit from God's general goodness to creation; nor is it that they fail to have some path to being forgiven by God. The problem is that they seem to have in some sense legitimate *grievances against God* and, as a result, have no path forward (short of dysfunctionally repressing their grievances) for participating in a positively meaningful way in their relationship with God. This is the problem that I aim to address in the present chapter.

My approach will be as follows. I will begin by briefly describing two scriptural portrayals of intensely conflicted divine–human relationships: God's relationship with Job, and God's relationship with the nation of Israel as described in the book of Lamentations. I will then seek to establish three conclusions. First, I will argue that, whatever else it might convey or accomplish, the theophany at the end of Job at least presents God as providing a tender loving response to Job that takes his grievances seriously and puts him on a path toward a repaired relationship with God. Second, I will argue that those very signs of God's love for Job and concern for his grievances are part of a broader pattern in the biblical portrayal of God's relationship with Israel, one manifest also in Lamentations; and I will argue that the fact that God is portrayed in these ways constitutes a positive sign—available to anyone who has access to these portrayals—that God is generally concerned with human grievances against God. Finally, I will argue that precisely the means available to both Job and the ancient Israelites for participating in a positively meaningful relationship with God are available to anyone who has the concept of God and who is willing and able to try to participate in such a relationship.

1.

Many passages of scripture poetically evoke the problems of evil and divine hiddenness, but none so poignantly as the Old Testament books of Job and Lamentations. Job presents us with the innocent sufferer *par excellence*, a man who undergoes with God's explicit permission the devastation of his possessions, livelihood, family, and physical health. Lamentations presents Daughter Zion, ravaged and torn, suffering humiliation and destruction beyond anything she might sensibly be said to deserve. The accusations against God in both books are pointed; God's love, goodness, and justice are sharply called into question.

Job's accusations eventually get a response from God, albeit (as most interpret it) not the sort of theodical answer we might want or expect. In Lamentations, the accusations against God are left to stand. God never makes an appearance, and no final justification is offered for the cruelties that the prophet lays at God's feet. Nevertheless, the idea that God loves Israel, even when Israel is being crushed and carried off into exile, is present throughout the Old Testament, including the pages of Lamentations. Nor is it present simply as a divine declaration in the face of contrary evidence; rather, it is presupposed and proclaimed by the prophets and psalmists and other spokesmen for Israel, often within the very same texts that bring accusations against God.[4]

---

[4] On this, cf. Walter Brueggemann's (2012) discussion of the tension between Israel's "core testimony" and her "counter-testimony."

But why should we agree with such proclamations? What sign do we have that God is at all concerned about Israel's grievances against God, and has provided a way for the divine–human relationship to remain positively meaningful? These questions are important for my purposes because, from a Christian point of view, the prophets' cries and complaints on behalf of Israel might, with little modification, be as easily spoken on behalf of the world. As God's chosen people, Israel rightly took herself to be entitled to God's loving concern; but the gospel of John reports that God loves the whole world. If we can find signs of divine concern for the grievances of afflicted Israel, so too we might find those same signs in God's relationship with a suffering world more broadly.

Let us begin by considering the divine–human relationship depicted in the book of Job. The book opens with a prologue in which we find God boasting to a character called "the satan," or "the accuser," about his servant Job, a man of unsurpassed piety and righteousness.[5] The accuser is unimpressed, saying that Job is faithful only because God has protected him from great suffering. In response to the thinly veiled challenge, God gives permission to the accuser to destroy Job's possessions and his children. So it goes; but Job remains pious, the accuser remains unimpressed. So God again turns Job over to the accuser's power, whereupon the accuser afflicts him with a disease that covers Job's entire body with sores. Job's wife challenges his persistence in piety and tells him to curse God and die; then "comforters" arrive to discuss with Job the source and cause of his suffering, their view being that there must be some sin in Job's life for which all of the calamities that have befallen him are just retribution. The book does not say as much, but it is hardly a stretch to think that these last events—the response from his wife and the arrival of his companions—only serve to complete Job's descent into a hell of suffering by assaulting his last remaining source of comfort, namely,

---

[5] The satan of the book of Job is not necessarily to be identified with the "Satan" of the New Testament. Something like the following explanation is typically given:

In the prologue of Job, the figure that incites God to afflict Job is not designated by a proper noun—"Satan"—but rather by a common noun preceded by the definite article—"the satan." It can also be translated "the accuser" or "the adversary." In the historical context in which the prologue was probably composed, such a figure would have been hired by a king as a sort of spy, whose job was to ferret out disloyalty to the throne within the king's realm.

(Brinks 2013: 372, following Tur-Sinai 1967: 41–5)

his communion with others and his confident assurance of his own righteous standing before God.[6]

Job's speeches throughout the book until God's appearance at the end are a mixture of lament, accusation against God, proclamation of his own innocence, rebuke of his friends, and demand for a hearing before God. Job's suffering is so intense that he expresses hatred for his own life and curses the day he was born—indeed, he would prefer to be strangled to death than to continue on in life (3:3–4; 7:15–16). Whereas the author of Psalm 8 marvels joyfully at the fact that God pays attention to human beings, Job, paralleling the psalmist's own language, marvels in frustration:[7]

> What are human beings, that you make so much of them,
> > that you set your mind on them,
> visit them every morning,
> > test them every moment?
> Will you not look away from me for a while,
> > let me alone until I swallow my spittle?
> If I sin, what do I do to you, you watcher of humanity?
> > Why have you made me your target?
> > Why have I become a burden to you? (7:17–20)

Whereas the author of Psalm 40 gratefully remarks that God has "inclined to [him] and heard his cry," lifted him out of the miry bog, and made his footsteps secure, Job, toward the end of his laments, accuses God of violently casting him into the mire, ignoring his cries, and tossing him about in the roar of a storm:[8]

> With violence he seizes my garment;
> > he grasps me by the collar of my tunic.
> He has cast me into the mire,
> > and I have become like dust and ashes.
> I cry to you and you do not answer me;
> > I stand, and you merely look at me.
> You have turned cruel to me;
> > with the might of your hand you persecute me.
> You lift me up on the wind, you make me ride on it,

---

[6] Cf. Stump 2012: 182–3.   [7] Fishbane 1992: 87–90.

[8] In contrast to the parallels with Psalm 8, I am not aware of any commentator who has suggested that there are genuine linguistic or thematic connections between Job 30 and Psalm 40; so the most that I can claim here is that there are some interesting superficial similarities.

and you toss me about in the roar of the storm.
I know that you will bring me to death,
and to the house appointed for all living. (30:18–23)

God eventually shows up to respond to Job's cries. But, famously, whatever else might be said to be going on in the climactic theophany, Job is not given any explicit defense of God's justice or goodness. Precisely where we might expect scripture to deliver a theodicy, we are given none. In fact, as in Lamentations, the book of Job seems to let the accusations stand. As most translations have it, Job does repent of something. But it is hardly clear that he repents of his accusations against God;[9] and, in any case, the book has God announcing at the end that Job alone has "spoken rightly" of God (42:7), suggesting that *if* Job repented of his accusations against God, he was wrong to do so.

Many answers to the problem of evil have nevertheless been extracted from the book. I won't try to survey them here, but I agree with most commentators that *if* delivering a theodicy is among the aims of Job, the theodicy that is given is both implausible and disappointing. The divine speeches are the most natural place to look for whatever theodicy the book has to offer. But, as most commentators agree, the upshot of the divine speeches is that God is powerful and completely in charge of creation whereas, by comparison, human beings are very small and of little account. If *that* content is intended to provide God's answer to the question, "How is it that you are justified in allowing innocent people like Job to suffer horribly?" then the answer seems just to be "might makes right." That is hardly plausible even as a general principle, much less a theodicy.

Plenty of commentators have extracted other, and better, theodical nuggets from the divine speeches; but, however creative, beautiful, and theologically appealing some of these might be, ultimately I think that they distort the text. As I read the divine speeches, they do seem designed primarily to convey God's tremendous power and dominion over creation; and it is precisely because this sort of content is both primary in the text and useless for theodicy that I do not think the aim of those speeches is to deliver or even to point us toward one.[10]

[9] Judgments about what Job repents of, or whether he repents at all, depend importantly on how one translates Job 42:6. On this, see Brinks 2013: 372. For some of the different options, see Balentine 2006: 692–701.

[10] Making matters worse, Job 2:3 has God remarking to the satan that he had "incited [God] against [Job], to destroy him *for no reason*" (my emphasis).

What, then, is their purpose? I have no answer to this question; but I do have a partial view about a much simpler question—namely, the question of what the speeches *accomplish* in the context of the entire theophany. In short, my view is that, whatever else it might have been intended to do, the theophany provides a powerful display of God's love for Job and concern for his grievances.

But how can it be so? Commentators who read the speeches as I do—as mainly conveying God's power and dominion—typically do not see God as displaying much by way of love for Job or concern for his grievances. The relatively few who see God as manifesting love toward Job typically read the speeches very differently. I want to close this section by briefly considering an interpretation of this second sort. Doing so will set the stage for the development of my own reading in Section 2.

In her own Gifford Lectures, published under the title *Wandering in Darkness*, Eleonore Stump argues that, far from simply displaying God's power and dominion over creation, the divine speeches in Job 38–41 display God's tender loving care for creation. God is depicted as birthing the seas, the rain, and the ice; leading and guiding the constellations; providing food for the lions and ravens; attending to the birthing cycles of the goats and deer, and paying attention to the growth of their young; playing with the great Leviathan on a leash; and so on. Some of the imagery used to convey these things is maternal. Much of it is vaguely anthropomorphizing—God *talks* to the stars, the elements, and the animals. She does not deny that the speeches convey God's power; but, she says, they portray God as "more than powerful." They portray God as lovingly, intimately engaged with all of creation and as "having a parental care toward all . . . creatures, even the inanimate ones" (Stump 2012: 190).

On Stump's view, moreover, what Job gets out of the divine speeches—what helps him to be satisfied after the divine speeches and leads him to repent of his accusations—is an explanation for his suffering, a theodicy. The explanation is not explicit, however, or even propositional; it is not a communicable story about why Job suffered.

The remark can, of course, be interpreted in a way consistent with God's having still been justified in permitting Job's suffering, and even with God's having permitted the whole episode for the sake of greater goods. Whether such an interpretation is plausible depends in part on what theological assumptions we are entitled to bring to the table. But it is certainly an *odd* remark to include in the text if the overall purpose of the book in its current, canonical form is to deliver a theodicy.

Rather, it is the sort of "explanation" that one gets, or can get, when one simply encounters a person who is presented in experience as both ideally parental and deeply loving.

Simply by encountering God as someone who loves creatures in a parental way, she thinks, Job can see that he too is loved by God. Moreover, in the same encounter he can also see that God operates on a key principle that all good parents operate on: "other things being equal, the outweighing benefit that justifies a parent in allowing some suffering to an innocent child of hers has to benefit the child primarily" (Stump: 191). Seeing all of this, she thinks, puts Job in possession of a theodicy. The justice, goodness, and love of God is secured in Job's mind; his complaint has been answered on its own terms.

Stump's interpretation of the divine speeches is careful, subtle, and deeply sensitive to all manner of textual cues as to the character of God's relationships with creatures—including not just Job and the animals, but the accuser as well. What is unique about it, however, is not that she sees genuine signs of God's care and concern for creation in those speeches, but that she thinks that this is (at least) as much the point of those speeches as the display of divine power, and that what these signs of care and concern are intended to convey is God's deep love and parental concern for all creatures and God's commitment to the just and loving principle of "no suffering without benefit to the sufferer."[11]

Stump's conclusions stand at some distance from the text, however, being the result not just of close attention to the language and imagery but also of some speculation as to what an author might aim to convey with such imagery. Unsurprisingly, others who similarly see an emphasis on care and concern for creation have taken away

---

[11] The benefit-to-the-sufferer principle is controversial. Marilyn McCord Adams is among those who endorse it. She says that God loves an individual human person only if God goes so far as to "defeat [not merely 'balance off'] any horrendous evil in which s/he participated by giving it positive meaning thorough organic unity with a great enough good *within the context of his/her life*" (Adams 1999: 31, emphasis in original). Given what she says about the distinction between defeating evil vs. balancing it off (Adams 1999: 21, 28–9), this implies that God loves individual human persons only if their participation in horrendous evils somehow ultimately contributes to *their* good. Among those who reject the principle are Michael Bergmann (2008: 390), Alvin Plantinga (2004: 23–4), and Peter van Inwagen (1988: 183–4). Many, however, endorse somewhat weaker principles—e.g., that any suffering that God causes us must be compensated by *some* benefit to us, so that our lives are, on the whole, good (Bergmann 2008: 390, Swinburne 1998: 230).

very different messages. Carol Newsom, for example, sees God as communicating concern for symbolically laden animals in a way that conveys a striking *absence* of special providential concern for human beings.[12] Michael Fox says that "[w]hatever else the Theophany means, it certainly seeks to induce humility" (2013: 21), the goal being to elicit a response of faith and loyalty from Job *even in the face of divine injustice.*

It is beyond my competence to say which interpretation of the divine speeches does most justice to the text. But, much as I appreciate the beauty of Stump's interpretation, I cannot bring myself to endorse it. Part of the reason is that I cannot set aside the fact that much of what God is said to be doing with creation involves taking sides with predators (e.g., hunting on behalf of the lion) that, as Newsom argues, are symbolic of godlessness and moral disorder, and interacting "unnervingly... in considerable sympathy with the emblems of chaos [e.g., the sea, the ostrich, Leviathan, behemoth]."[13] Even if we grant Stump the background assumptions required to support her reading, I find it hard to imagine the author of Job expecting his ancient readers to look past all of this symbolism and see the theodical message that Stump takes to be the content of God's response to Job's accusations. Why present God as speaking from a *whirlwind* and as emphasizing not only God's playful relationship with Leviathan but also God's power to "fill his skin with spikes and his head with spears" if the point of the theophany was to reveal the loving face of a heavenly parent and to convey that God allows no suffering without benefit to the sufferer?[14]

Ultimately, I do not *need* to resist Stump's interpretation in order to make my case. In fact, if she is correct, my task with respect to the book of Job is, in a way, already accomplished: this, I might say—what I have just presented from Stump—is how God shows love to Job. But I do not want to rest my case on it, partly because I cannot myself endorse it, but also because I think that my case is stronger if my reading of the text is more in line with the majority interpretation of the divine speeches.

As I understand it, the majority interpretation sees the primary content as asserting God's power and dominion over creation. Within that majority, some also see signs of God's loving and providential

---

[12] Newsom 2003: 244–52.   [13] Newsom 2003: 246–7.
[14] For additional concerns about Stump's reading of Job, see Brinks 2013.

concern for creation; others do not. My own understanding of what is accomplished by the theophany is consistent with all of this. It is also, as shall emerge, consistent with divergent interpretations of Job's response—ones that see Job as genuinely humbled and repentant, ones that see him as cagily mouthing repentance while cautiously maintaining an attitude of protest, and even ones that see him openly maintaining a position of defiance.[15]

2.

One of the oldest representations of God in scripture is the one found in the "Song of the Sea," the poem in Exodus 15 that describes God's victory over Pharaoh's army. In that text, God is a mighty warrior who strides onto the battlefield and unleashes his burning anger against Israel's oppressors, terrifying them, setting them atremble, and ultimately casting them into the sea. The poet asks, "Who among the gods is like you, Lord? Who is like you—majestic in holiness, awesome in glory, working wonders?" The implied answer, plainly enough, is "Nobody. Nobody at all."

The Song of the Sea portrays God in highly anthropomorphic terms. God is a mighty man writ large—not explicitly the transcendent, omnipotent deity of classical theism but, even so, a champion capable of taking all comers, of defeating all foes, human or divine, on earth or in heaven. Other parts of scripture exalt God even further. Second Isaiah represents a kind of pinnacle in this regard. There too, the author asks to whom God might be compared; but in that text God is far beyond a "mighty man of war." God is one before whom entire nations are but a drop from a bucket, as dust on the scales, as nothing—indeed, *less* than nothing. Who has measured the waters in his hand, marked off the heavens with his fingers, weighed the mountains in a scale? God alone. Who counsels God? Nobody.

One rendering of God's second speech to Job puts roughly the same rhetorical question in God's own mouth right at the end of the divine discourse on Leviathan: "Who can stand before me? Who

---

[15] See, e.g., Curtis 1979, as well as the discussion in Fox 2013: 18–21.

can confront me and be safe? Under the whole heaven, who?"[16] Remarkably, however, the obvious answer—not only implied, but dramatically displayed in the narrative—is not *nobody*, but rather *Job*, the one who has, throughout the preceding thirty-two chapters, challenged God to a disputation.[17]

Who can stand before God and be safe? Whatever else is conveyed by the divine speeches, and regardless of how one ultimately decides to understand the rhetorical questions at the end of the discourse on Leviathan, *this* question is manifestly at least part of the subtext underlying God's speeches to Job. On the assumption that the display of divine power and dominion comprises the primary content of those speeches, it does not defy credibility to suppose that the main point of those speeches was to raise this question and to convey its startling answer.[18] As Claus Westermann observes, the answer that Job received to his accusations and challenges was hardly what Job expected; but, he notes, "none of that alters the basic fact that God does answer him. One could almost say that the *fact* of God's answering gets overlooked in the consideration of *what* God says."[19] The

---

[16] This is Westermann's rendering (1981: 119–20). More typical is to emend the Hebrew, supplying third-person pronouns in place of the first-person ones so as to make these questions a continuation of the rhetorical questions pertaining to Leviathan: Who can stand before *him (i.e., Leviathan)*? Who can confront *him* and be safe? But even if one rejects Westermann's rendering, the question is still tacitly posed by God; for, on the more traditional rendering, God, having just described his own taming of Leviathan, asks who can stand before *it*. Only God, of course; but then, *a fortiori*, who at all can stand before God?

[17] Westermann 1981: 120.

[18] Just how startling the answer is depends a bit on when Job was written. The book of Job is manifestly in dialogue with other scriptural texts; and the portions of Second Isaiah just mentioned seem to be among those. Dating Job in relation to those texts, however, is a vexed matter; so it is sometimes difficult to tell which way the dialogue goes—whether the author of Job is alluding to Second Isaiah, for example, or the other way around. At present, the majority of opinions on the dates of the relevant texts suggest that, to the extent that there is influence at all between them, the parts of Job on which I am focusing would have been influenced by the particular psalms and portions of Second Isaiah with which they seem to interact, rather than vice versa. (Cf., e.g., Brinks Rea 2010: ch. 1 and Fishbane 1992.) I will proceed here under the assumption that this opinion is correct. So far as I can tell, my partial interpretation of the theophany does not depend on that assumption. But the portrayal of Job as emerging safe from his encounter with God does seem more powerful under the assumptions I am making than it might be under different assumptions. One might well imagine early readers with Psalms and Second Isaiah firmly in mind finding the outcome of the theophany quite startling indeed, whereas it might not be nearly so if Job was a much earlier text than those others.

[19] Westermann 1981: 105.

exalted Lord of the Universe, the subduer of the sea, the tamer of mighty Behemoth and Leviathan, has appeared in response to a summons from Job, a mere pile of dust and ashes; *and Job has remained safe.*

The rhetorical questions in the divine speeches do not impart new knowledge to Job; their answers are obvious. But what was never obvious—what Job could not possibly have known or expected in advance of the encounter—is that a man could accuse the almighty creator of cruelty and injustice, summon God to a hearing, have God appear in the fullness of power and glory, and be left standing at the end of it all. Whatever *other* knowledge or information Job might have gotten from the theophany, this may be the most striking.[20]

The effect—and the theological significance—of this basic fact is only intensified when one attends to the overall form of the theophany in light of some of the imagery from Job's own words. Recall that, toward the end of his own accusatory speeches, Job describes himself as having "become like dust and ashes" (Job 30:6). In the same place, too, he accuses God of tossing him about as in a storm: "You lift me up on the wind," he says; "you make me ride on it, and you toss me about in the roar of the storm." When God finally appears, God

---

[20] One might ask how this interpretation comports with Job 19:24–6:

> O that my words were written down!
> O that they were inscribed in a book!
> O that with an iron pen and with lead
>   they were engraved on a rock forever!
> For I know that my Redeemer lives,
> and that at the last he will stand upon the earth;
> and after my skin has been thus destroyed,
>   then in my flesh I shall see God,
> whom I shall see on my side,
>   and my eyes shall behold, and not another.

It might seem natural to read these verses as expressing Job's expectation—indeed *knowledge*—that, subsequent to the destruction of his flesh that he is now undergoing, he will ultimately *and in this life* be lifted up, restored to wholeness, and vindicated before God. And this might look to be inconsistent with a reading of the theophany according to which Job has no prior expectation of emerging unharmed from an encounter with God. In fact, however, this is neither the only possible interpretation, nor the most plausible; and among the contested questions in the interpretation of these verses are (a) whether verse 25 is to be translated so as to express *knowledge* that Job's redeemer lives, or merely *hope of seeing his redeemer* while he (Job) remains alive; (b) whether the redeemer is God; and (c) whether the encounter anticipated in verse 26 is an encounter in this life, or post mortem. For discussion of these and other issues, see Balentine 2006: 305–7, Clines 1989: 457–70, and Tur-Sinai 1967: 304–5.

does arrive in the midst of a storm; and God's words roar forth from it: "Brace yourself like a man; I will question you and you shall answer me" (Job 38:3, NIV). But Job does not ride the storm; he is not tossed. God's speeches come from a whirlwind, the greatest possible threat to the corporeal integrity of a pile of dust and ash. Yet in that encounter (even if not the events that led up to it) Job remains safe.[21]

Suppose that, despite all appearances from the prologue, God has perfectly good reasons for permitting Job's suffering or, at any rate, that God's permission of those sufferings is fully consistent with God's being perfectly good and loving.[22] Even so, given his own state of ignorance about God's reasons, together with the fact that human beings have no revelation-independent means of verifying their opinions about God's nature, Job is rightly confused and angry, doubtful about divine justice and mercy. His theological

---

[21] I do not presume that Job was a historical figure; nor do I presume that the book of Job presupposes any particular theory about religious experience. Nevertheless, it is of interest to ask how we ought to imagine the theophany in light of the theory of divine encounters that I offered in Chapters 6–7. On that account, there would have been a whirlwind—this would have been the natural stimulus for Job's experience— but there would have been no voice audible to just any observer who might have been present. It is natural, then, to imagine the divine speeches as being content delivered to Job as a result of the combination of his own background theology together with the experience of standing in the terrifying presence of a whirlwind.

On this way of envisioning things, it is altogether natural that *divine power* would be the primary content; and, again, it would be precisely in light of the fact that Job was brought to stand before a whirlwind, after all his suffering and all of his talk about being tossed on the storm and reduced to dust and ashes, and to receive therein a revelation of divine power and dominion *and* to emerge unscathed that the total experience would have such intense personal theological significance. It hardly strains credulity to imagine a pious sufferer having an experience like that and feeling at the end of it that, whatever he might have suffered, *somehow* he is loved and cared for by God. It hardly strains credulity to imagine a pious sufferer having an experience like that and emerging satisfied.

Neither does it strain credulity to imagine a sufferer having an experience like that and remaining defiant, however; nor is it hard to imagine such a one being thoroughly intimidated, and responding with cautious, perhaps even partially insincere repentance. Any of the responses that have been attributed to Job are psychologically credible in light of my interpretation; that is, I think, part of its virtue. Importantly, too, the nature of Job's response is irrelevant to the question whether, on my interpretation, the theophany is an expression of divine love toward Job.

[22] I think that this is the right supposition to make; but my interpretation does not depend on it. If the book of Job indeed represents God as admitting to being incited to destroy Job for no reason, it portrays God as less than perfect, and as suffering a mighty failure of empathy toward Job. But all of the signs of love toward Job that I will go on to identify here still seem to me to be signs of *love*, even on this alternative interpretation of the divine remark at Job 2:3.

commitments and religious devotion are quite reasonably shaken to the core. He is right to lament; he is right to protest; he is right to demand a hearing from God. In the face of all of this, what is *the most* loving response God could make?

There are, in fact, many things God might do to communicate love to Job. Which is best—*whether* there is a best—depends on facts about God and God's personality to which we have very little access, and on facts about Job that are underspecified by the text. But *a* loving response—a dramatic, tender response—is to confront Job with a powerful image of Job's safety in the presence of God, to remind Job of just how mighty God is, and then to convey, through the image of a pile of dust *invited* to brace himself for a disputation with the whirlwind and then left standing firm, that Job is safe with God, that Job can demand an account from God, bring all of his rage and frustration and protest to lay at the feet of the terrible almighty, and not be laid low but rather be invited to stand up and emerge unharmed.

Moreover, Job does not simply emerge unharmed. Job gets something out of God. The book ends with God expressing approval of Job, apparently validating his laments and accusations by saying that Job alone has spoken rightly of God, and providing Job with new family and possessions in greater measure than what he had lost. As many commentators have observed, such a restoration of family and wealth could hardly compensate for or defeat the badness of Job's earlier losses. As a general rule, for example, coming to have new children in no way makes up for the deaths of one's previous children; and the same may be true, even if only to a lesser extent, of Job's other losses. So we might doubt that what Job gets at the end is anything close to a complete restoration of his earlier happiness or a categorical defeat of all of his sufferings. His life would still be marked, and deeply so, by his ordeal. But we need not deny this fact in order to see, in the conclusion of the book of Job, a communication of divine love.

On the assumption that God's reasons for permitting Job's sufferings were fully consistent with divine love and perfect goodness, the badness of all that Job suffered *will* be defeated at the end of all things. We need not suppose (implausibly, anyway) that *what* defeats that badness is the replacement of Job's possessions and family. What is plain to see, however, is that Job has spent the better part of a biblical book accusing God and, in the end, has successfully subpoenaed God to his own court, stood firm in the presence of God, offered no *unambiguous* repentance or recantation, received explicit divine validation, and then received a reward. What is plain to see, in other words, is that God—the one before whom the very nations are as a drop from a bucket, as dust on the scales, as nothing (indeed less than nothing)—has submitted to Job, the pile of dust and ashes.[23]

3.

Who can contend with God and be safe? To whom will God submit? Job, for one. But his is not the only name on the list. Jacob wrestled with God and wrested away a blessing. Abraham and Moses disagreed with, challenged, and even presumed to counsel God, and more than once did God accommodate them. Gideon twice demanded a sign from God as a condition of his obedience, and God delivered. Moving to the New Testament, everyone who attempted to stone Jesus, everyone who argued with and condemned Jesus, and everyone who participated in his humiliation and crucifixion contended successfully not with a mere man, but with God; and God submitted to it all. Not everyone on this list emerged from their encounter absolutely unscathed. Jacob was left with a limp. Moses was deprived of the chance to walk into the promised land. Even so, it is nothing short of shocking that the God who is described in the sorts of terms that we find in the Song of the Sea, the majestic verses of Isaiah 40, and the divine speeches of Job should also be portrayed so often in scripture as tolerating and even encouraging human protest, and then submitting in response. It is easy to forget that "he who struggles with God" is the very meaning of the name divinely bestowed upon the namesake of God's chosen nation, Israel.[24]

---

[23] My reading of what is going on in the divine speeches at the end of Job resonates in many ways with Marilyn McCord Adams's (2003). They are not the *same* reading by any means; but they are importantly similar, particularly in their emphasis on the value and divine acceptance of Job's protest.

[24] I am focusing here on scriptural examples of people struggling with God for reasons that should be obvious; but Anson Laytner (1990) documents a full-blooded Jewish tradition of arguing with God stretching from biblical times on into the twentieth century, and concludes his study with a personal reflection on the spiritual importance of this tradition in his own life as an "agnostic mystic."

There is something deeply puzzling about the idea that it might be legitimate to protest against a perfect deity. It is hard to see how it could make sense to complain about the ways of God, to accuse God of injustice or a failure of mercy, if one thinks that God's ways are the embodiment of perfection in knowledge, power, love, and goodness.[25] All the more so, then, it is difficult to see what sense it could make for a perfect deity to *authorize* and even *invite* lamentation and protest speech—especially what we might call *impious* protest, or protest that does not arise out of steadfast faith and hope in God's goodness and mercy, but rather calls those or other perfections into question, or even presupposes their absence. Yet, given traditional Christian views about the nature and inspiration of scripture, and given the volume and diversity of lamentation and protest discourse in scripture, it seems that God has done precisely that.[26]

One possibility is that the divine authorization of protest speech is a tacit condemnation of perfect being theology: God is, in effect, *telling us* through the authorization of certain kinds of protest speech that God is not perfect. As I have already noted, some think that this is part of what is conveyed by the divine speeches to Job;[27] some think that this is the correct conclusion to draw in light of the content of Lamentations;[28] and many have thought that it is implicit in the Old

---

[25] I think that this simple fact goes a long way toward explaining why lament and protest have tended to have a relatively small and uncomfortable place in Christian theology and worship. On the role of lament and protest in Christian worship, see Billings 2015: chs. 3 and 4, Brueggemann 1986, and Moffat 2013. It is perhaps instructive to compare Christian approaches to lament and protest with the Jewish "arguing with God" tradition documented by Laytner (1990).

[26] Some theologians and biblical scholars maintain that the only kind of protest that is in fact authorized in scripture is pious protest. (Cf. Billings 2015: 45, and Calvin 1998: 321–2, 396.) But it seems to me that this view is not credible. It is most plausible when the texts primarily in view are the psalms of lament, and when Job is read under the assumption that Job's response to God is one of genuine repentance rather than cagy, insincere repentance or outright rejection. (Cf. Billings 2015: 25–9, and ch. 3.) It is harder to affirm when Lamentations is primarily in view, or when Job is read under assumptions less traditional but currently more widely accepted among biblical scholars. (Harder, but obviously not impossible. Cf. Calvin 1998 and Harrison 1973: 225, and also 202, 218–19, and 221.)

[27] See Fox 2013 and references therein.

[28] Brueggemann 2012; O'Connor 2002. For a reading of Lamentations that strongly contrasts with those offered by O'Connor and Brueggemann, see Harrison 1973.

Testament portrayal of God.[29] Another possibility is that God is perfect but the canon as we have it is not entirely divinely inspired.[30] Neither of these two options, however, is attractive from the point of view of traditional Christian belief; so I shall set them aside.

Another possibility is that lament and protest are acceptable in the divine–human relationship because, in short, God loves us and we can benefit in significant ways from being allowed to bring our protests before God. For example, suffering people struggling to maintain faith in the face of divine silence might cope better with their circumstances if they have the freedom to vent, unfiltered, all of their anger, frustration, mistrust, and sadness upon God. Allowing this would surely be a mercy, and one that, if recognized, could go some distance toward mending God's relationships with such people. Perhaps also the divine authorization of lament and protest is given for "soul-making" purposes. Drawing on early twentieth-century developments in psychology, Walter Brueggemann observes that when children are allowed and encouraged to assert their own desires and opinions in the face of what they take to be unjust or unreasonable treatment by adults, they come to develop a healthier, more robust sense of their own selves as free and independent beings than they would if they were always forced into submission.[31] There is also evidence that lament and protest (broadly construed) are important components in the process of recovering from trauma; and, conversely, the suppression of lament and protest (again, broadly construed) is a common tactic of abusers of various kinds.[32]

There is also a further benefit, one that commonly goes ignored in the literature on these topics. Contending with God in a mode of

---

[29] See, e.g., Blumenthal 1993, Crenshaw 2013, and Hazony 2012: 98, 304 n. 120. Of course, the idea goes back as far as Marcion (Harnack 1990: chs. 4 and 5, esp. p. 58).

[30] Of course, "the canon" means different things in the mouths of different people: Jews, Roman Catholics, and Presbyterians, for example, recognize different texts as canonical; and examples here could be multiplied. But my claim here does not depend on any particular claim about which books are canonical; for most Christians (and many adherents of other theistic religions), within the texts they recognize as canonical there will be some that seem to authorize protest against God, and one possible explanation for them—regardless of their view about which texts are canonical—will be that "the canon" as they have it is not entirely divinely inspired.

[31] Brueggemann 1986: 60–1. See also Middleton 2016: 57.

[32] Cf. Herman 2015: esp. chs. 3 and 4. Thanks to Kathryn Pogin for the pointer, and to both Kathryn Pogin and Michelle Panchuk for helpful conversations on this point.

lament or protest can be a way for someone whose relationship with
God is intensely conflicted to continue participating in the relationship in a positively meaningful way.[33] Not all relationships ought to
be continued, for not all relationships are of positive value. But
(assuming the truth of traditional Christian doctrine) a relationship
with God is of maximal value and will ultimately be recognized as
such; so continuing it—as opposed to irrevocably severing it—is
ultimately guaranteed to be worthwhile. In light of this, it seems
that one participates *in a relationship with God* in a positively meaningful way just if one participates in such a way as to avoid irrevocably
severing it and to promote (deliberately or not) its improvement and
one's own recognition of its value.

When one has serious grievances against God, there are powerful
obstacles to such participation. One may not want to continue the
relationship; one might be emotionally incapable of more traditional
modes of prayer and worship; one might be strongly inclined to make
choices that are inconsistent with improving the relationship or
promoting one's own recognition of its value. But, often enough,
lament and protest will remain accessible ways of continuing one's
relationship with God and, deliberately or not, promoting its
improvement. They are behaviors that one can engage in just by
trying to do so, assuming one has the concept of God, regardless of
the state of one's confidence in God's existence, character, or dispositions toward oneself. They are, furthermore, ways of drawing near to
God despite one's own pain and despite the conflict that mars
one's relationship with God. They are alternatives to abandoning
one's relationship with God; and, importantly, they are alternatives to
abject submission to suffering, silence, and an unintelligible divine
value scheme.

---

[33] Westermann gestures in this direction:

[A] consequence of the refusal to incorporate accusations against God in the life
of prayer is that, when faced with terrible catastrophes, the human being will
simply deny God, both publicly and privately. One finds oneself no longer
capable, at all, of praying to the God who allows such things to happen. In the
place of turning away from God like this, the Bible knows of another possibility:
the one who holds up the incomprehensible against God manages still, in that
very process, to hold firmly to God.   (1994: 93)

Cf. also Westermann 1982: 171–3, and Laytner 1990: esp. Ch. 1 and the "Personal
Afterword."

We have, then, much to gain from the divine authorization of lament and protest. Surely this is part of the story about why God authorizes that kind of speech. But I doubt that it can be the whole story. Lamentations is a raw, visceral outcry against the apparent injustice of God. On the view just described, we benefit from this book being in the canon, but there is no meaningful sense in which *those very accusatory words* are validated by God. God perhaps tolerates Lamentations for our sake; but, on the view that I have been describing, God does not validate the perspective from which its accusatory words arise.

The view I favor, however, maintains that lament and protest are not just tolerated by God for the sake of benefits like those I've just mentioned; they are *validated* by God as reasonable and acceptable modes of interaction. Perhaps in some contexts God even *prefers* for us to interact with God this way. (Here, to take just one example, we might think of Abraham disputing with God over the fate of Sodom and Gomorrah.) The psalms of lament are in the psalter as much for our use in worship as the psalms of praise; the accusatory words of Lamentations may, in some contexts, be appropriated by individuals or communities in private prayer or public worship in just the same ways that more familiar words of gratitude or repentance from elsewhere in scripture are routinely appropriated. This is not, how-ever, to suggest that God agrees with—affirms the propositional content of—those words, even if we sometimes do. Validation, as I understand it here, does not imply endorsement.

What, then, does it mean to say that God "validates" lament and protest and the perspectives from which they arise? Roughly this: God recognizes that, given what we can know about the range of possible goods and evils and the logical and causal relations among them, given what we are able to understand about the nature of love and virtue, and given other constraints imposed by human cognitive limitations, lament, protest, and outright accusation against God are sometimes reasonable responses on the part of people who love their fellow creatures and love the good insofar as they are able to understand it.

These are not, of course, the only reasonable responses. One might, for example, begin by adopting the stance of the skeptical theist— someone who deals with the problem of suffering simply by acknow-ledging that a perfect being might permit evils, even horrendous evils, somehow for the sake of worthwhile goods that are unknowable or incomprehensible to cognitively limited creatures like us. In adopting this stance, one might then choose neither to lament nor protest God's permission of suffering (even if one laments over the sufferings themselves), but to affirm instead, in faith, the fact that all evil and suffering will ultimately be defeated as God accomplishes God's good purposes in the world. I do not by any means want to suggest that there is anything wrong with this sort of response to evil and suffering, nor do I mean to suggest that lament and protest are somehow better. But not everyone can enter into the perspective of the skeptical theist. Perhaps not everyone *should* do so—some, after all, take it to be a fundamentally misguided response to the problem of suffering.[34] And even if one can embrace skeptical theism, one still might be unable to maintain unwavering confidence that all bad things, no matter how horrendous, can ultimately be defeated. For all such people and more, one way in which God can show love to them and can honor their love for the good and the commitment to justice and mercy that leads them even to confront the almighty creator and demand a change of circumstance is to encourage them to bring their laments and protests before God and to validate (in the sense

---

[34] Objections to skeptical theism abound. For a sampling, see Maitzen 2013, O'Connor 2013, and Wilks 2013, as well as my own reply (Rea 2013). Relatedly, Nicholas Wolterstorff rejects both soul-making and free will theodicies because neither does justice to biblical revelation from God. "The root of the difficulty," he writes toward the end of his discussion of free will theodicies:

> for the person who judges himself or herself answerable to the biblical speech of God, is that the God of the Bible has told us too much. If we hadn't been told that it was God's intent that we should live until full of years, then no problem. If we hadn't been told that it was God's intent that we should flourish, then no problem. If we hadn't been told that it was God's intent that we should flourish here on earth in the community of persons, then no problem. If we hadn't been told that it was God's intent that each and every one of us should flourish until full of years, then no problem. It's the speech of the biblical God that leads us to see that suffering and life-duration have gone awry with reference to God's creating and maintaining intent. If we could dispense with answering to that speech, it would be possible to devise a point of view which fits together such suffering and brevity of life as we find in our world with the divine intent; many have done exactly that. (2002: 226–7)

One might think that what Wolterstorff says here speaks just as much against skeptical theism as it does against theodicies that explicitly affirm that suffering is part of God's plan, permitted to achieve greater goods. Perhaps, then, such a person *should not* embrace skepticism; and, notably, the stance that Wolterstorff himself recommends is one that involves protest (albeit alongside God, rather than against God).

described above) the perspectives from which they arise. It is in this way, I think, that God has shown love to the church and to the world by providentially arranging for texts like Job and Lamentations to become parts of the canon.[35]

4.

The invitation to protest a perfectly loving being is only puzzling until we recognize that God can validate the protest without endorsing its content, not in a patronizing way but in a way that fully respects the origins of the protest in a well-considered, thoughtful love for the good as it can be understood by human beings. Validating protest can be an important way in which God shows love to those who occupy the perspective of the protester. And this perspective is, broadly speaking, precisely that which is occupied by anyone in what I have described as an intensely conflicted relationship with God.

I have said that *often enough*, those who occupy such a perspective will be able, through lament and protest, to participate in a positively meaningful way in their relationship with God. I have also suggested that such people can, if they are willing, experience the love of God through their recognition that God accepts, encourages, validates, and may in some cases even submit to the demands of their protest. To the extent that this is possible, it seems also clear that these intensely conflicted relationships can yet be positively meaningful.

But some kinds of human suffering pose significant obstacles even to this mode of relationship with God. *Religious trauma* is a prime example. Michelle Panchuk defines religious trauma as "a traumatic experience perceived by the subject to be caused by the divine being, religious community, religious teaching, religious symbols, or religious practices that transforms the individual, either epistemically

---

[35] Admittedly, this act of divine love will be received only if one is able to understand the relevant texts as authorizing lament and protest (both pious and impious). But this is just one instance of a larger difficulty, itself an instance of divine hiddenness—namely, that *much* of what God has to communicate to humanity can be received (from a Christian point of view) only if one has access to the proper interpretation of biblical texts. And, of course, my response to the question of how a loving God could permit instances of divine hiddenness like that is contained in other chapters of the present book.

or not-merely-cognitively, in such a way that their capacity to participate in religious life is significantly diminished."[36] She offers as examples both a case of a young girl subjected to serious physical abuse at the hands of religiously motivated parents, and a young boy sexually abused by a rabbi. She goes on to note that survivors of such trauma may well experience various post-traumatic symptoms, at least some of which might have "a religious trigger or object." For example, a survivor "may come to believe that God is untrustworthy or that religious communities are unsafe ... [or] might experience intrusive memories triggered by religious practices, feel extreme fear, distrust, or revulsion toward the divine being, or internalize a deep sense of self-hatred as the result of religious doctrines."[37] To the extent that such things occur, it might seem that the survivor of religious trauma will be unable to participate in a relationship with God just by trying. Rather, such participation, even by way of lament and protest, might be possible only after substantial psychological healing.

Moreover, even if lament and protest are psychologically possible for some victims of religious trauma, one might think that the very nature of the trauma is such as to cut them off from the potential benefits of relating to God in those ways. Imagine a parent standing by silently while one of his or her children, acting in his or her name, seriously abuses another of his or her children. In a case like this, it is incumbent upon the parent to somehow distance himself or herself from the abuser's action; for, absent such distancing, it would seem entirely reasonable for the victim to conclude from the parent's silence that the parent endorses, or at least doesn't object to, the abuse that has been delivered in his name. In such a context, it is hard to see how a parent who responds with a (mere!) invitation to lament and protest could possibly be experienced as loving; and it might also be hard to see how continuing to participate in the relationship by way of lament and protest could be seen as positively meaningful.[38]

This is a powerful objection to the view I have been developing in this chapter. But I believe it can be addressed. Part of my response is to insist, again, that it is not by way of the *mere* invitation to lament and protest that God expresses love to human beings, but rather by way of validating the perspective of the person offering lament and

---

[36] Panchuk 2018.   [37] Panchuk 2018.
[38] Thanks to Michelle Panchuk both for raising the objection and for very helpful discussion of it.

protest. In the example just described, if the parent could be seen as validating the child's protest, that would serve to create the much-needed distance between the parent and the abuse. But this is only part of my response; the rest comes by way of a clarification and a concession.

First, the clarification: to say that someone *can* participate in a relationship with God by way of lament and protest is not to deny that some steps might be required to clear the way first. "Can" claims are notoriously ambiguous in this way. Consider the question whether I can participate in a *conversational* relationship with God *just by trying*. If I am asleep, I cannot; I would have to wake up first. And yet it is also true that I can; for I will inevitably have some waking hours in my life. If I am hard at work on a complicated mathematical problem, perhaps I cannot; I would have to stop working on the problem first. But at the very same time it is true that I can, because I can voluntarily stop working on the problem in order to converse with God.

Likewise for many victims of religious trauma as regards relating to God through lament and protest. Some will inevitably have moments when their trauma-induced obstacles dissipate and they can, without emotional or physical side effects, relate to God in these ways. For others, there may be choices they can make—choices that are genuinely psychologically available and not repugnant to them—that would enable them to engage in lament or protest. In both cases, then, we have people who in one sense cannot engage in a relationship with God just by trying, but in another sense *can* do so.

Perhaps, too, such people can even experience love from God in the midst of their protest. For at the times when they can protest, it may also be open to them to entertain the idea that God is good, that God genuinely loves them and is committed to their ultimate well-being, and that every bad thing that God permits will ultimately be defeated within the context of the lives of those who suffer from it; and it may likewise be open to them to entertain the idea that God has authorized lament and protest for their sake, in an effort to show them love. In many contexts, simply entertaining such ideas will be enough to make possible an experience of divine love.[39]

---

[39] One might object, in light of the conclusions I defended in Chapter 5, that entertaining these thoughts will be cold comfort (or worse) in conjunction with the thought that God might be permitting the horrors they suffer for reasons having nothing at all to do with their own ultimate good, for the sake of God's own

Once all of this is clear, the class of people cut off from the possibility and benefits of relating to God even by way of lament and protest might look a lot smaller than it initially seemed to be. That said, however, I cannot rule out the possibility that, although what I have just said may be true for *many* victims of religious trauma, it may yet not be true for *all* victims of religious trauma. What, then, of them?

Here is the concession: I acknowledge that some people in conflicted relationships with God may be unable to participate in that relationship by way of lament and protest. So if there is any sense in which they can participate in a positively meaningful relationship with God, it will have to be in some other way—one not obstructed by the obstacles raised by the effects of their trauma. In my view, the "way" in question is precisely that which is open to those who lack even the concept of God: they are able to *seek* God, in a sense that I will explain in Chapter 9, and the seeking by itself will suffice (for a time) for participation in a positively meaningful relationship with God.

non-anthropocentric projects. But to raise this objection is, I think, simply to ignore one of the most crucial points in Chapter 5—namely, that although I say that God may permit sufferings in our lives *for the sake of* goods having nothing to do with our good or the good of any other human being, there is no reason to doubt that, loving us as God does, God will arrange for those sufferings to be defeated within the context of our lives, thus guaranteeing that even lives marked by horrendous evil will nonetheless be great goods, on the whole, to those who have them. Thanks to Reader 2 for encouraging me, even if in a rather colorful way, to deal with this objection.

9

The Scandal of Particularity

Chapters 7 and 8 have provided reason to think that a great many people—particularly those who have the concept of God, access to the Christian scriptures and liturgies of the church, and the capacity to engage God relationally by way of either worship or protest—are in a position to participate in a positively meaningful relationship with God just by trying to do so, and this even if their belief in God is no longer rational or is seriously cast into doubt. These conclusions help to undercut the idea that divine hiddenness supports negatively valenced analogies about divine love over traditional, positively valenced ones. Nevertheless, as I have acknowledged along the way, certain classes of people slip through the cracks.

Many people throughout history have lacked access to the Christian scriptures and liturgies. In his most recent defense of the hiddenness problem, Schellenberg rests much on the idea that many have lacked even the concept of God.[1] Moreover, as I noted toward the end of Chapter 8, some people who have both the concept of God and access to scripture and liturgy are nevertheless unable to relate to God even by way of protest, much less by way of worship. As I see it, these facts, together with others like them, comprise a version of the "scandal of particularity": the apparently problematic fact that access to information about the good news of the gospel and to the appropriate means (according to Christian doctrine) for engaging with and worshiping God have not been universally distributed to humankind, but have rather been available only to particular groups of human beings at any given time.

---

[1] Schellenberg 2015b: ch. 6.

As with the other kinds of problems I have been considering in the last few chapters, the scandal of particularity does not license an *inference* to the conclusion that there is no perfectly loving God; but it does constitute a further source of doubt about the appropriateness of traditional, positively valenced analogies for characterizing God's love. It suggests that God, if God exists at all, is more aptly characterized as a negligent or inept lover, one who either willfully or because of a kind of incompetence bestows good things only upon his favorite children, leaving the rest out in the cold (or worse).

My goal in this chapter is to respond to this concern. I shall do so by arguing that we have no good reason to doubt that anyone capable of participating in personal relationships—regardless of whether they have the Christian concept of God—is both in a position to *try* to participate in a relationship with God, and actually to do so just by trying. At first glance, this conclusion might look to be a solution to the hiddenness problem that is independent of what I offered in earlier chapters; but, for reasons I shall explain later, I do not want to defend it as such. Within the context of the present book, its main job is simply to undermine one further reason for thinking that negatively valenced characterizations of divine love are more apt than traditional ones.

The chapter unfolds as follows. I begin by identifying sufficient conditions on trying to participate in a relationship with God, and arguing that these conditions can be satisfied even by someone who lacks the Christian concept of God. Next, I explain why simply trying to participate in a relationship with God by itself suffices for participating in a relationship with God. If I am right, it follows directly that anyone who can try to participate in a relationship with God can participate in such a relationship just by trying. I then close with a discussion of some objections.

1.

I take as my starting point one of the most famous sayings from Jesus's Sermon on the Mount:

> Ask and it will be given you; search and you will find; knock and the door will be opened for you. For everyone who asks receives, and

everyone who searches finds, and for everyone who knocks, the door will be opened. Is there anyone among you who, if your child asks for bread, will give a stone? Or if the child asks for a fish, will give a snake?[2]

It is hard to know exactly what Jesus meant by these words, especially since all three promises are, on the face of it, frequently violated in experience. Believers *often* ask without receiving what they ask for, search without finding, and knock in some sense or other without ever encountering anything they would recognize as an open door. So either Jesus spoke falsely, or this saying does not mean what it superficially seems to mean.

Some commentators decline to take a position on the meaning of these promises, noting simply that they impose no explicit restrictions on the kinds of requests that God can be expected to grant, the kinds of quests God might be expected to bring to completion, or the kinds of doors we might expect God to open.[3] Among those who do take a position, it is common to treat all three as expressing roughly the same *contextually restricted* promise: if we seek and pray for the right sorts of things, or for good things, or for things pertaining to the kingdom of God, then we can count on God to give us those things.[4]

I have no specific interpretation of my own to defend; I mention the variety of possibilities just to make the following point: on the plausible and traditional assumption that a relationship with God is both good for us to seek and highly relevant to the furtherance of the kingdom of God, this saying is, *even on its more restricted readings*, naturally understood to be promising that those who ask for a relationship with God will be given one, that those who seek God will find God, and that those who knock upon God's door will be granted a response. This is the promise on which I want to focus in what follows.

The hiddenness problem is fueled in part by the fact that even this more restricted promise seems not to be fulfilled in experience. Many people seem to themselves and others to be seeking God without finding, desiring a relationship with God without being given one, knocking, in some sense, but only in vain. Worse, though, is the fact that many people—particularly those who lack the concept of God

---

[2] Matt. 7:7–10.   [3] Hagner 1993: 172–5.
[4] See, e.g., Blomberg 1992: 129–30, Hare 1993: 78–9, Keener 1997: 158–61, and Witherington 2006: 156–60.

and those who, by virtue of religious trauma or other forms of suffering, have lost the capacity even to entertain thoughts of God without experiencing negative consequences—seem not even to be *able* to seek God. Worse still, where religious trauma is involved we seem to find people who *did* ask, seek, or knock but can do so no longer because their initial efforts were met with horror and suffering.[5]

Strictly speaking, Jesus's saying does not say that seeking is a *necessary* condition on having a relationship with God. But, even so, it is hard to see how God's "love" for someone could possibly be understood on analogy with the best of human loves if God both delivers a promise like this one but also allows people to be in a position where they are not even *able* to seek a relationship with God. In this way, then, Jesus's "ask, search, knock" saying seems only to exacerbate the hiddenness problem. Rather than comforting us in the face of merely apparent divine hiddenness, it seems only to emphasize God's hiddenness and to remind us that many fall outside the scope of the love that is supposed to guarantee the fulfillment of these promises.

In fact, however, I think the appearances are misleading. In particular, I think that there is no good reason to doubt that everyone—literally everyone—capable of personal relationships is able to seek God; and I think that there are plausible conceptions of *seeking God* and *participating in a relationship with God* according to which everyone who *tries* to seek God immediately succeeds in participating in a personal relationship with God. Moreover, in light of all of this, I think that there is no reason to doubt that everyone who seeks God is guaranteed of finding God in a salvific way. In what follows, I will defend these claims and then draw out the consequences of my answer for the Schellenberg problem and other problems about divine hiddenness.

2.

Searching for something, in the sense relevant here, is an intentional act. It is, of course, entirely natural to talk about heat-seeking missiles searching for their targets, or about computers or computer programs

---

[5] On the concept and spiritual effects of religious trauma, see Panchuk 2018, and the discussion at the end of Chapter 8, pp. 157–9.

searching for data on a disk drive, and this despite the fact that inanimate things cannot act intentionally. Likewise, it is entirely natural to talk about certain kinds of animals to which we would not wish to ascribe intentional action as searching for food, seeking mates, and so on. Behavior of this sort seems just to be a certain kind of goal-directed activity: an animal seeks a mate just if its behavior is directed toward the goal of finding a mate; a heat-seeking missile searches for its target just if its movements are governed by the goal of bringing the missile closer to a particular source of infrared radiation; and so on. Seeking or searching for God, however, is different; and so from here on when I talk about seeking or searching, what I will have in mind is just the kind of seeking or searching that counts as intentional action by an agent.

In this latter sense, searching for something is a matter of intentionally acting in ways that one takes to be directed toward the goal of finding it. One cannot search for something by accident (except maybe by intentionally searching for it under a description that one does not realize applies to it); and if one does not believe that one's intended actions are directed toward the goal of finding a thing, then, whatever else one may be doing, one is not searching for it. But, at the same time, one does not have to *know* or even *justifiably believe* that one's actions are directed toward the goal of finding something in order to count as searching for it. Someone with wholly unreasonable beliefs about where to find a thing might still count as searching for it just by virtue of intentionally acting on those beliefs.

If this account of searching is correct, then searching for something implies an intention to find it, or at least to try to find it. This latter intention, in turn, involves conceptualization. We search for things under descriptions, and the descriptions involve concepts. So, for example, if I undertake what I think of as a search for my car keys, or for the fastest route from St. Andrews to Loch Ness, or for the fountain of youth, my intentions are aptly described (from the outside, even if not by *me*) as intentions to discover whether, where, or by what the descriptions *my car keys*, *the fastest route to Loch Ness*, or *the fountain of youth* are satisfied.

Accordingly, searching for something implies having a concept of it. This is not to say that that it implies having a concept whose *content* is that very thing; for the thing in question might not exist. But it does require having a concept whose content is a property or cluster of properties whose exemplification implies that the object of the search exists. This is perhaps why it appears that people who lack the concept of God, or people who cannot entertain that concept without serious emotional or physical consequences, seem cut off from searching for God.

In fact, however, the appearance is misleading. The reason is simply that, strictly speaking, there is no such thing as *the* concept of God. What Schellenberg calls "the concept of God" is in fact just one among many concepts by way of which one might search for God. Still, it is common to talk as if there is just one concept of God, and to use the term "the concept of God" to refer to something like the classical theistic concept—a concept whose content includes, perhaps among other things, the concepts of omnipotence, omniscience, and perfect goodness. Let us, for convenience, name this concept "CG."

Despite its descriptive inaccuracy, I will continue to use the label "the concept of God" to refer to CG. But let us also say that something is *a concept of God* just if God is the content of the concept or it is a concept that could only be satisfied by a being who would, if it existed, be God. So any of the following might be concepts of God, despite being different concepts from CG: *the creator of the universe, the highest being, the cause of my experience last night, the perfect lover of my soul, whoever it is that my friend David worships.*[6] Moreover, even though some of these concepts (e.g., *the cause of my experience last night*) only count as concepts of God under very particular circumstances, it seems clear that when any of these concepts *does* count as a concept of God, it is possible to search for God by searching for whatever satisfies it. For this reason, then, it is possible to search for God even if one cannot entertain the concept, CG, that some people call *the concept of God.*

---

[6] It should be obvious why a concept like *the cause of my experience last night* might be, but is not necessarily, a concept of God. But what about *the creator of the universe*? Why say only that this *might* be a concept of God? The reason, in short, is that I do not think that, necessarily, anyone who has (e.g.) a concept of *the creator of the universe* has a concept that can only be satisfied by the being that Christians intend to refer to with the name "God." (Recall that "God," in this book, functions as a name rather than a title. See Chapter 3, p. 31, n. 7.) If God exists, then *the creator of the universe* will almost certainly be a concept of God for the simple reason that God will almost certainly be its content (by virtue of being, by far, its best candidate referent). But if God does not exist, or if one's creator-concept is sufficiently detailed and deviant, God will not be its content and it might be a concept that could be satisfied by some other being.

There is, of course, no way to *prove* that everyone who is capable of participating in personal relationships is able to entertain at least one concept of God. But given the wide variety of concepts that are or at least can be concepts of God, it is hard to see why we would doubt it. So I conclude that there is no good reason to doubt that everyone capable of personal relationships is able to seek God.

3.

What does it mean to *try* to seek God? Given what I have said about the nature of seeking, it follows that trying to seek God is just a matter of trying to perform actions that one believes, rightly or wrongly, to be directed somehow toward the goal of ultimately finding God. It is an interesting and controversial question whether one can try to seek God without at the same time *desiring* to seek God, or to find God.[7] I will not take a position on this question; but it does seem impossible to try to seek God without at least being *receptive* to finding God.

I am borrowing the notion of receptivity from Terence Cuneo's work;[8] and, although I do not understand it in exactly the same way he does, our conceptions of it are not far off from one another. For Cuneo, receptivity is an attitude. I prefer to think of it as a stance or disposition that may or may not include attitudes like desire, interest, attraction, and so on. For purposes here, let us say that someone is receptive to finding God just if she is not indifferent to finding God, is disposed to welcome it (at least under certain circumstances), and has not consciously ruled it out as something to be resisted, avoided, or for all practical purposes not to be sought after or pursued.[9]

One is receptive to that which one desires, then; but one may also be receptive to objects or experiences that one does not in fact desire but nonetheless wants to desire, or finds interesting or attractive in ways and to degrees that do not quite rise to the level of desire. When someone joins an online dating service, for example, presumably one

---

[7] Cf. Mele 1990, Adams 1991, Mele 1991, and Adams 1994.

[8] Cf. Cuneo 2017.

[9] Perhaps, then, receptivity to God and to a relationship with God is the same as what Schellenberg would call "nonresistance" to God; but I cannot find conclusive textual support in Schellenberg's work for this claim.

does not at that very moment desire to date any one of the other members, much less all of them; but, at the same time, neither is she indifferent to the prospect, nor, in the typical case, has she at that point ruled out dating any of them. Her disposition, at that point, is one of receptivity. One can also be receptive to objects or experiences with which one has no acquaintance and to which one has given no thought. An adopted child might be receptive to a relationship with her biological mother even if she does not know that she is adopted, and even if she does not have the conceptual resources to distinguish between biological and adoptive motherhood.

If all of this is correct, then one can be receptive to God and to a relationship with God even if one has never entertained the concept of God (CG, that is) or is unable for other reasons to entertain it. Moreover, a person receptive to God can count as trying to seek God simply by trying to take steps that she believes, rightly or wrongly, to be directed toward finding something that she (knowingly or not) conceptualizes by way of a concept of God; and she can do this even if she has never given any thought to CG, and has no idea that God is in fact the object of her (attempted) search. In fact, a bit of reflection reveals that simply *trying* to seek God—given that trying to seek God implies receptivity toward God—will itself count as seeking God.

Suppose, for example, that a prehistoric cave dweller decides to try to search for the creator of the universe. Although she does not realize it, the concept *creator of the universe* is a concept of God;[10] so, given all that I have said, in trying to take steps that she believes are directed toward the goal of finding the creator, she will count as trying to seek God. But now suppose that, for whatever reason, whenever she so much as tries to do the things that, in her mind, count as seeking the creator, she fails. She continues to try, but she also continues to fail. Eventually she gives up. Is she, then, someone who never actually

---

[10] Assuming God exists, anyway, and modulo the qualifications in note 6. The assumption that God exists is legitimate in the present context because I am trying to address the concern that *God* has allowed prehistoric persons, among others, to be in a situation where they are unable to seek God by virtue of lacking a concept of God. True, if there is reason to think that the creator concepts (and every other candidate concept of God) that could be formed by such persons would not have God as their content, or would not be such that only God could satisfy them, then I would have a hard time denying that they are unable to seek God. But I see no reason to think that this situation obtains, or is even remotely probable. Instead, it seems to me to be *very* likely that, however mistaken such early creator concepts might have been, still God would be their best candidate referent.

sought God but only tried to do so? No. Whatever else we might say about her efforts, clearly we should grant that she not only tried to seek God, but *did* seek God. She just did not get very far in her quest.[11]

Suppose one has no idea how to find God, and so one has no beliefs about what specific actions might take finding God as their goal. Is it impossible for such a person to try to seek God? It might seem so, if I am right that trying to seek God is a matter of trying to do things that one *believes* to be directed somehow toward the goal of finding God. But the appearance is misleading.

Suppose I find myself alone in the middle of a forest, I want to try to search for my hiking companions, but I have absolutely no idea how to do this—I don't know where they might be; I don't know whether I am more likely to run across them by walking or staying put; I am (let us suppose) unable to signal with light or noise. Still, I can arbitrarily select a course of action and simply assign it the goal of finding my companions, and this will count as trying (successfully) to search for them. It is hard to see how I could *assign* an act of mine the goal of finding my companions without desiring or intending to find my companions; but, in any case, it seems that in this situation acting on the desire or intention to find my companions will be sufficient for assigning that goal to my act. So, where I have no idea how to go about finding my companions, simply acting on the desire or intention to find them will suffice both for trying to search for them *and* for actually searching for them. Likewise in the case of searching for God.[12]

Trying to seek God, then, is remarkably easy. It requires receptivity to a relationship with God and either a desire to find something that one conceptualizes by way of a concept of God, or an intention (motivated by a desire to find God, or not) to take actions that one

---

[11] Matters would be different, of course, if the person were trying to take steps that she believed to be directed toward the goal of finding the creator while at the same time being unqualifiedly disposed to resist actually finding the creator. Suppose, for example, she has been commanded upon pain of death to try to search for the creator. One could imagine her trying to obey the command by taking the steps in question, even if she unqualifiedly desires not to find the creator. As I understand *trying to seek*, however, an activity like this would not count as trying to seek God; for trying to seek God implies receptivity toward God. Insofar as it implies receptivity, then, merely trying to seek God will itself count as seeking God.

[12] For a different take on seeking God by way of desire for (without belief in) God, see Perlmutter 2016.

believes to be directed toward the goal of finding something that one conceptualizes by way of a concept of God. These seem to be conditions that can be satisfied by anyone capable of having the relevant desires and forming the relevant intentions—anyone, it would seem, who is capable of participating in personal relationships at all, and who has and can entertain *a* concept of God, even if not CG.

At any rate, there is no good reason to *doubt* that these conditions can be satisfied by anyone capable of participating in personal relationships; and, given the range of activities that can be believed to be directed toward the goal of finding something that someone conceptualizes by way of a concept of God, there likewise seems to be no reason to doubt that whatever other necessary conditions there are on trying to seek, these can also be satisfied by anyone capable of participating in personal relationships. Furthermore, as I have already said, trying to seek God itself counts as seeking God. So there is likewise no reason to doubt that anyone capable of participating in personal relationships is able to seek God.

4.

How does one participate in a personal relationship? I cannot hope to identify necessary and sufficient conditions on such a vague and messy concept as *relationship participation*; but I can at least identify a *sufficient* condition for participation in a personal relationship *with* God, and that is all that I will need for my limited purposes here.

Let us begin by considering friendship between human beings. Being in such a relationship obviously does not require constant interaction; nor does it even require spatial proximity. One does not cease to be in a friendship with someone simply by traveling out of town and not getting in touch for a while. I have friends with whom I have lost contact and with whom, because of distance in time and space, I have no definite intentions of interacting in the future. But I do not, on those grounds, believe my relationships with these people to be broken. I am still (so far as I am aware) in a friendship with them; and the reason seems just to be that we became friends at some point and, since that time, we have each (so far as I am aware) remained receptive to future friendly interaction with one another. I do not claim that continued receptivity is *necessary* for the continuation of a friendship; but it does seem to be sufficient, even in cases where we would say that the friendship is conflicted or otherwise problematic.[13]

Being in a friendship is not the same as *participating* in it, however. My friends and I with whom I have lost contact are probably still *in* a friendship together, but it would be odd at best to say that we are participating in the friendship. It is hard to say exactly what the difference is between these friendships and the ones in which I am currently participating; but the answer has something to do with the difference in expectations for and intentions regarding interaction in the future. If my relationship with one of my friends with whom I have lost contact were to change, so that there were mutually laid plans or mutual expectations for interaction in the near future, it would be appropriate to say that we had resumed participation in the friendship. Likewise, if there were no plan or expectation for interaction in the near future, but we were at least taking steps to bring about an opportunity for interaction in the distant future, it would make sense to say that we had resumed participation in the friendship. Perhaps other conditions would suffice as well. The point here is just that receptivity and desire on their own are not enough for participation in a friendship; but either of those together with mutual action directed toward the goal of bringing about friendly interaction are sufficient.

Personal relationships with God are often understood on analogy with friendships or filial relationships or both. Accordingly, our intuitions about what suffices for participation in those sorts of relationships ought to tell us something about what it would take on our end to participate in (something analogous to) a personal relationship with God.[14] Here too, receptivity and desire seem not to be enough. But it does seem that receptivity or desire in conjunction with *trying* to act in a way directed toward the goal of bringing about interaction would suffice for doing our part to participate in a

---

[13] This is not, of course, to say that mere receptivity is sufficient for the friendship to continue unchanged, or for it to retain its original level of depth and intimacy. My point is just that, so long as receptivity remains intact, it seems incorrect to say that the friendship has come to an end.

[14] Modulo, of course, the limits imposed by divine transcendence upon what our intuitions can tell us about God.

relationship with God.[15] And if God is also receptive and is acting in some way toward the goal of future interaction, then, in that case, we are participating *with God* in a personal relationship.

I assume that God is always both receptive to and desirous of some kind of positive personal relationship with every capable human being; and I also assume that God is always engaged in action that is somehow directed toward the goal of future (positive) interaction with every human being. As I have explained in earlier chapters, I do not think that these assumptions *follow* from the fact that God is perfectly loving; but they are at least suggested by it, and by the various analogies traditionally used to illustrate God's love. So, from a Christian point of view, it seems reasonable to take these assumptions for granted unless and until we have evidence that they are false (which, I think, we do not). And if they are correct, then the various claims that I have made and defended in this chapter together imply that it is possible to participate in a relationship with God *just by trying to seek God*. Insofar as trying to participate in a personal relationship with God is just one way among many of trying to seek God, it follows too that it is possible to participate in a personal relationship with God just by trying to do so.

I do not, of course, intend to suggest that merely trying to seek God suffices immediately for having an optimal, unconflicted, or salvific relationship with God. Nor do I intend to suggest that trying to seek God is somehow wholly up to us, with all the Pelagian or semi-Pelagian consequences that would bring with it. Rather, all I intend to claim is that merely trying to seek God suffices to begin our part of the relational process apparently envisioned in the biblical injunction to "draw near to God and He will draw near to you," an injunction which is easily understood to be consistent with the traditional view that even "our part" in the process is vitally dependent upon God's help.

One further consequence of what I have said in this chapter is that it is possible to participate in a relationship with God without *knowing* that one is doing so and, indeed, without knowing or even believing that God *exists*. This conclusion might look promising as a solution to the hiddenness problem that works independently of the solution I offered in Chapters 3–5. I think that there is some merit to

---

[15] Note that I understand "interaction" broadly, so that (for example) silent communion or union will count as interaction no less than more overt modes of personal engagement.

this idea; but, for reasons that shall emerge in Section 5, I do not want to rest any weight on it.

5.

I want to close by considering two objections to what I have been arguing in this chapter. The first concerns the claim that one can participate in a relationship with God without believing that God exists. How can this be possible? How could one participate in a personal relationship while not even believing that the other party exists?

Several people have maintained that either non-conceptual awareness of God or what we might call "deviant" conceptual awareness of God might serve as an adequate basis (apart from belief) for a personal relationship with God.[16] William Wainwright, for example, suggests that someone who loves the good might thereby, unknowingly, love God;[17] and in loving and pursuing the good, such a person might also have a kind of personal relationship with God. In a similar vein, Ted Poston and Trent Dougherty suggest that experience of God might serve as the basis for a personal relationship with God even if one has no belief to the effect that God is the source or stimulus for the experience.[18] Independently of the hiddenness literature, John Hick has long defended the view that each of the world's great religions is an equally valid "response to the Real" (where "the Real" is whatever it is that is *in fact* the proper object of religious devotion).[19] In defending this view, Hick tacitly affirms the idea that, if God is the Real, one can participate in a relationship with God by worshipfully *responding* to God even if one is not responding to God *as such*, under a suitably accurate concept of God.

In contrast to the views just described, my own view is that not even *awareness* of God is required for participation in a personal relationship with God. It seems to me that if God is watching over and, in subtle providential ways, guiding or responding to someone

---

[16] In addition to the others who will be cited in this paragraph, see also Evans 2006 and Cuneo 2013.

[17] Wainwright 2002.   [18] Poston and Dougherty 2007.

[19] See, e.g., Hick 2005.

who is looking for God but who does not yet have belief in God (or even CG, "the" concept of God), that person is, unwittingly, participating in a relationship with God. It seems that if, at the end of all things and in the midst of a fully explicit relationship with God, one were to look back on one's life and see that one's quest for God had been providentially watched over and guided by God, and that God had in subtle ways been responding to things that one was doing, one would naturally conclude that one's personal relationship with God and one's own participation in it had begun with the quest, rather than only with its fulfillment. At that stage, one's relationship with God would, obviously, not be all one might hope for in a personal relationship; it is not, at that stage, what the Christian tradition would unite in calling a *salvific* relationship with God; it is in many other ways inadequate. But it seems to me to be a personal relationship of some sort nonetheless, and one in which both God and the seeker are participating, each in their own way.

As Schellenberg points out in responding to Wainwright, relationships with God that involve non-conceptual or deviant conceptual awareness are importantly different from the kind of explicit or conscious relationship with God that figures in the hiddenness argument.[20] Consequently, establishing that people can participate in such relationships with God—or in relationships with God that involve no awareness of God whatsoever—just by trying, even when they lack CG or are otherwise unable to form rational belief in God, will not suffice on its own as a response to the Schellenberg problem.

Even so, however, I do not think that this conclusion is *irrelevant* to the Schellenberg problem. As we saw in Chapter 1, Schellenberg argues that a perfectly loving God would *never* permit nonresistant nonbelief because such a deity would *always* be open to conscious, reciprocally interactive relationship; and so (because belief seems to be necessary for that kind of relationship) God would always provide sufficient grounds for belief to every person capable of a relationship with God.[21] But is it really so clear that a perfectly loving God would not only be always open to *some kind* of relationship with human beings, but also to the particular kind of conscious relationship that is the focus of the Schellenberg problem? I would say "no." I think this

---

[20] Schellenberg 2005a: 207–8.

[21] On the question whether belief is necessary for conscious relationship, however, see Howard-Snyder 2015: 138.

independently of other arguments that I have given in this book; that is why I say that there is some merit to the idea that the conclusion that one can participate in a relationship with God without believing in, or being consciously aware of, God can stand alone as a solution to the Schellenberg problem. But I also acknowledge that this view is hard to *defend* without at the same time appealing either to divine transcendence, as I did in Chapters 3–4, or to the fact (defended in Chapter 5) that divine love is not the same as ideal human love. It is for this reason that I do not want to rest any weight on it as a response to the Schellenberg problem.

I do, however, want to rest weight on it as a response to the claim that the existence of people who lack the concept of God, or are for other reasons unable to entertain that concept, lends, all by itself, support to negatively valenced analogies about divine love. As I see it, everyone who is capable of personal relationships is able to try to seek God; and everyone who is at least receptive to a relationship with God and is willing to try to seek God (under some concept or other) automatically thereby enters into a personal relationship with God. I see no reason to doubt, furthermore, that God subtly encourages people receptive to a relationship with God to try to seek; and I want here also to rest weight on the promise that everyone who seeks God finds a (salvific) relationship with God.

From the point of view of Christian orthodoxy, it is hard to argue with taking Jesus at his word—at least in cases where we have no decisive evidence that his word simply cannot be taken at face value. And in this case, I think we do have no decisive evidence that Jesus's word cannot be taken at face value. Even those who believe in hell, and that salvation comes only to those who explicitly believe in Jesus (two claims on which I will take no position here), cannot rule out the possibility that those who sought God in this life without ever managing to find belief in Jesus will have some opportunity in the afterlife to do so. And if seeking God by itself counts as participating in a personal relationship with God, it is hard to defend the claim that God is unloving toward such people simply by virtue of not providing a *conscious* or *explicit, reciprocal* relationship without presupposing that we can know more about the nature of perfect love than I have argued that we can.

The second objection is that the view I am developing here once again seems to leave the deeply traumatized behind. Suppose it is true that everyone is able to try to seek God—even people who, because of trauma, cannot entertain the traditional concept of God or embrace the idea that it might be satisfied. Still, God has left many of us, maybe most, in a position where we *have* to seek God in order to find a positively meaningful relationship with God; and, in the case of the religiously traumatized, it looks as if God has raised obstacles to their seeking by allowing religious institutions and the people affiliated with them to be sources of trauma in their lives.

Recall the rhetorical question that follows Jesus's invitation to ask, search, and knock:

> For everyone who asks receives, and everyone who searches finds, and for everyone who knocks, the door will be opened. Is there anyone among you who, if your child asks for bread, will give a stone? Or if the child asks for a fish, will give a snake?

This intent of the analogy is apparently to drive home the depth of divine love and concern for the needs of human beings. But reflection on religious trauma puts a bitter spin on it; for the religiously traumatized seem to be candidates, if anyone is, for being people who *did* ask for bread and fish from God only to receive snakes and stones in return.[22] In short, then, religious trauma dramatically reinforces negatively valenced analogies about divine love; and, despite whatever progress has been made by showing that the religiously traumatized can still seek God, not enough progress is made by that conclusion to undercut some of the important—and scriptural— negative analogies that might be drawn.

The challenge posed by religious trauma is not one that I think *mere* theism—theism unsupplemented by substantial further doctrines about what God is or might be doing in the world—can meet. The religiously traumatized have understandable and, in my opinion, fully justified (in light of their evidence) grievances against God; and, as I noted in Chapter 8, to the extent that it looks as if God does not care about those grievances and is not moved to validate or address them in some way, it will be hard to maintain the idea that divine love is most aptly characterized on analogy with the best of human loves. I have already argued that the divine authorization of protest is helpful on this score; but one might think that still more is needed. I do not know what resources other religious traditions would have to

---

[22] I owe this point, and this way of putting it, to Michelle Panchuk (2018).

meet such a demand; but Christians, at any rate, can appeal to the cross.

Discussions of the salvific work of Christ most commonly focus on Christ's atoning work, understanding it as a way in which God's grievances against us are addressed. In fact, many discussions—particularly when the penal substitutionary view of the atonement is in view—proceed as if human beings have no legitimate grievances against God, and that God's grievances against us are severe enough to justify God's subjecting even those who never manage to live out their childhood to eternal conscious torment. In light of this, it is certainly understandable that the idea that Christ's salvific work is meant in part to address human grievances against God would go largely unconsidered.

In the early 1990s, in a manuscript that was never subsequently published, Jesse Hobbs argued that the suffering and death of Christ were, at least in part, a kind of divine apology for all of the evils in the world.[23] This sort of view is untenable on the assumption that God is morally perfect; for, presumably, a morally perfect being would never do anything for which genuine apology is appropriate. But a morally perfect being might well sorrow over the pain inflicted on uncomprehending creatures by the pursuit of good ends that are ultimately beyond their ken; and such a being might take dramatic steps to validate the complaints that arise out of it, to identify not only with human victims of horrendous evil but also with the perpetrators, and to secure for people a blessed life at the end of all things—all with the aim of *defeating*, rather than merely compensating, the badness of the evils they have suffered. This, in basic outline, is Marilyn McCord Adams's understanding of the work of Christ; and if it is correct, then all of this, too, is part of the story about God's efforts in reconciling with the religiously traumatized.[24]

It is not my intention here to defend Adams's theory in all of its details; nor do I mean to suggest that Adams's is the only soteriological theory that can do the work that I am wanting to do here. The parts of her theory that are most helpful in the present context are, first, the part that posits the *defeat* of all evil (rather than mere

[23] This is, at any rate, how I remember it. But I have no access to the manuscript now, and so perhaps my memory is somehow doing Hobbs an injustice. If so, then the idea here is likely one of my own invention.

[24] See Adams 2006. See also Adams 2003: esp. 48–9 n. 4.

compensation, or accomplishment of outweighing greater goods) as one of the goals and effects of Christ's work and, second, the part that has God, in Christ, identifying both with sufferers of religious trauma as well as with the perpetrators. The defeat of evil is important for reasons already discussed in earlier chapters.[25] Identifying through his own suffering with victims puts God in a kind of solidarity with victims; and identifying in his own suffering with perpetrators allows victims to see in the salvific work of Christ both a divine acknowledgment that God has participated somehow as a perpetrator of horrors and that the badness of these horrors, and of participation in them, merits some kind of condemnation. This kind of acknowledgment falls short of apology or penance, since it includes no actual admission of guilt; so it is an acknowledgment that can in principle be given by a morally perfect being. And it is the sort of acknowledgment, too, that can fit within a variety of different stories about what else, exactly, happens in and is accomplished by the salvific work of Christ.

One might object that Christ's identification with victims in this life is limited in two important ways: first, the fact that Christ, as God incarnate, is never subject to the sort of abject powerlessness at the hands of others to which, say, a prisoner of war or a five-year-old abuse victim might be subject; and, second, by virtue of the salvific work accomplished by Christ's suffering and death, he is never subject to the sort of *meaningless* horrific suffering to which some people are subject.[26] These considerations are indeed persuasive; but I do not think that they ultimately undermine the points that I am making.

In response to the first limitation, we might note that it would be implausible to insist that trauma victims can identify with one another only if their traumas are identical; and it would be rash to underestimate the sense of powerlessness that an incarnate *deity* might experience upon finding himself bound by his own love and goodness for others to submit to *whatever* kind of torture and death the human beings around him were aiming to dish out. In response to the second limitation, we might observe that the "limitation" in question is naturally understood just to be the fact that the badness of Christ's suffering is defeated by the broader circumstances in

---

[25] See Chapter 5, pp. 82–3 and Chapter 8, pp. 159–60.
[26] Thanks to Michelle Panchuk for pressing this point.

which it is embedded. But, as I see it, Christians ought to affirm the same of *everyone's* suffering, the difference being only that, in the case of other horrendous evils, we just don't know what exactly the defeating circumstances are.

6.

In Chapter 1, I asked, "What are we to make of the hiddenness of God?" I have not answered this question by providing God's *reason* for remaining hidden; in fact, I have argued that we cannot expect to find the reason but, for multiple different reasons, neither can we rationally infer from God's hiddenness either that God does not love us or that God does not exist. But, as I have noted multiple times along the way, *this* response to the hiddenness problem leaves us with a lingering problem: the question of how we can continue to cling to the idea that divine love is properly understood on analogy with the most excellent of human loves. My answer, over the course of the past four chapters, has come to this: we can tell reasonable stories that cultivate skepticism toward the idea that divine love is more aptly understood by way of negative analogies than through positive ones, and cultivate both hope and optimism that, at the end of all things and in the wake of the ultimate defeat of all evil and suffering, we will see that even the most positive analogies that have been used to characterize God's love fall far short of capturing its greatness. The stories that I have told have relied at various points on what Christians take to be God's revelation to humanity; but, for the most part, very similar stories could as easily have been told as merely speculative defenses of theism. Accordingly, I conclude that neither the believing Christian nor the "mere natural theologian" need be moved either to atheism or to a kind of non-personal deism by consideration of the phenomenon of divine hiddenness.

References

Adams, Frederick. 1991. "He Doesn't Really Want to Try." *Analysis* 51:109–12.

Adams, Frederick. 1994. "Trying, Desire, and Desiring to Try." *Canadian Journal of Philosophy* 24:613–26.

Adams, Marilyn McCord. 1990. "Horrendous Evils and the Goodness of God." In *The Problem of Evil*, edited by Marilyn McCord Adams and Robert Merrihew Adams, 209–21. Oxford: Oxford University Press.

Adams, Marilyn McCord. 1999. *Horrendous Evils and the Goodness of God.* Ithaca, NY: Cornell University Press.

Adams, Marilyn McCord. 2003. "In Praise of Blasphemy!" *Philosophia* 30:33–49.

Adams, Marilyn McCord. 2006. *Christ and Horrors: The Coherence of Christology.* Current Issues in Theology. Cambridge: Cambridge University Press.

Adams, Robert Merrihew. 1984. "Saints." *Journal of Philosophy* 81:392–401.

Alston, William P. 1989a. "Can We Speak Literally of God?" In *Divine Nature and Human Language*, 39–63. Ithaca, NY: Cornell University Press.

Alston, William P. 1989b. "Irreducible Metaphors in Theology." In *Divine Nature and Human Language*, 17–38. Ithaca, NY: Cornell University Press.

Alston, William P. 1991. *Perceiving God: The Epistemology of Religious Experience.* Ithaca, NY: Cornell University Press.

Alston, William P. 2003a. "Religious Experience Justifies Religious Belief." In *Contemporary Debates in Philosophy of Religion*, edited by Michael L. Peterson and Raymond VanArragon, 135–45. Malden, MA: Wiley-Blackwell.

Alston, William P. 2003b. "Reply to Fales." In *Contemporary Debates in Philosophy of Religion*, edited by Michael L. Peterson and Raymond VanArragon, 158–61. Malden, MA: Wiley-Blackwell.

Anderson, Gary A. 1991. *A Time to Mourn, a Time to Dance: The Expression of Grief and Joy in Israelite Religion.* University Park, PA: Pennsylvania State University Press.

Anderson, Robert. 1897. *The Silence of God.* New York: Dodd, Mead, and Company.

Ávila, Teresa of. 1976. *The Collected Works of St. Teresa of Ávila.* Translated by Otilio Rodriguez and Kieran Kavanaugh. 2nd edition. Vol. 1. Washington: ICS Publications.

Ávila, Teresa of. 1980. *The Collected Works of St. Teresa of Ávila.* Translated by Otilio Rodriguez and Kieran Kavanaugh. Vol. 2. Washington, DC: ICS Publications.

Baillie, John. 1939. *Our Knowledge of God.* New York: Scribner.

Balentine, Samuel. 1983. *The Hidden God: The Hiding of the Face of God in the Old Testament.* Oxford: Oxford University Press.

Balentine, Samuel E. 2006. *Job.* Macon, GA: Smyth & Helwys Publishing.

Barth, Karl. 1957. *Church Dogmatics, Vol. 2, Part 1: The Doctrine of God.* Edited by G. W. Bromiley and T. F. Torrance. Translated by T. H. L. Parker and J. L. M. Haire. London: T&T Clark.

Bealer, George. 1996. "On the Possibility of Philosophical Knowledge." *Philosophical Perspectives* 10:1–34.

Bealer, George. 1998. "Intuition and the Autonomy of Philosophy." In *Rethinking Intuition,* edited by Michael R. Depaul and William Ramsey, 201–40. Lanham, MD: Rowman & Littlefield.

Beilby, James. 2004. "Divine Aseity, Divine Freedom: A Conceptual Problem for Edwardsian-Calvinism." *Journal of the Evangelical Theological Society* 47:647–58.

Bellah, Robert N. 2011. *Religion in Human Evolution: From the Paleolithic to the Axial Age.* Cambridge, MA: Belknap Press.

Bergmann, Michael. 2008. "Skeptical Theism and the Problem of Evil." In *The Oxford Handbook of Philosophical Theology,* edited by Thomas P. Flint and Michael C. Rea, 374–99. Oxford: Oxford University Press.

Bergmann, Michael. 2012. "Commonsense Skeptical Theism." In *Reason, Metaphysics, and Mind: New Essays on the Philosophy of Alvin Plantinga,* edited by Kelly James Clark and Michael Rea, 9–30. New York: Oxford University Press.

Bergmann, Michael, Michael J. Murray, and Michael C. Rea, eds. 2011. *Divine Evil? The Moral Character of the God of Abraham.* Oxford/New York: Oxford University Press.

Billings, J. Todd. 2015. *Rejoicing in Lament: Wrestling with Incurable Cancer and Life in Christ.* Grand Rapids, MI: Brazos Press.

Blackaby, Richard and Henry T. Blackaby. 2014. *Experiencing God.* Revised and expanded. Nashville, TN: B&H Publishing Group.

Blomberg, Craig. 1992. *Matthew.* New American Commentary, vol. 22. Nashville, TN: Broadman Press.

Blumenthal, David R. 1993. *Facing the Abusing God: A Theology of Protest.* Louisville, KY: Westminster John Knox Press.

Brenneman, Todd M. 2016. "The Applause of Heaven: Max Lucado and the Cutesy in American Evangelicalism." *Journal of the American Academy of Religion* 84:617–40.

Brinks, C. L. 2013. "On Nail Scissors and Toothbrushes: Responding to the Philosophers' Critiques of Historical Biblical Criticism." *Religious Studies* 49:357–76.

Brinks Rea, C. L. 2010. *The Thematic, Stylistic, and Verbal Similarities Between Isaiah 40–55 and the Book of Job*. PhD thesis, University of Notre Dame.

Brother Lawrence. 1977. *The Practice of the Presence of God*. Translated by John J. Delaney. Reissue edition. Garden City, NY: Image.

Brown, David. 2004. *God and Enchantment of Place: Reclaiming Human Experience*. Oxford: Oxford University Press.

Brownstein, Michael. 2016. "Implicit Bias." In *The Stanford Encyclopedia of Philosophy*, edited by Edward N. Zalta. Spring 2016. <http://plato.stanford.edu/archives/spr2016/entries/implicit-bias/>.

Brueggemann, Walter. 1986. "The Costly Loss of Lament." *Journal for the Study of the Old Testament* 36:57–71.

Brueggemann, Walter. 2012. *Theology of the Old Testament: Testimony, Dispute, Advocacy*. Minneapolis, MN: Fortress Press.

Burnett, Joel S. 2010. *Where is God? Divine Absence in the Hebrew Bible*. Minneapolis, MN: Fortress Press.

Burrell, David. 1973. *Analogy and Philosophical Language*. New Haven, CT: Yale University Press.

Bush, Stephen S. 2014. *Visions of Religion: Experience, Meaning, and Power*. New York: Oxford University Press.

Bynum, Caroline Walker. 1982. "Jesus as Mother and Abbot as Mother: Some Themes in Twelfth-Century Cistercian Writing." In *Jesus as Mother: Studies in the Spirituality of the High Middle Ages*, 110–69. Berkeley, CA: University of California Press.

Calvin, John. 1998. *Commentaries on the Book of the Prophet Jeremiah and the Lamentations, Pt. 1–4*. Translated by John Owen. Calvin's Commentaries: 19. Grand Rapids, MI: Baker Book House.

Camp, Elisabeth. 2006a. "Contextualism, Metaphor, and What Is Said." *Mind and Language* 21:280–309.

Camp, Elisabeth. 2006b. "Metaphor and that Certain 'Je Ne Sais Quoi.'" *Philosophical Studies* 129:1–25.

Caputo, John D. 1992. "How to Avoid Speaking of God: The Violence of Natural Theology." In *Prospects for Natural Theology*, edited by Eugene Thomas Long, 128–50. Washington, DC: Catholic University of America Press.

Clines, David J. A. 1989. *Job. 1–20*. Vol. 17. Word Biblical Commentary. Dallas, TX: Word Books.

Coakley, Sarah. 2009. "Dark Contemplation and Epistemic Transformation: The Analytic Theologian Re-Meets Teresa of Ávila." In *Analytic Theology: New Essays in the Philosophy of Theology*, edited by Oliver D. Crisp and Michael C. Rea, 280–312. Oxford/New York: Oxford University Press.

Cooper, David Edward. 1986. *Metaphor*. New York: Basil Blackwell.

Cox, D. Michael. 2015. "Neither Literal nor Metaphorical: Divine Body Traditions, Indispensable Pictures and Wittgensteinian 'Secondary Sense.'" *Modern Theology* 31:445–68.

Crenshaw, James L. 2013. "Comments on 'Animal Sacrifices.'" In *Divine Evil? The Moral Character of the God of Abraham*, edited by Michael Bergmann, Michael J. Murray, and Michael C. Rea, 138–43. Oxford/ New York: Oxford University Press.

Crisp, Oliver D. and Michael C. Rea, eds. 2009. *Analytic Theology: New Essays in the Philosophy of Theology*. Oxford/New York: Oxford University Press.

Crummett, Dustin. 2015. "We Are Here to Help Each Other." *Faith and Philosophy* 32:45–62.

Cuneo, Terence. 2013. "Another Look at Divine Hiddenness." *Religious Studies* 49:151–64.

Cuneo, Terence. 2016. *Ritualized Faith: Essays on the Philosophy of Liturgy*. Oxford: Oxford University Press.

Cuneo, Terence. 2017. "The Inaccessibility of Religion Problem." *Ergo* 4:669–91.

Curtis, John Briggs. 1979. "On Job's Response to Yahweh." *Journal of Biblical Literature* 98:497–511.

Dalferth, Ingolf. 2001. "Representing God's Presence." *International Journal of Systematic Theology* 3:237–56.

Dalferth, Ingolf. 2006. *Becoming Present: An Inquiry into the Christian Sense of the Presence of God*. Leuven: Peeters Publishers.

D'Aquili, Eugene G. and Andrew B. Newberg. 1998. "The Neuropsychological Basis of Religions, or Why God Won't Go Away." *Zygon* 33:187–201.

Davis, Caroline Franks. 1989. *The Evidential Force of Religious Experience*. Oxford: Clarendon Press.

Dougherty, Trent. 2014a. "Phenomenal Conservatism, Skeptical Theism, and Probabilistic Reasoning." In *Skeptical Theism: New Essays*, edited by Trent Dougherty and Justin P. McBrayer, 21–31. Oxford: Oxford University Press.

Dougherty, Trent. 2014b. *The Problem of Animal Pain: A Theodicy For All Creatures Great And Small*. London: Palgrave Macmillan.

Dougherty, Trent. 2016. "Reflections on the Deep Connection between Problems of Evil and Problems of Divine Hiddenness." *European Journal of Philosophy of Religion* 8:65–84.

Dougherty, Trent and Ross Parker. 2015. "Hiddenness of God." *Routledge Encyclopedia of Philosophy Online*. <https://www.rep.routledge.com/articles/thematic/hiddenness-of-god/v-1>.

Draper, Paul. 2008. "The Problem of Evil." In *The Oxford Handbook of Philosophical Theology*, edited by Thomas P. Flint and Michael C. Rea, 332–51. Oxford: Oxford University Press.

Draper, Paul and Trent Dougherty. 2013. "Explanation and the Problem of Evil." In *The Blackwell Companion to the Problem of Evil*, edited by

Justin P. McBrayer and Daniel Howard-Snyder, 67–82. Malden, MA: Wiley-Blackwell.

Dumsday, Travis. 2012. "Divine Hiddenness as Divine Mercy." *Religious Studies* 48:183–98.

Evans, C. Stephen. 2006. "Can God Be Hidden and Evident at the Same Time? Some Kierkegaardian Reflections." *Faith and Philosophy* 23:241–53.

Fales, Evan. 1996. "Scientific Explanations of Mystical Experiences: II. The Challenge to Theism." *Religious Studies* 32 (September):297–313.

Fales, Evan. 2003. "Do Mystics See God?" In *Contemporary Debates in Philosophy of Religion*, edited by Michael L. Peterson and Raymond VanArragon, 145–58. Malden, MA: Wiley-Blackwell.

Fishbane, Michael. 1992. "The Book of Job and Inner-Biblical Discourse." In *The Voice from the Whirlwind: Interpreting the Book of Job*, edited by Leo G. Perdue and W. Clark Gilpin, 86–98. Nashville, TN: Abingdon Press.

Forman, Robert K. C. 1990. "Introduction: Mysticism, Constructivism, and Forgetting." In *The Problem of Pure Consciousness: Mysticism and Philosophy*, 3–49. Oxford: Oxford University Press.

Fox, Michael V. 2013. "God's Answer and Job's Response." *Biblica* 94:1–23.

Frankfurt, Harry G. 2004. *The Reasons of Love*. Princeton, NJ: Princeton University Press.

Friedman, Richard Elliott. 1995. *The Disappearance of God: A Divine Mystery*. Boston, MA: Little, Brown and Company.

Garcia, Laura L. 2002. "St. John of the Cross and the Necessity of Divine Hiddenness." In *Divine Hiddenness: New Essays*, edited by Daniel Howard-Snyder and Paul Moser, 83–97. Cambridge: Cambridge University Press.

Geller, S. A. 2000. "The God of the Covenant." In *One God or Many? Concepts of Divinity in the Ancient World*, edited by Barbara Neveling Porter, 273–319. Chebeague, ME: CDL Press.

Gellman, Jerome I. 2001. *Mystical Experience of God: A Philosophical Inquiry*. Aldershot: Ashgate.

Green, Adam. 2009. "Reading the Mind of God: Alston, Shared Attention, and Mystical Experience." *Religious Studies* 45:455–70.

Hagner, Donald A. 1993. *Matthew. 1–13*. Word Biblical Commentary. Dallas, TX: Word Books.

Hampson, Daphne. 1996. *After Christianity*. Valley Forge, PA: Trinity Press International.

Hanson, Norwood R. 2002. "Seeing and Seeing As." In *Philosophy of Science: Contemporary Readings*, edited by Yuri Balashov and Alexander Rosenberg, 321–39. London: Routledge.

Hare, Douglas R. A. 1993. *Matthew*. Interpretation, a Bible Commentary for Teaching and Preaching. Louisville, KY: John Knox Press.

Harnack, Adolf von. 1990. *Marcion: The Gospel of the Alien God*. Translated by J. E. Steely and L. Bierma. Durham, NC: Labyrinth.

Harrison, R. K. 1973. *Jeremiah and Lamentations: An Introduction and Commentary*. Downers Grove, IL: Intervarsity Press.

Hazony, Yoram. 2012. *The Philosophy of Hebrew Scripture*. New York: Cambridge University Press.

Hector, Kevin. 2011. *Theology Without Metaphysics: God, Language and the Spirit of Recognition*. Cambridge: Cambridge University Press.

Herman, Judith L. 2015. *Trauma and Recovery: The Aftermath of Violence—From Domestic Abuse to Political Terror*. Revised edition. New York: Basic Books.

Hick, John. 1968. "Religious Faith as Experiencing-As." *Royal Institute of Philosophy Lectures* 2:20–35.

Hick, John. 2000. "Ineffability." *Religious Studies* 36:35–46.

Hick, John. 2005. *An Interpretation of Religion: Human Responses to the Transcendent*. 2nd edition. New Haven, CT: Yale University Press.

Holland, R. F. 1965. "The Miraculous." *American Philosophical Quarterly* 2:43–51.

Howard-Snyder, Daniel. 2009. "Epistemic Humility, Arguments from Evil, and Moral Skepticism." *Oxford Studies in Metaphysics* 2:16–57.

Howard-Snyder, Daniel. 2015. "Divine Openness and Creaturely Nonresistant Nonbelief." In *Hidden Divinity and Religious Belief*, edited by Adam Green and Eleonore Stump, 126–38. Cambridge: Cambridge University Press.

Howard-Snyder, Daniel. 2017. "Panmetaphoricism." *Religious Studies* 53:25–49.

Howard-Snyder, Daniel and Paul Moser, eds. 2002. *Divine Hiddenness: New Essays*. Cambridge: Cambridge University Press.

Huxley, Aldous. 1945. *The Perennial Philosophy*. Harper Collins.

James, William. 1902. *The Varieties of Religious Experience: A Study in Human Nature*. New York: The Modern Library.

Jantzen, Grace. 1988. *Julian of Norwich : Mystic and Theologian*. New York: Paulist Press.

Jantzen, Grace. 1989. "Mysticism and Experience." *Religious Studies* 25:295–315.

Jenkins, C. S. I. 2015. "What Is Love? An Incomplete Map of the Metaphysics." *Journal of the American Philosophical Association* 1:349–64.

Jenson, Robert. 1992. "'The Father, He...'" In *Speaking the Christian God: The Holy Trinity and the Challenge of Feminism*, edited by Alvin F. Kimel Jr. Grand Rapids, MI: Eerdmans.

Johnson, Elizabeth A. 1984. "The Incomprehensibility of God and the Image of God as Male and Female." *Theological Studies* 45:441–65.

Jones, Tamsin. 2011. *A Genealogy of Marion's Philosophy of Religion: Apparent Darkness*. Bloomington, IN: Indiana University Press.

Jordan, Jeff. 1994. "Religious Experience and Naturalistic Explanations." *Sophia* 33:58–73.

Jordan, Jeff. 2012. "The Topography of Divine Love." *Faith and Philosophy* 29:53–69.

Jordan, Jeff. 2015. "The Topography of Divine Love: A Reply to Thomas Talbott." *Faith and Philosophy* 32:182–7.

Katz, Steven T. 1978. "Language, Epistemology, and Mysticism." In *Mysticism and Philosophical Analysis*, 22–74. New York: Oxford University Press.

Kaufmann, Yehezkel. 1972. *The Religion of Israel: From its Beginnings to the Babylonian Exile*. Translated by Moshe Greenberg. New York: Schocken Books.

Kavanaugh, Kieran, ed. 1988. *John of the Cross: Selected Writings*. New edition. New York: Paulist Press.

Keener, Craig S. 1997. *Matthew*. IVP New Testament Commentary Series, vol. 1. Downers Grove, IL: InterVarsity Press.

Kohák, Erazim. 1984. *The Embers and the Stars: A Philosophical Inquiry into the Moral Sense of Nature*. Chicago, IL: University Of Chicago Press.

Korpel, Marjo C. A. and Johannes C. de Moor. 2011. *The Silent God*. Leiden: Brill.

Kugel, James L. 2008. *How to Read the Bible: A Guide to Scripture, Then and Now*. Reprint edition. New York: Free Press.

Kukla, André. 2005. *Ineffability and Philosophy*. Oxford: Routledge.

Kvanvig, Jonathan. 2002. "Divine Hiddenness: What is the Problem?" In *Divine Hiddenness: New Essays*, edited by Daniel Howard-Snyder and Paul Moser, 149–63. Cambridge: Cambridge University Press.

Langton, Rae and David Lewis. 1998. "Defining 'Intrinsic.'" *Philosophy and Phenomenological Research* 58:333–45.

Lawler, Michael G. 1987. *Symbol and Sacrament: A Contemporary Sacramental Theology*. New York: Paulist Press.

Laytner, Anson. 1990. *Arguing with God: A Jewish Tradition*. Northvale, NJ: Jason Aronson Inc.

Levenson, Jon D. 1994. *Creation and the Persistence of Evil*. Reprint edition. Princeton, NJ: Princeton University Press.

Lomelino, Jason. 2012. *Jesus Burgers: True Stories of Love, Redemption and Miracles in a College Town*. Santa Barbara, CA: Sea Hill Press, Inc.

Lucado, Max. 1995. *A Gentle Thunder*. Nashville, TN: Thomas Nelson.

Luhrmann, T. M. 2011. "Hallucinations and Sensory Overrides." *Annual Review of Anthropology* 40:71–85.

Luhrmann, T. M. 2012. *When God Talks Back: Understanding the American Evangelical Relationship with God*. New York: Knopf.

Machery, Edouard. 2015. "Cognitive Penetrability: A No Progress Report." In *The Cognitive Penetrability of Perception: New Philosophical*

Perspectives, edited by John Zeimbekis and Athanassios Raftopoulos, 59–74. Oxford: Oxford University Press.

MacPherson, Fiona. 2012. "Cognitive Penetration of Colour Experience: Rethinking the Issue in Light of an Indirect Mechanism." *Philosophy and Phenomenological Research* 84:24–62.

MacPherson, Fiona. 2015. "Cognitive Penetration and Nonconceptual Content." In *The Cognitive Penetrability of Perception: New Philosophical Perspectives*, edited by John Zeimbekis and Athanassios Raftopoulos, 331–58. Oxford: Oxford University Press.

Maitzen, Stephen. 2006. "Divine Hiddenness and the Demographics of Theism." *Religious Studies* 42:177–91.

Maitzen, Stephen. 2013. "The Moral Skepticism Objection to Skeptical Theism." In *The Blackwell Companion to The Problem of Evil*, edited by Justin P. McBrayer and Daniel Howard-Snyder, 444–57. Oxford: Wiley.

Marion, Jean-Luc. 1994. "Metaphysics and Phenomenology: A Relief for Theology." Translated by Thomas A. Carlson. *Critical Inquiry* 20:572–91.

Marion, Jean-Luc. 2012. *God Without Being*. 2nd edition. Translated by Thomas A. Carlson. Chicago, IL: University Of Chicago Press.

Marsh, Jason. 2013. "Darwin and the Problem of Natural Nonbelief." *The Monist* 96:349–76.

McCall, Thomas H. 2015. *An Invitation to Analytic Christian Theology*. Downers Grove, IL: IVP Academic.

McDowell, John. 1996. *Mind and World*. 2nd edition. Cambridge, MA: Harvard University Press.

McFague, Sallie. 1987. *Models of God: Theology for an Ecological, Nuclear Age*. Philadelphia, PA: Fortress Press.

McKim, Robert. 1990. "The Hiddenness of God." *Religious Studies* 26:141–61.

McKim, Robert. 2001. *Religious Ambiguity and Religious Diversity*. Oxford: Oxford University Press.

Mele, Alfred R. 1990. "He Wants to Try." *Analysis* 50:251–3.

Mele, Alfred R. 1991. "He Wants to Try Again: A Rejoinder." *Analysis* 51:225–8.

Middleton, J. Richard. 2016. "God's Loyal Opposition: Psalmic and Prophetic Protest as a Paradigm for Faithfulness in the Hebrew Bible." *Canadian-American Theological Review* 5:51–65.

Milazzo, G. Tom. 1991. *The Protest and the Silence: Suffering, Death, and Biblical Theology*. Minneapolis, MN: Fortress Press.

Mittleman, Alan. 2015. "The Problem of Holiness." *Journal of Analytic Theology* 3:29–46.

Moffat, Donald P. 2013. "The Profit and Loss of Lament: Rethinking Aspects of the Relationship Between Lament and Penitential Prayer." In *Spiritual*

Complaint: The Theology and Practice of Lament, edited by Miriam Bier and Tim Bulkeley, 88–101. Eugene, OR: Pickwick Publications.

Morris, Thomas V. 1988. "The Hidden God." *Philosophical Topics* 16:5–21.

Moser, Paul. 2002. "Cognitive Idolatry and Divine Hiding." In *Divine Hiddenness: New Essays*, edited by Daniel Howard-Snyder and Paul Moser, 120–48. Cambridge: Cambridge University Press.

Moser, Paul. 2008. *The Elusive God: Reorienting Religious Epistemology.* Cambridge: Cambridge University Press.

Muffs, Yochanan. 2009. *Personhood of God: Biblical Theology, Human Faith and the Divine Image.* Woodstock, VT: Jewish Lights.

Murphy, Mark. 2014. "Toward God's Own Ethics." In *Challenges to Religious and Moral Belief*, edited by Michael Bergmann and Patrick Kain, 154–71. Oxford: Oxford University Press.

Murphy, Mark. 2017. *God's Own Ethics: Norms of Divine Agency and the Argument from Evil.* Oxford: Oxford University Press.

Murray, Michael. 2002. "Deus Absconditus." In *Divine Hiddenness: New Essays*, edited by Daniel Howard-Snyder and Paul Moser, 62–82. Cambridge: Cambridge University Press.

Newsom, Carol A. 2003. *The Book of Job: A Contest of Moral Imaginations.* Oxford: Oxford University Press.

Nietzsche, Friedrich. 1997. *Daybreak: Thoughts on the Prejudices of Morality.* Edited by Maudemarie Clark and Brian Leiter. Translated by R. J. Hollingdale. Cambridge: Cambridge University Press.

Nygren, Anders. 1969. *Agape and Eros.* New York: Harper & Row.

O'Connor, David. 2013. "Theistic Objections to Skeptical Theism." In *The Blackwell Companion to The Problem of Evil*, edited by Justin P. McBrayer and Daniel Howard-Snyder, 468–81. Oxford: Wiley.

O'Connor, Kathleen H. 2002. *Lamentations and the Tears of the World.* Maryknoll, NY: Orbis Books.

Oord, Thomas. 2010. *The Nature of Love: A Theology.* St. Louis, MO: Chalice Press.

Otto, R. 1958. *The Idea of the Holy.* Translated by John W. Harvey. 2nd edition. New York: Oxford University Press.

Panchuk, Michelle. 2018. "The Shattered Spiritual Self and the Sacred: Philosophical Reflections on Religious Trauma, Worship, and Deconversion." *Res Philosophica* 96.

Parker, Ross. 2013. "Deep and Wide: A Response to Jeff Jordan on Divine Love." *Faith and Philosophy* 30:444–61.

Payne, S. 1990. *John of the Cross and the Cognitive Value of Mysticism: An Analysis of Sanjuanist Teaching and its Philosophical Implications for Contemporary Discussions of Mystical Experience.* Dordrecht: Kluwer.

Peckham, John. 2015a. *The Concept of Divine Love in the Context of the God–World Relationship.* New York: Peter Lang.

Peckham, John. 2015b. *The Love of God: A Canonical Model.* Downers Grove, IL: IVP Academic.

Perlmutter, Julian. 2016. "Desiring the Hidden God: Knowledge Without Belief." *European Journal of Philosophy of Religion* 8:51–64.

Perrine, Timothy and Stephen J. Wykstra. 2014. "Skeptical Theism, Abductive Atheology, and Theory Versioning." In *Skeptical Theism: New Essays*, edited by Trent Dougherty and Justin P. McBrayer, 142–63. Oxford/New York: Oxford University Press.

Pinnock, Clark H., Richard Rice, John Sanders, William Hasker, and David Basinger. 1994. *The Openness of God: A Biblical Challenge to the Traditional Understanding of God.* Downers Grove, IL: IVP Academic.

Plantinga, Alvin. 2000. *Warranted Christian Belief.* New York: Oxford University Press.

Plantinga, Alvin. 2004. "Supralapsarianism, or 'O Felix Culpa.'" In *Christian Faith and the Problem of Evil*, edited by Peter van Inwagen, 1–25. Grand Rapids, MI: Eerdmans.

Poston, Ted and Trent Dougherty. 2007. "Divine Hiddenness and the Nature of Belief." *Religious Studies* 43:183–98.

Proudfoot, Wayne. 1987. *Religious Experience.* Berkeley, CA: University of California Press.

Pseudo-Dionysius. 1987. *Pseudo-Dionysius: The Complete Works.* Translated by Colm Luibheid. New York: Paulist Press.

Ratzsch, Del. 2003. "Perceiving Design." In *God and Design: The Teleological Argument and Modern Science*, edited by Neil A. Manson, 125–45. London: Routledge.

Rea, Michael. 2002. *World without Design: The Ontological Consequences of Naturalism.* Oxford: Clarendon Press.

Rea, Michael. 2009a. "Narrative, Liturgy, and the Hiddenness of God." In *Metaphysics and God: Essays in Honor of Eleonore Stump*, edited by Kevin Timpe, 76–96. New York: Routledge.

Rea, Michael. 2009b. "The Trinity." In *The Oxford Handbook of Philosophical Theology*, edited by Thomas P. Flint and Michael Rea, 403–29. Oxford: Oxford University Press.

Rea, Michael. 2011a. "Divine Hiddenness, Divine Silence." In *Philosophy of Religion: An Anthology*, edited by Louis Pojman and Michael Rea, 6th edition, 266–75. Boston, MA: Cengage.

Rea, Michael. 2011b. "Hylomorphism and the Incarnation." In *The Metaphysics of the Incarnation*, edited by Anna Marmodoro and Jonathan Hill, 134–52. Oxford: Oxford University Press.

Rea, Michael. 2013. "Skeptical Theism and the 'Too-Much-Skepticism' Objection." In *The Blackwell Companion to The Problem of Evil*, edited by Justin P. McBrayer and Daniel Howard-Snyder, 482–506. Oxford: Wiley.

Rea, Michael. 2015. "Hiddenness and Transcendence." In *Hidden Divinity and Religious Belief*, edited by Adam Green and Eleonore Stump, 210–25. Cambridge: Cambridge University Press.

Reimer, Marga, and Elisabeth Camp. 2006. "Metaphor." In *The Oxford Handbook of Philosophy of Language*, edited by Ernest Lepore and Barry C. Smith, 845–63. Oxford: Oxford University Press.

Rendtorff, Rolf. 1993. "The Paradigm is Changing: Hopes—and Fears," *Biblical Interpretation* 1:34–53.

Rowe, William. 1962. "The Meaning of 'God' in Tillich's Theology." *Journal of Religion* 42:274–86.

Sanders, John. 1998. *The God Who Risks: A Theology of Providence*. Downers Grove, IL: Intervarsity Pr.

Sanders, James. 2005. *Torah and Canon*, 2nd edition. Eugene, OR: Cascade Books.

Sartre, Jean Paul. 1956. *Being and Nothingness*. Translated by Hazel Barnes. New York: Washington Square Press Books.

Schellenberg, J. L. 1993. *Divine Hiddenness and Human Reason*. Ithaca, NY: Cornell University Press.

Schellenberg, J. L. 2002. "What the Hiddenness of God Reveals: A Collaborative Discussion." In *Divine Hiddenness: New Essays*, edited by Daniel Howard-Snyder and Paul Moser, 33–61. Cambridge: Cambridge University Press.

Schellenberg, J. L. 2003. "Divine Hiddenness Justifies Atheism." In *Contemporary Debates in Philosophy of Religion*, edited by Michael L. Peterson and Raymond VanArragon, 30–41. Malden, MA: Wiley-Blackwell.

Schellenberg, J. L. 2004. "'Breaking Down the Walls that Divide': Virtue and Warrant, Belief and Nonbelief." *Faith and Philosophy* 21:195–213.

Schellenberg, J. L. 2005a. "The Hiddenness Argument Revisited (I)." *Religious Studies* 41:201–15.

Schellenberg, J. L. 2005b. "The Hiddenness Argument Revisited (II)." *Religious Studies* 41:287–303.

Schellenberg, J. L. 2007. *The Wisdom to Doubt: A Justification of Religious Skepticism*. Ithaca, NY: Cornell University Press.

Schellenberg, J. L. 2010. "The Hiddenness Problem and the Problem of Evil." *Faith and Philosophy* 27:45–60.

Schellenberg, J. L. 2015a. "Divine Hiddenness and Human Philosophy." In *Hidden Divinity and Religious Belief*, edited by Adam Green and Eleonore Stump, 13–32. Cambridge: Cambridge University Press.

Schellenberg, J. L. 2015b. *The Hiddenness Argument: Philosophy's New Challenge to Belief in God*. New York: Oxford University Press.

Schifferdecker, Kathryn. 2008. *Out of the Whirlwind: Creation Theology in the Book of Job*. Cambridge, MA: Harvard University Press.

Siegel, Susanna. 2006. "Which Properties Are Represented in Perception?" In *Perceptual Experience*, edited by Tamar S. Gendler and John Hawthorne, 481–503. Oxford: Oxford University Press.

Smith, Mark S. 2002. *The Early History of God: Yahweh and the Other Deities in Ancient Israel*. 2nd edition. Grand Rapids, MI: Eerdmans.

Sommer, Benjamin D. 1999. "Revelation at Sinai in the Hebrew Bible and in Jewish Theology." *The Journal of Religion* 79: 422–51.

Sommer, Benjamin D. 2011. *The Bodies of God and the World of Ancient Israel*. Cambridge: Cambridge University Press.

Soskice, Janet Martin. 1985. *Metaphor and Religious Language*. Oxford: Clarendon Press.

Soskice, Janet Martin. 1992. "Can a Feminist Call God 'Father'?" In *Speaking the Christian God: The Holy Trinity and the Challenge of Feminism*, edited by Alvin F. Kimel Jr., 81–94. Grand Rapids, MI: Eerdmans.

Soskice, Janet Martin. 2002. "The Gift of the Name: Moses and the Burning Bush." In *Silence and the Word: Negative Theology and Incarnation*, edited by Oliver Davies and Denys Turner, 61–75. Cambridge: Cambridge University Press.

Speaks, Jeff. 2018. *The Greatest Possible Being*. Oxford: Oxford University Press.

Stace, W. T. 1960. *Mysticism and Philosophy*. Philadelphia, PA: Lippincott.

Stokes, Dustin. 2014. "Cognitive Penetration and the Perception of Art." *Dialectica* 68:1–34.

Stump, Eleonore. 2011. "The Non-Aristotelian Character of Aquinas's Ethics: Aquinas on the Passions." *Faith and Philosophy* 28:29–43.

Stump, Eleonore. 2012. *Wandering in Darkness: Narrative and the Problem of Suffering*. Oxford: Oxford University Press.

Stump, Eleonore. 2016. *The God of the Bible and the God of the Philosophers*. Milwaukee, WI: Marquette University Press.

Stump, Eleonore. 2018. *At-Onement*. Oxford: Oxford University Press.

Swinburne, Richard. 1998. *Providence and the Problem of Evil*. Oxford: Clarendon Press.

Swinburne, Richard. 2004. *The Existence of God*. 2nd edition. Oxford: Clarendon Press.

Talbott, Thomas. 2013. "The Topography of Divine Love: A Response to Jeff Jordan." *Faith and Philosophy* 30:302–16.

Taliaferro, Charles. 2012. "Transcending Place and Time: A Response to David Brown on Enchantment, Epistemology, and Experience." In *Theology, Aesthetics, and Culture: Responses to the Work of David Brown*, edited by Robert MacSwain and Taylor Worley, 103–14. Oxford: Oxford University Press.

Taves, Ann. 2009. "Channeled Apparitions: On Visions that Morph and Categories that Slip." *Visual Resources* 25:137–52.

Taves, Ann. 2016. *Revelatory Events: Three Case Studies of the Emergence of New Spiritual Paths.* Princeton, NJ: Princeton University Press.

Teresa, Mother. 2007. *Come Be My Light: The Private Writings of the Saint of Calcutta.* Edited by Brian Kolodiejchuk. New York: Doubleday.

Terrien, Samuel L. 1978. *The Elusive Presence: Toward a New Biblical Theology.* San Francisco, CA: Harper & Row.

Ticciati, Susannah. 2013. *A New Apophaticism: Augustine and the Redemption of Signs.* Leiden: Brill.

Timpe, Kevin. 2014. "Trust, Silence, and Liturgical Acts." In *Skeptical Theism: New Essays*, edited by Trent Dougherty and Justin P. McBrayer, 264–74. Oxford: Oxford University Press.

Torrance, Alan. 2001. "Is Love the Essence of God." In *Nothing Greater, Nothing Better: Theological Essays on the Love of God*, edited by Kevin Vanhoozer, 114–37. Grand Rapids, MI: Eerdmanns.

Trakakis, Nick. 2015. "The Hidden Divinity and What it Reveals." In *Hidden Divinity and Religious Belief*, edited by Adam Green and Eleonore Stump, 192–209. Cambridge: Cambridge University Press.

Turner, Denys. 1998. *The Darkness of God: Negativity in Christian Mysticism.* Cambridge: Cambridge University Press.

Turner, Denys. 2004. *Faith, Reason and the Existence of God.* New York: Cambridge University Press.

Tur-Sinai, Naphtali. 1967. *The Book of Job: A New Commentary.* Jerusalem: Kiryath Sepher.

Uffenheimer, Benjamin. 1986. "Myth and Reality in Ancient Israel." In *The Origins and Diversity of Axial Age Civilizations*, edited by S. N. Eisenstadt, 135–68. Albany, NY: SUNY Press.

Unger, Johan. 1976. *On Religious Experience: A Psychological Study.* Uppsala: Uppsala University Press.

Urban, Wilbur. 1940. "A Critique of Professor Tillich's Theory of the Religious Symbol." *Journal of Liberal Religion* 2:34–6.

van Inwagen, Peter. 1988. "The Magnitude, Duration, and Distribution of Evil: A Theodicy." *Philosophical Topics* 16:161–87.

van Inwagen, Peter. 2002. "What is the Problem of the Hiddenness of God?" In *Divine Hiddenness: New Essays*, edited by Daniel Howard-Snyder and Paul Moser, 24–32. Cambridge: Cambridge University Press.

Van Woudenberg, René. 1998. "Panmetaphoricism Examined." *Philosophy and Rhetoric* 31 (4):231–47.

Vorgrimler, Herbert. 1992. *Sacramental Theology.* Translated by Linda Maloney. Collegeville, MN: The Liturgical Press.

Wainwright, William. 2002. "Jonathan Edwards and the Hiddenness of God." In *Divine Hiddenness: New Essays*, edited by Daniel Howard-Snyder and Paul Moser, 98–119. Cambridge: Cambridge University Press.

Wainwright, William J. 1981. *Mysticism: A Study of Its Nature, Cognitive Value, and Moral Implications*. Madison: University of Wisconsin Press.

Wenham, Gordon J. 1970. "Trends in Pentateuchal Criticism Since 1950," *The Churchman* 84:210–20.

Wenham, Gordon J. 1999. "Pondering the Pentateuch: The Search for a New Paradigm." In *The Face of Old Testament Studies: A Survey of Contemporary Approaches*, edited by David W. Baker and Bill T. Arnold. Grand Rapids, MI: Baker Books.

Wessling, Jordan. 2012. "The Scope of God's Supreme Love." *Philosophia Christi* 14:335–51.

Westermann, Claus. 1981. *The Structure of the Book of Job: A Form-Critical Analysis*. Philadelphia, PA: Fortress Press.

Westermann, Claus. 1982. *Elements of Old Testament Theology*. Atlanta, GA: John Knox Press.

Westermann, Claus. 1994. *Lamentations: Issues and Interpretation*. Translated by Charles Muenchow. Minneapolis, MN: Fortress Press.

White, Thomas Joseph, ed. 2010. *The Analogy of Being: Invention of the Antichrist or Wisdom of God?* Grand Rapids, MI/Cambridge: Eerdmans.

Wilks, Ian. 2013. "The Global Skepticism Objection to Skeptical Theism." In *The Blackwell Companion to The Problem of Evil*, edited by Justin P. McBrayer and Daniel Howard-Snyder, 458–67. Oxford: Wiley.

Witherington, Ben, III. 2006. *Matthew*. Smyth & Helwys Bible Commentary. Macon, GA: Smyth & Helwys Pub.

Wolf, Susan. 1982. "Moral Saints." *Journal of Philosophy* 79:419–39.

Wolterstorff, Nicholas. 2002. "The Silence of the God Who Speaks." In *Divine Hiddenness: New Essays*, edited by Daniel Howard-Snyder and Paul Moser, 215–28. Cambridge: Cambridge University Press.

Wynn, Mark. 2009. "Towards a Broadening of the Concept of Religious Experience: Some Phenomenological Considerations." *Religious Studies* 45:147–66.

Wynn, Mark. 2013. *Renewing the Senses: A Study of the Philosophy and Theology of the Spiritual Life*. Oxford: Oxford University Press.

Yadav, Sameer. 2015. *The Problem of Perception and the Experience of God: Toward a Theological Empiricism*. Minneapolis, MN: Fortress Press.

Index

Printed and bound by CPI Group (UK) Ltd, Croydon, CR0 4YY